Century 21
Accounting

General Journal
11e | Working Papers
Chapters 1-17

Claudia Bienias Gilbertson, CPA
Retired
North Hennepin Community College
Brooklyn Park, Minnesota

Mark W. Lehman, CPA, CFE
Associate Professor Emeritus
Richard C. Adkerson School of Accountancy
Mississippi State University
Starkville, Mississippi

 CENGAGE

Australia • Brazil • Mexico • Singapore • United Kingdom • United States

**Century 21 Accounting:
Multicolumn Journal, 11th Edition
Working Papers, Volume 1**
**Claudia Bienias Gilbertson,
Mark W. Lehman**

SVP, GM Skills & Global Product Management:
Jonathan Lau

Product Director: Matthew Seeley

Product Manager: Nicole Robinson

Senior Director, Development: Marah Bellegarde

Product Development Manager: Juliet Steiner

Senior Content Developer: Darcy Scelsi

Product Assistant: Deborah Handy

Vice President, Marketing Services:
Jennifer Ann Baker

Director, Product Marketing: Jeremy Walts

Senior Production Director: Wendy Troeger

Director, Production: Andrew Crouth

Senior Content Project Manager: Betty Dickson

Managing Art Director: Jack Pendleton

Media Producer: Jim Gilbert

Senior Digital Content Specialist:
Jaclyn Hermesmyer

Cover image(s): Shutterstock.com

For product information and technology assistance, contact us at
Cengage Learning Customer & Sales Support, 1-800-354-9706.

For permission to use material from this text or product,
submit all requests online at **www.cengage.com/permissions.**

Further permissions questions can be e-mailed to
permissionrequest@cengage.com.

Library of Congress Control Number: 2018930681

Student Edition ISBN-13: 978-1-337-62323-0

Cengage Learning
20 Channel Center Street
Boston, MA 02210
USA

Cengage Learning is a leading provider of customized learning solutions with employees residing in nearly 40 different countries and sales in more than 125 countries around the world. Find your local representative at: **www.cengage.com.**

Cengage Learning products are represented in Canada by Nelson Education, Ltd.

For your course and learning solutions, visit **www.cengage.com/school**

To learn more about Cengage Learning, visit **www.cengage.com**

Notice to the Reader

Publisher does not warrant or guarantee any of the products described herein or perform any independent analysis in connection with any of the product information contained herein. Publisher does not assume, and expressly disclaims, any obligation to obtain and include information other than that provided to it by the manufacturer. The reader is expressly warned to consider and adopt all safety precautions that might be indicated by the activities described herein and to avoid all potential hazards. By following the instructions contained herein, the reader willingly assumes all risks in connection with such instructions. The publisher makes no representations or warranties of any kind, including but not limited to, the warranties of fitness for particular purpose or merchantability, nor are any such representations implied with respect to the material set forth herein, and the publisher takes no responsibility with respect to such material. The publisher shall not be liable for any special, consequential, or exemplary damages resulting, in whole or part, from the readers' use of, or reliance upon, this material.

Printed in the United States of America
Print Number: 01   Print Year: 2018

TO THE STUDENT

These *Working Papers* are to be used in the study of Chapters 1–17 of CENTURY 21 ACCOUNTING, 11E. Forms are provided for:

1. Study Guides
2. Work Together Exercises
3. On Your Own Exercises
4. Application Problems
5. Mastery Problems
6. Challenge Problems
7. Source Documents Problems
8. Reinforcement Activities 1 and 2

Printed on each page is the number of the problem in the textbook for which the form is to be used. Also shown is a specific instruction number for which the form is to be used.

You may not be required to use every form that is provided. Your teacher will tell you whether to retain or dispose of the unused pages.

The pages are perforated so they may be removed as the work required in each assignment is completed. The pages will be more easily detached if you crease the sheet along the line of perforations and then remove the sheet by pulling sideways rather than upward.

TABLE OF CONTENTS

Working Papers for Chapter 1
Starting a Proprietorship: Changes That Affect the Accounting Equation • 1

Working Papers for Chapter 2
Analyzing Transactions into Debit and Credit Parts • 19

Working Papers for Chapter 3
Journalizing Transactions • 35

Working Papers for Chapter 4
Posting to a General Ledger • 55

Working Papers for Chapter 5
Cash Control Systems • 91

Working Papers for Chapter 6
Work Sheet and Adjusting Entries for a Service Business • 125

Working Papers for Chapter 7
Financial Statements for a Proprietorship • 143

Working Papers for Chapter 8
Recording Closing Entries and Preparing a Post-Closing Trial Balance for a Service Business • 159

Working Papers for Chapter 9
Accounting for Purchases and Cash Payments • 197

Working Papers for Chapter 10
Accounting for Sales and Cash Receipts • 239

Working Papers for Chapter 11
Accounting for Transactions Using a General Journal • 271

Working Papers for Chapter 12
Preparing Payroll Records • 311

Working Papers for Chapter 13
Accounting for Payroll and Payroll Taxes • 349

Working Papers for Chapter 14
Accounting for Uncollectible Accounts Receivable • 393

Working Papers for Chapter 15
Preparing Adjusting Entries and a Trial Balance • 423

Working Papers for Chapter 16
Financial Statements and Closing Entries for a Corporation • 465

Working Papers for Chapter 17
Financial Statement Analysis • 499

Name	Perfect Score	Your Score
Identifying Accounting Terms	27 Pts.	
Identifying Account Concepts and Practices	18 Pts.	
Analyzing How Transactions Change an Accounting Equation	10 Pts.	
Analyzing How Transactions Change Owner's Equity in an Accounting Equation	12 Pts.	
Total	65 Pts.	

Part One—Identifying Accounting Terms

Directions: Select the one term in Column I that best fits each definition in Column II. Print the letter identifying your choice in the Answers column.

Column I	Column II	Answers
A. account	**1.** The process of planning, recording, analyzing, and interpreting financial information. (p. 6)	**1.** _____
B. account balance	**2.** A planned process designed to compile financial data and summarize the results in accounting records and reports. (p. 6)	**2.** _____
C. account title	**3.** Financial reports that summarize the financial condition and operations of a business. (p. 6)	**3.** _____
D. accounting	**4.** A formal report that shows what an individual owns, what an individual owes, and the difference between the two. (p. 7)	**4.** _____
E. accounting equation	**5.** Anything of value that is owned. (p. 7)	**5.** _____
F. accounting system	**6.** An amount owed. (p. 7)	**6.** _____
G. asset	**7.** The difference between personal assets and personal liabilities. (p. 7)	**7.** _____
H. business ethics	**8.** The difference between assets and liabilities. (p. 7)	**8.** _____
I. business plan	**9.** The principles of right and wrong that guide an individual in making decisions. (p. 8)	**9.** _____
J. capital account	**10.** The use of ethics in making business decisions. (p. 8)	**10.** _____
K. creditor	**11.** A business that performs an activity for a fee. (p. 10)	**11.** _____
L. equities	**12.** A business owned by one person. (p. 10)	**12.** _____
M. equity	**13.** A formal written document that describes the nature of a business and how it will operate. (p. 10)	**13.** _____
N. ethics	**14.** Generally Accepted Accounting Principles. The standards and rules that accountants follow while recording and reporting financial activities. (p. 11)	**14.** _____
O. expense	**15.** Financial rights to the assets of a business. (p. 13)	**15.** _____
P. financial statements	**16.** The amount remaining after the value of all liabilities is subtracted from the value of all assets. (p. 13)	**16.** _____
Q. GAAP	**17.** The equation showing the relationship among assets, liabilities, and owner's equity. (p. 13)	**17.** _____
R. liability	**18.** Any business activity that changes assets, liabilities, or owner's equity. (p. 14)	**18.** _____
S. net worth statement	**19.** A record that summarizes all the transactions pertaining to a single item in the accounting equation. (p. 14)	**19.** _____
T. owner's equity	**20.** The name given to an account. (p. 14)	**20.** _____
U. personal net worth	**21.** The difference between the increases and decreases in an account. (p. 14)	**21.** _____

Column I	Column II	Answers
V. proprietorship	**22.** An account used to summarize the owner's equity in a business. (p. 14)	**22.** _____
W. revenue	**23.** A person or business to whom a liability is owed. (p. 16)	**23.** _____
X. sale on account	**24.** An increase in equity resulting from the sale of goods or services. (p. 18)	**24.** _____
Y. service business	**25.** A sale for which payment will be received at a later date. (p. 18)	**25.** _____
Z. transaction	**26.** The cost of goods or services used to operate a business. (p. 19)	**26.** _____
AA. withdrawals	**27.** Assets taken from the business for the owner's personal use (p. 20)	**27.** _____

Part Two—Identifying Account Concepts and Practices

Directions: Place a *T* for True or an *F* for False in the Answers column to show whether each of the following statements is true or false.

Answers

1. Accounting is the language of business. (p. 6)   **1.** _____

2. A creditor would favor a positive net worth. (p. 7)   **2.** _____

3. The principles of right and wrong that guide an individual in making personal decisions is called business ethics. (p. 8)   **3.** _____

4. Keeping personal and business records separate is an application of the business entity concept. (p. 11)   **4.** _____

5. Generally Accepted Accounting Principles, GAAP, allows for flexibility in reporting. (p. 11)   **5.** _____

6. Recording business costs in terms of hours required to complete projects is an application of the unit of measurement concept. (p. 11)   **6.** _____

7. Assets such as cash and supplies have value because they can be used to acquire other assets or be used to operate a business. (p. 13)   **7.** _____

8. The relationship among assets, liabilities, and owner's equity can be written as an equation. (p. 13)   **8.** _____

9. The accounting equation does not have to be in balance to be correct. (p. 13)   **9.** _____

10. When a company pays insurance premiums in advance to an insurer, it records the payment as a liability because the insurer owes future coverage. (p. 15)   **10.** _____

11. When items are bought and paid for later, this is referred to as buying on account. (p. 16)   **11.** _____

12. When cash is paid on account, a liability is increased. (p. 16)   **12.** _____

13. When cash is received from a sale, the total amount of both assets and owner's equity is increased. (p. 18)   **13.** _____

14. The accounting concept Realization of Revenue is applied when revenue is recorded at the time goods or services are sold. (p. 18)   **14.** _____

15. When cash is paid for expenses, the business has more equity. (p. 19)   **15.** _____

16. If two amounts are recorded on the same side of the accounting equation, the equation will no longer be in balance. (p. 20)   **16.** _____

17. When a company receives cash from a customer for a prior sale, the transaction increases the cash account balance and increases the accounts receivable balance. (p. 20)   **17.** _____

18. A withdrawal decreases owner's equity. (p. 20)   **18.** _____

Part Three—Analyzing How Transactions Change an Accounting Equation

Directions: For each of the following transactions, select the two accounts in the accounting equation that are changed. Decide if each account is increased or decreased. Place a "+" in the column if the account is increased. Place a "−" in the column if the account is decreased.

Transactions

1–2. Received cash from owner Nicole McGraw as an investment. (p. 14)

3–4. Paid cash for supplies. (p. 15)

5–6. Paid cash for insurance. (p. 15)

7–8. Bought supplies on account from Hyde Park Office Supplies. (p. 16)

9–10. Paid cash on account to Hyde Park Office Supplies. (p. 16)

Trans. No.	Assets			=	Liabilities	+	Owner's Equity
	Cash	+ Supplies	+ Prepaid Insurance	=	Accts. Pay.— Hyde Park Office supplies	+	Nicole McGraw, Capital
1–2							
3–4							
5–6							
7–8							
9–10							

Part Four—Analyzing How Transactions Change Owner's Equity in an Accounting Equation

Directions: For each of the following transactions, select the two accounts in the accounting equation that are changed. Decide if each account is increased or decreased. Place a "+" in the column if the account is increased. Place a "−" in the column if the account is decreased.

Transactions

1–2. Received cash from sales. (p. 18)

3–4. Sold services on account to New U Fitness. (p. 18)

5–6. Paid cash for rent. (p. 19)

7–8. Paid cash for telephone bill. (p. 19)

9–10. Received cash on account from New U Fitness. (p. 20)

11–12. Paid cash to owner A. Conrad for personal use. (p. 20)

Trans. No.	Assets				=	Liabilities	+	Owner's Equity
	Cash +	Accts. Rec.— New U Fitness +	Supplies +	Prepaid Insurance =		Accts. Pay.— Hardcore Fitness Supplies +		A. Conrad, Capital
1–2								
3–4								
5–6								
7–8								
9–10								
11–12								

Across

1. A record that summarizes all the transactions pertaining to a single item in the accounting equation.

2. An increase in equity resulting from the sale of goods or services.

5. An account used to summarize the owner's equity in a business.

8. Anything of value that is owned.

11. Any business activity that changes assets, liabilities, or owner's equity.

13. The name given to an account.

14. An amount paid for the use of money for a period of time.

15. The cost of goods or services used to operate a business.

17. Someone who owns, operates, and takes the risk of a business venture.

18. The principles of right and wrong that guide an individual in making decisions.

19. An amount owed.

20. A formal written document that describes the nature of a business and how it will operate.

Down

1. The difference between the increases and decreases in an account.

3. The difference between assets and liabilities.

4. Assets taken from the business for the owner's personal use.

6. The process of planning, recording, analyzing, and interpreting financial information.

7. Interest paid on an original amount deposited in a bank plus any interest that has been paid.

9. A business that performs an activity for a fee.

10. A business owned by one person.

12. A person or business to whom a liability is owed.

16. Financial rights to the assets of a business.

1-1 WORK TOGETHER, p. 9

Completing a net worth statement

Completing a net worth statement

1-2 WORK TOGETHER, p. 17

Determining how transactions change an accounting equation

Trans. No.	Assets	=	Liabilities	+	Owner's Equity
1					
2					
3					
4					

Determining how transactions change an accounting equation

Trans. No.	Assets	=	Liabilities	+	Owner's Equity
1					
2					
3					
4					
5					

1-3 WORK TOGETHER, p. 22

Determining how transactions change an accounting equation

Trans. No.	Assets				=	Liabilities	+	Owner's Equity
	Cash +	Accts. Rec.—Harmon Co. +	Supplies +	Prepaid Insurance =		Accts. Pay.—Corona Supplies +		Nathaniel Conrad, Capital
1								
2								
3								
4								
5								

Determining how transactions change an accounting equation

Trans. No.	Assets				=	Liabilities	+	Owner's Equity
	Cash +	Accts. Rec.— Bethany Center +	Supplies +	Prepaid Insurance =		Accts. Pay.— McGrew Supplies +		Bryan Arnett, Capital
1								
2								
3								
4								
5								

1-1 **APPLICATION PROBLEM (LO2), p. 25**

Preparing a net worth statement

Lauren Juliana	
Net Worth Statement	
Assets	
Cash	
Jewelry	
Total Assets	
Liabilities	
Knapp College	
Ashley's Boutique	
Buzz Electronics	
Total Liabilities	
Owner's Equity (Net Worth)	
Assets − Liabilities = Net Worth	

Completing the accounting equation

Assets	=	Liabilities	+	Owner's Equity
15,650		11,475		
11,000				6,000
		2,000		3,300
12,000				7,000
125,000		69,000		
		1,875		15,750
35,000		13,000		
6,000				2,500
		139,000		4,650
17,000		2,800		
42,000				17,000
8,750		2,980		
		47,000		24,000
67,000				32,000
73,000		41,000		
		93,000		7,700
49,325				10,020
		21,250		2,800

1-2.2 APPLICATION PROBLEM (LO4, 5), p. 26

Determining how transactions change an accounting equation

Trans. No.	Assets			=	Liabilities		+	Owner's Equity
	Cash +	Supplies +	Prepaid Insurance =		Accts. Pay.— Knapp Co. +	Accts. Pay.— Hickman Mowing +		Bethany Hartman, Capital
Beg. Bal. 1	0 +5,000	0	0		0	0		0 +5,000
New Bal. 2	5,000	0	0		0	0		5,000
New Bal. 3								
New Bal. 4								
New Bal. 5								
New Bal. 6								
New Bal. 7								
New Bal. 8								
New Bal.								

Determining how revenue, expense, and withdrawal transactions change an accounting equation

Trans. No.	Assets				=	Liabilities	+	Owner's Equity
	Cash +	Accts. Rec.—Eden Wedding Planners	+ Supplies +	Prepaid Insurance =		Accts. Pay.—Shutter Supplies	+	Shannon O'Bryan, Capital
Beg. Bal. 1	725 −400	0	200	300		200		1,025 −400 (expense)
New Bal. 2	325	0	200	300		200		625
New Bal. 3								
New Bal. 4								
New Bal. 5								
New Bal. 6								
New Bal. 7								
New Bal. 8								
New Bal.								

1-M MASTERY PROBLEM (LO4, 5, 6), p. 27

Determining how transactions change an accounting equation

Trans. No.	Assets				= Liabilities +	Owner's Equity
	Cash +	Accts. Rec.— Dr. Shephard +	Supplies +	Prepaid Insurance =	Accts. Pay.— Paws & Claws Co. +	Peter Gentry, Capital
Beg. Bal. 1	2,500 −500	0	200	100	1,300	1,500 −500 (expense)
New Bal. 2	2,000	0	200	100	1,300	1,000
New Bal. 3						
New Bal. 4						
New Bal. 5						
New Bal. 6						
New Bal. 7						
New Bal. 8						
New Bal. 9						
New Bal. 10						
New Bal. 11						
New Bal. 12						
New Bal. 13						
New Bal.						

Determining how transactions change an accounting equation

1.

Trans. No.	Assets				=	Liabilities	+	Owner's Equity
	Cash	+	Accts. Rec.—4Kids Daycare	+	Supplies	+	Prepaid Insurance	=	Accts. Pay.—Ashley Tech Services	+	Linda Liu, Capital
Beg. Bal. 1	7,542	1,265	1,100	600	3,145	7,362
New Bal. 2						
New Bal. 3						
New Bal. 4						
New Bal.						

2.

_____

_____

_____

_____

_____

_____

_____

_____

_____

_____

_____

_____

_____

_____

_____

Part One—Identifying Accounting Terms

Directions: Select the one term in Column I that best fits each definition in Column II. Print the letter identifying your choice in the Answers column.

Column I	Column II	Answers
A. accounts payable	**1.** An accounting device used to analyze transactions. (p. 33)	**1.** _____
B. accounts receivable	**2.** An amount recorded on the left side of an account. (p. 33)	**2.** _____
C. chart of accounts	**3.** An amount recorded on the right side of an account. (p. 33)	**3.** _____
D. credit	**4.** The side of the account that is increased. (p. 33)	**4.** _____
E. debit	**5.** A list of accounts used by a business (p. 36)	**5.** _____
F. normal balance	**6.** Amounts to be paid in the future for goods or services already acquired. (p. 39)	**6.** _____
G. T account	**7.** Amounts to be received in the future due to the sale of goods or services. (p. 44)	**7.** _____

Part Two—Analyzing Transactions into Debit and Credit Parts

Directions: Analyze each of the following transactions into debit and credit parts. Print the letter identifying your choice in the proper Answers columns.

Account Titles

A. Cash
B. Accts. Rec.—Parkview Company
C. Supplies

D. Prepaid Insurance
E. Accts. Pay.—City Supplies
F. N. Lee, Capital
G. N. Lee, Drawing

H. Sales
I. Advertising Expense

	Answers	
	Debit	**Credit**
1–2. Received cash from owner as an investment. (p. 36)	1. _____	2. _____
3–4. Paid cash for supplies. (p. 37)	3. _____	4. _____
5–6. Paid cash for insurance. (p. 38)	5. _____	6. _____
7–8. Bought supplies on account from City Supplies. (p. 39)	7. _____	8. _____
9–10. Paid cash on account to City Supplies. (p. 40)	9. _____	10. _____
11–12. Received cash from sales. (p. 43)	11. _____	12. _____
13–14. Sold services on account to Parkview Company. (p. 44)	13. _____	14. _____
15–16. Paid cash for advertising. (p. 45)	15. _____	16. _____
17–18. Received cash on account from Parkview Company. (p. 46)	17. _____	18. _____
19–20. Paid cash to owner for personal use. (p. 47)	19. _____	20. _____

Part Three—Identifying Changes in Accounts

Directions: For each of the following items, select the choice that best completes the statement. Print the letter identifying your choice in the Answers column.

Answers

1. The values of all things owned (assets) are on the accounting equation's (A) left side (B) right side (C) credit side (D) none of these. (p. 32)

1. _____

2. The values of all equities or claims against the assets (liabilities and owner's equity) are on the accounting equation's (A) left side (B) right side (C) debit side (D) none of these. (p. 32)

2. _____

3. An amount recorded on the left side of a T account is a (A) debit (B) credit (C) normal balance (D) none of these. (p. 33)

3. _____

4. An amount recorded on the right side of a T account is a (A) debit (B) credit (C) normal balance (D) none of these. (p. 33)

4. _____

5. The normal balance side of any asset account is the (A) debit side (B) credit side (C) right side (D) none of these. (p. 33)

5. _____

6. The normal balance side of any liability account is the (A) debit side (B) credit side (C) left side (D) none of these. (p. 33)

6. _____

7. The normal balance side of an owner's capital account is the (A) debit side (B) credit side (C) left side (D) none of these. (p. 33)

7. _____

8. Debits must equal credits (A) in a T account (B) on the equation's left side (C) on the equation's right side (D) for each transaction. (p. 36)

8. _____

9. Decreases in an asset account are shown on a T account's (A) debit side (B) credit side (C) left side (D) none of these. (p. 37)

9. _____

10. Increases in an asset account are shown on a T account's (A) debit side (B) credit side (C) right side (D) none of these. (p. 37)

10. _____

11. Increases in any liability account are shown on the T account's (A) debit side (B) credit side (C) left side (D) none of these. (p. 39)

11. _____

12. Decreases in any liability account are shown on a T account's (A) debit side (B) credit side (C) right side (D) none of these. (p. 40)

12. _____

13. Increases in a revenue account are shown on a T account's (A) debit side (B) credit side (C) left side (D) none of these. (p. 43)

13. _____

14. The normal balance side of any revenue account is the (A) debit side (B) credit side (C) left side (D) none of these. (p. 43)

14. _____

15. Increases in an expense account are shown on a T account's (A) debit side (B) credit side (C) right side (D) none of these. (p. 45)

15. _____

16. The normal balance side of any expense account is the (A) debit side (B) credit side (C) right side (D) none of these. (p. 45)

16. _____

17. The normal balance side of an owner's drawing account is the (A) debit side (B) credit side (C) right side (D) none of these. (p. 47)

17. _____

18. Increases in an owner's drawing account are shown on a T account's (A) debit side (B) credit side (C) right side (D) none of these. (p. 47)

18. _____

Across

5. An accountant who combines accounting and investigating skills to uncover suspected fraudulent business activity, or to prevent such activity.

6. Amounts to be paid in the future for goods or services already acquired.

7. An amount recorded on the left side of an account.

8. An amount recorded on the right side of an account.

Down

1. A list of accounts used by a business.

2. The side of an account that is increased is called the normal balance of the account.

3. Amounts to be received in the future due to the sale of goods or services.

4. An accounting device used to analyze transactions.

2-1 WORK TOGETHER, p. 35

Determining the increase and decrease and the normal balance sides for accounts

Determining the increase and decrease and the normal balance sides for accounts

2-2 WORK TOGETHER, p. 42

Analyzing transactions into debit and credit parts

Mar. 1. _____

Mar. 6. _____

Mar. 3. _____

Mar. 9. _____

Mar. 4. _____

Analyzing transactions into debit and credit parts

June 2.

June 8.

June 4.

June 9.

June 5.

2-3 WORK TOGETHER, p. 49

Analyzing revenue, expense, and withdrawal transactions into debit and credit parts

Mar. 11.

Mar. 16.

Mar. 13.

Mar. 19.

Mar. 14.

Chapter 2 Analyzing Transactions into Debit and Credit Parts • **27**

Analyzing revenue, expense, and withdrawal transactions into debit and credit parts

June 12.

June 14.

June 15.

June 18.

June 19.

2-1 APPLICATION PROBLEM (LO2, 3), p. 52

Determining the increase, decrease, and normal balance side for accounts

1	2	Increase Side		Decrease Side		Account's Normal Balance	
		3	4	5	6	7	8
Account	Account Classification	Debit	Credit	Debit	Credit	Debit	Credit
Cash	Asset	↑			↓	✔	

Analyzing transactions into debit and credit parts

June 1.

Cash	
10,000.00	

Sawyer Helfrey, Capital	
	10,000.00

June 2.

June 4.

June 5.

June 8.

2-3 APPLICATION PROBLEM (LO5), p. 53

Analyzing revenue, expense, and withdrawal transactions into debit and credit parts

June 11.

June 18.

June 12.

June 19.

June 14.

Analyzing transactions into debit and credit parts

2-C   CHALLENGE PROBLEM (LO4, 5), p. 54

Analyzing transactions recorded in T accounts

1	2	3	4	5	6
Trans. No.	Accounts Affected	Account Classification	Entered in Account as a Debit	Credit	Description of Transaction
1	Cash	Asset	✔		Received cash from owner as an investment
	Kelsey Guerrero, Capital	Owner's Equity		✔	
2					
3					
4					
5					
6					
7					
8					
9					
10					
11					
12					
13					

Study Guide 3

Name	Perfect Score	Your Score
Identifying Accounting Terms	10 Pts.	
Identifying Accounting Concepts and Practices	20 Pts.	
Recording Transactions in a General Journal	20 Pts.	
Total	50 Pts.	

Part One—Identifying Accounting Terms

Directions: Select the one term in Column I that best fits each definition in Column II. Print the letter identifying your choice in the Answers column.

Column I	Column II	Answers
A. check	1. A form for recording transactions in chronological order. (p. 58)	1._____
B. double-entry accounting	2. Recording transactions in a journal. (p. 58)	2._____
C. entry	3. Information for each transaction recorded in a journal. (p. 59)	3._____
D. invoice	4. The recording of debit and credit parts of a transaction. (p. 59)	4._____
E. journal	5. A business paper from which information is obtained for a journal entry. (p. 59)	5._____
F. journalizing	6. A business form ordering a bank to pay cash from a bank account. (p. 60)	6._____
G. memorandum	7. A form describing the goods or services sold, the quantity, the price, and the terms of sale. (p. 60)	7._____
H. receipt	8. An invoice used as a source document for recording a sale on account. (p. 60)	8._____
I. sales invoice	9. A business form giving written acknowledgement for cash received. (p. 61)	9._____
J. source document	10. A form on which a brief message is written to describe a transaction. (p. 61)	10._____

Part Two—Identifying Accounting Concepts and Practices

Directions: Place a *T* for True or an *F* for False in the Answers column to show whether each of the following statements is true or false.

1. Information in a journal includes the debit and credit parts of each transaction recorded in one place. (p. 59)

  1. _____

2. The Objective Evidence accounting concept requires that there be proof that a transaction did occur. (p. 59)

  2. _____

3. Examples of source documents include checks, sales invoices, receipts, and memorandums. (p. 59)

  3. _____

4. A memorandum is the source document used when items are paid in cash. (p. 61)

  4. _____

5. A receipt is the source document for cash received from transactions other than sales. (p. 61)

  5. _____

6. A calculator tape is the source document for daily cash sales. (p. 61)

  6. _____

7. The accounts affected when cash is received from the owner as an investment are Cash and Sales. (p. 62)

  7. _____

8. When cash is paid for supplies, the Cash account is debited. (p. 63)

  8. _____

9. When cash is used to pay for insurance, the asset account Prepaid Insurance increases. (p. 65)

  9. _____

10. The source document used when supplies are ordered by telephone on account is a memorandum. (p. 66)

  10. _____

11. The source document used when supplies bought on account are paid for is a receipt. (p. 67)

  11. _____

12. When cash is received from sales, both the Cash account and the Sales account are increased. (p. 70)

  12. _____

13. The source document *sales invoice* is abbreviated as S in a journal entry. (p. 71)

  13. _____

14. When services are sold on account, an asset account and a liability account are affected. (p. 71)

  14. _____

15. The accounts affected when paying cash for equipment rental are Equipment Rental Expense and Cash. (p. 72)

  15. _____

16. When cash is received on account, one asset account increases and another asset account decreases. (p. 73)

  16. _____

17. The accounts affected when paying cash to the owner for a withdrawal of equity are the capital account and Cash. (p. 74)

  17. _____

18. If there is only one blank line remaining on a journal page, it is standard practice to split the entry and record the second line of the entry on the next page. (p. 76)

  18. _____

19. To correct an error in a journal, simply erase the incorrect item and write the correct item in the same place. (p. 78)

  19. _____

20. If an error is detected in a journal entry after several additional journal entries have been made, the entry should be corrected by drawing a line through the incorrect parts and writing the correct parts on the same line above the error. (p. 78)

  20. _____

Part Three—Recording Transactions in a General Journal

Directions: Analyze each of the following transactions into debit and credit parts and choose account titles from the list below. Print the letters identifying your choices in the proper Answers columns.

Account Titles

A. Accounts Payable—Casey Company
B. Accounts Receivable— T. Sundeen

C. Advertising Expense
D. Cash
E. David Dumire, Capital
F. David Dumire, Drawing

G. Prepaid Insurance
H. Sales
I. Supplies
J. Utilities Expense

	Answers	
	Debit	**Credit**
1–2. Received cash from owner, David Dumire, as an investment. (p. 62)	1. _____	2. _____
3–4. Paid cash for supplies. (p. 63)	3. _____	4. _____
5–6. Paid cash for insurance. (p. 65)	5. _____	6. _____
7–8. Bought supplies on account from Casey Company. (p. 66)	7. _____	8. _____
9–10. Paid cash on account to Casey Company. (p. 67)	9. _____	10. _____
11–12. Received cash from sales. (p. 70)	11. _____	12. _____
13–14. Sold services on account to T. Sundeen. (p. 71)	13. _____	14. _____
15–16. Paid cash for advertising expense. (p. 72)	15. _____	16. _____
17–18. Received cash on account from T. Sundeen. (p. 73)	17. _____	18. _____
19–20. Paid cash to owner, David Dumire, for a withdrawal of equity. (p. 74)	19. _____	20. _____

Across

3. A form on which a brief message is written to describe a transaction.

4. Recording transactions in a journal.

5. A form describing the goods or services sold, the quantity, the price, and the terms of sale.

7. A business form ordering a bank to pay cash from a bank account.

8. An invoice used as a source document for recording a sale on account. It is also referred to as a sales ticket or a sales slip.

Down

1. A form for recording transactions in chronological order.

2. A business paper from which information is obtained for a journal entry.

6. A business form giving written acknowledgement for cash received.

9. Information for each transaction recorded in a journal.

3-1, 3-2, 3-3, and 3-4　WORK TOGETHER, pp. 64, 69, 75, and 80

3-1 Journalizing entries in a general journal
3-2 Journalizing entries in a general journal
3-3 Journalizing transactions that affect owner's equity in a general journal
3-4 Journalizing transactions and starting a new journal page

GENERAL JOURNAL   PAGE

	DATE	ACCOUNT TITLE	DOC. NO.	POST. REF.	DEBIT	CREDIT	
1							1
2							2
3							3
4							4
5							5
6							6
7							7
8							8
9							9
10							10
11							11
12							12
13							13
14							14
15							15
16							16
17							17
18							18
19							19
20							20
21							21
22							22
23							23
24							24
25							25
26							26
27							27
28							28
29							29
30							30
31							31
32							32
33							33

GENERAL JOURNAL

PAGE

	DATE		ACCOUNT TITLE	DOC. NO.	POST. REF.	DEBIT	CREDIT	
1								1
2								2
3								3
4								4
5								5
6								6
7								7
8								8
9								9
10								10
11								11
12								12
13								13
14								14
15								15
16								16
17								17
18								18
19								19
20								20
21								21
22								22
23								23
24								24
25								25
26								26
27								27
28								28
29								29
30								30
31								31
32								32
33								33

Name _____ Date _____ Class _____

3-1 Journalizing entries in a general journal
3-2 Journalizing entries in a general journal
3-3 Journalizing transactions that affect owner's equity in a general journal
3-4 Journalizing transactions and starting a new journal page

GENERAL JOURNAL

PAGE _____

	DATE	ACCOUNT TITLE	DOC. NO.	POST. REF.	DEBIT	CREDIT	
1							1
2							2
3							3
4							4
5							5
6							6
7							7
8							8
9							9
10							10
11							11
12							12
13							13
14							14
15							15
16							16
17							17
18							18
19							19
20							20
21							21
22							22
23							23
24							24
25							25
26							26
27							27
28							28
29							29
30							30
31							31
32							32
33							33

GENERAL JOURNAL

PAGE

	DATE		ACCOUNT TITLE	DOC. NO.	POST. REF.		DEBIT		CREDIT		
1											1
2											2
3											3
4											4
5											5
6											6
7											7
8											8
9											9
10											10
11											11
12											12
13											13
14											14
15											15
16											16
17											17
18											18
19											19
20											20
21											21
22											22
23											23
24											24
25											25
26											26
27											27
28											28
29											29
30											30
31											31
32											32
33											33

Name _____ Date _____ Class _____

3-1   **Journalizing transactions in a general journal (LO3, 4)**

3-2   **Journalizing buying insurance, buying on account, and paying on account in a general journal (LO3, 4, 5)**

3-3   **Journalizing transactions that affect owner's equity and receiving cash on account in a general journal (LO3, 4, 5, 6, 7)**

3-4.1   **Starting a new journal page (LO3, 4, 5, 6, 7, 8)**

GENERAL JOURNAL   PAGE

	DATE	ACCOUNT TITLE	DOC. NO.	POST. REF.	DEBIT	CREDIT	
1							1
2							2
3							3
4							4
5							5
6							6
7							7
8							8
9							9
10							10
11							11
12							12
13							13
14							14
15							15
16							16
17							17
18							18
19							19
20							20
21							21
22							22
23							23
24							24
25							25
26							26
27							27
28							28
29							29
30							30
31							31
32							32
33							33

GENERAL JOURNAL   PAGE

	DATE	ACCOUNT TITLE	DOC. NO.	POST. REF.	DEBIT	CREDIT	
1							1
2							2
3							3
4							4
5							5
6							6
7							7
8							8
9							9
10							10
11							11
12							12
13							13
14							14
15							15
16							16
17							17
18							18
19							19
20							20
21							21
22							22
23							23
24							24
25							25
26							26
27							27
28							28
29							29
30							30
31							31
32							32
33							33

3-4.2 APPLICATION PROBLEM, p. 85

Journalizing transactions (LO3, 4, 5, 6, 7)

GENERAL JOURNAL   PAGE _____

	DATE	ACCOUNT TITLE	DOC. NO.	POST. REF.	DEBIT	CREDIT	
1							1
2							2
3							3
4							4
5							5
6							6
7							7
8							8
9							9
10							10
11							11
12							12
13							13
14							14
15							15
16							16
17							17
18							18
19							19
20							20
21							21
22							22
23							23
24							24
25							25
26							26
27							27
28							28
29							29
30							30
31							31
32							32
33							33

Journalizing transactions and starting a new journal page (LO3, 4, 5, 6, 7, 8)

GENERAL JOURNAL

PAGE

	DATE		ACCOUNT TITLE	DOC. NO.	POST. REF.	DEBIT	CREDIT	
1								1
2								2
3								3
4								4
5								5
6								6
7								7
8								8
9								9
10								10
11								11
12								12
13								13
14								14
15								15
16								16
17								17
18								18
19								19
20								20
21								21
22								22
23								23
24								24
25								25
26								26
27								27
28								28
29								29
30								30
31								31
32								32
33								33

3-M **MASTERY PROBLEM (concluded)**

GENERAL JOURNAL   PAGE

	DATE	ACCOUNT TITLE	DOC. NO.	POST. REF.	DEBIT	CREDIT	
1							1
2							2
3							3
4							4
5							5
6							6
7							7
8							8
9							9
10							10
11							11
12							12
13							13
14							14
15							15
16							16
17							17
18							18
19							19
20							20
21							21
22							22
23							23
24							24
25							25
26							26
27							27
28							28
29							29
30							30
31							31
32							32
33							33

Journalizing transactions from source documents (LO2, 3, 4, 5, 6, 7)

Receipt No. 1	Receipt No. 1	Form _1_
Date _June 1_ , 20--	Date _June 1_ 20--	
From _Henry White_	Rec'd from _Henry White_	
For _Investment_	For _Investment_	
	Four thousand and no/100 Dollars	
$ 4,000 00	Amount $ 4,000 00	
	Henry White	
	Received by	

No. 1		Form _2_
Date _June 3_	20-- $ _300.00_	
To _Worldwide Supply Company_		
For _Supplies_		
BALANCE BROUGHT FORWARD	0	00
AMOUNT DEPOSITED 6 1 20-- Date	4,000	00
SUBTOTAL	4,000	00
AMOUNT THIS CHECK	300	00
BALANCE CARRIED FORWARD	3,700	00

No. 2		Form _3_
Date _June 5_	20-- $ _600.00_	
To _NW Management Company_		
For _June rent_		
BALANCE BROUGHT FORWARD	3,700	00
AMOUNT DEPOSITED		
SUBTOTAL Date	3,700	00
AMOUNT THIS CHECK	600	00
BALANCE CARRIED FORWARD	3,100	00

No. 1	Form _4_
MEMORANDUM	

_Bought supplies on account from
Atlas Supplies, $300.00_

Signed: _Henry White_   Date: _June 8,_   20--

3-S SOURCE DOCUMENTS PROBLEM (continued)

No. 3   Form _5_
Date _June 9_   20-- $ _80,00_
To _Statewide Electric_

For _Electric bill_

BALANCE BROUGHT FORWARD	3,100	00
AMOUNT DEPOSITED		
SUBTOTAL Date	3,100	00
AMOUNT THIS CHECK	80	00
BALANCE CARRIED FORWARD	3,020	00

No. 4   Form _6_
Date _June 11_   20-- $ _300,00_
To _Atlas Supplies_

For _Payment on account_

BALANCE BROUGHT FORWARD	3,020	00
AMOUNT DEPOSITED		
SUBTOTAL Date	3,020	00
AMOUNT THIS CHECK	300	00
BALANCE CARRIED FORWARD	2,720	00

Form _7_

June 12, 20--
_T12_

```
         0.00*
       100.00+
       500.00+
       600.00*
```

White's Repair Service 11203 Pacific Blvd NW Albany, OR 97321-7726	SALES INVOICE	Form _8_

SOLD TO: J.Puckett
4456 Main Street SW
Albany, OR 97321-4456

No. 1

Date _6/15/--_

Terms _30 days_

DESCRIPTION	Amount
Repair Water Heater	$ 1,100.00
Total	$ 1,100.00

No. 5	Form _9_
Date _June 16_ 20-- $ _300.00_	
To _Oakridge Insurance CO._	
For _Insurance_	

BALANCE BROUGHT FORWARD	2,720	00
AMOUNT DEPOSITED 6 12 20--	600	00
SUBTOTAL	3,320	00
AMOUNT THIS CHECK	300	00
BALANCE CARRIED FORWARD	3,020	00

Form _10_

June 19, 20--
T19

0.00*
300.00
115.00+
285.00+
700.00*

No. 6	Form _11_
Date _June 23_ 20-- $ _50.00_	
To _Sunrise Delivery Co._	
For _Miscellaneous expense_	

BALANCE BROUGHT FORWARD	3,020	00
AMOUNT DEPOSITED 6 19 20--	700	00
SUBTOTAL	3,720	00
AMOUNT THIS CHECK	50	00
BALANCE CARRIED FORWARD	3,670	00

Form _12_

June 26, 20--
T26

0.00*
515.00+
386.00+
901.00*

No. 7	Form _13_
Date _June 29_ 20-- $ _37.00_	
To _Seaside Cleaning Company_	
For _Miscellaneous expense_	

BALANCE BROUGHT FORWARD	3,670	00
AMOUNT DEPOSITED 6 26 20--	901	00
SUBTOTAL	4,571	00
AMOUNT THIS CHECK	37	00
BALANCE CARRIED FORWARD	4,534	00

3-S SOURCE DOCUMENTS PROBLEM (continued)

Receipt No. 2	Receipt No. 2	Form _14_
Date _June 29_, 20--	Date _June 29_ 20--	
From _J. Puckett_	Rec'd from _J. Puckett_	
For _On account_	For _On account_	
	One thousand one hundred and ⁿᵒ/100 _____ Dollars	
	Amount $ 1,100 00	
$ 1,100 00	_Henry White_	
	Received by	

No. 8		Form _15_
Date _June 29_ 20-- $ _110.00_		
To _Salem Telephone CO._		
For _Cell phone bill_		
BALANCE BROUGHT FORWARD	4,534	00
AMOUNT DEPOSITED 6 29 20--	1,100	00
SUBTOTAL ___Date	5,634	00
AMOUNT THIS CHECK	110	00
BALANCE CARRIED FORWARD	5,524	00

No. 9		Form _16_
Date _June 30_ 20-- $ _2,000.00_		
To _Henry White_		
For _Owner withdrawl of equilty_		
BALANCE BROUGHT FORWARD	5,524	00
AMOUNT DEPOSITED		
SUBTOTAL ___Date	5,524	00
AMOUNT THIS CHECK	2,000	00
BALANCE CARRIED FORWARD	3,524	00

	Form _17_
June 30, 20--	0.00*
T30	350.00+
	350.00*

GENERAL JOURNAL

PAGE

	DATE		ACCOUNT TITLE	DOC. NO.	POST. REF.	DEBIT	CREDIT	
1								1
2								2
3								3
4								4
5								5
6								6
7								7
8								8
9								9
10								10
11								11
12								12
13								13
14								14
15								15
16								16
17								17
18								18
19								19
20								20
21								21
22								22
23								23
24								24
25								25
26								26
27								27
28								28
29								29
30								30
31								31
32								32
33								33

3-S **SOURCE DOCUMENTS PROBLEM (concluded)**

GENERAL JOURNAL

PAGE

	DATE	ACCOUNT TITLE	DOC. NO.	POST. REF.	DEBIT	CREDIT	
1							1
2							2
3							3
4							4
5							5
6							6
7							7
8							8
9							9
10							10
11							11
12							12
13							13
14							14
15							15
16							16
17							17
18							18
19							19
20							20
21							21
22							22
23							23
24							24
25							25
26							26
27							27
28							28
29							29
30							30
31							31
32							32
33							33

Journalizing transactions using a variation of the general journal (LO3, 4, 5, 6, 7)

GENERAL JOURNAL   PAGE

	DEBIT	DATE	ACCOUNT TITLE	DOC. NO.	POST. REF.	CREDIT	
1							1
2							2
3							3
4							4
5							5
6							6
7							7
8							8
9							9
10							10
11							11
12							12
13							13
14							14
15							15
16							16
17							17
18							18
19							19
20							20
21							21
22							22
23							23
24							24
25							25
26							26
27							27
28							28
29							29
30							30
31							31
32							32
33							33

Name		Perfect Score	Your Score
	Identifying Accounting Terms	8 Pts.	
	Identifying Accounting Concepts and Practices	21 Pts.	
	Analyzing Posting from a Journal to a General Ledger	16 Pts.	
	Total	45 Pts.	

Part One—Identifying Accounting Terms

Directions: Select the one term in Column I that best fits each definition in Column II. Print the letter identifying your choice in the Answers column.

Column I	**Column II**	**Answers**
A. account number	1. A ledger that contains all accounts needed to prepare financial statements. (p. 94)	1. _____
B. correcting entry	2. The number assigned to an account. (p. 94)	2. _____
C. file maintenance	3. A group of accounts. (p. 94)	3. _____
D. general ledger	4. The procedure for arranging accounts in a general ledger, assigning account numbers, and keeping records current. (p. 95)	4. _____
E. ledger	5. Writing an account title and number on the heading of an account. (p. 96)	5. _____
F. opening an account	6. Transferring information from a journal entry to a ledger account. (p. 98)	6. _____
G. posting	7. Determining that the amount of cash agrees with the balance of the Cash account in the accounting records. (p. 107)	7. _____
H. proving cash	8. An additional journal entry made to correct an incorrect journal entry. (p. 109)	8. _____

Part Two—Identifying Account Concepts and Practices

Directions: Place a *T* for True or an *F* for False in the Answers column to show whether each of the following statements is true or false.

1. Because an account form has columns for the debit and credit balance of an account, it is often referred to as the balance-ruled account form. (p. 93)

   1. _____

2. The asset division accounts for Delgado Web Services are numbered in the 200s. (p. 94)

   2. _____

3. The cash account for Delgado Web Services is the first asset account and is numbered 110. (p. 94)

   3. _____

4. The third division of the chart of accounts for Delgado Web Services is the owner's equity division. (p. 94)

   4. _____

5. The first digit of account numbers for accounts in the owner's equity ledger division is 4. (p. 94)

   5. _____

6. The last two digits in a 3-digit account number indicate the general ledger division of the account. (p. 94)

   6. _____

7. When adding a new expense account between accounts numbered 510 and 520, the new account is assigned the account number 515. (p. 95)

   7. _____

8. Delgado Web Services arranges expense accounts in chronological order in its general ledger. (p. 95)

   8. _____

9. The two steps for opening an account are writing the account title and recording the balance. (p. 96)

   9. _____

10. Each amount in the Debit and Credit columns of a general journal is posted to the account written in the Account Title column. (p. 98)

    10. _____

11. The only reason for the Post. Ref. columns of the journal and general ledger is to indicate which entries in the journal still need to be posted if posting is interrupted. (p. 98)

    11. _____

12. There are five steps in posting an amount from the debit column of a general journal. (p. 98)

    12. _____

13. If a debit is posted to an asset account, the amount of the debit will be subtracted from the previous account balance to determine the new account balance. (p. 98)

    13. _____

14. If a credit is posted to a liability account, the amount of the credit will be subtracted from the previous account balance to determine the new account balance. (p. 99)

    14. _____

15. After a journal has been posted, the Post. Ref. column is completely filled in with account numbers. (p. 102)

    15. _____

16. Errors discovered before entries are posted must be corrected with a correcting entry. (p 109)

    16. _____

17. If an error requires a correcting entry, a memorandum is prepared as the source document describing the correction to be made. (p. 109)

    17. _____

18. If the payment of cash for rent was journalized and posted in error as a debit to Miscellaneous Expense instead of Rent Expense, the correcting entry will include a credit to Cash. (p. 109)

    18. _____

19. If an error in posting is made but not discovered until additional postings have been made to the account, the correct posting should be made on the next available line in the correct account. (p. 110)

    19. _____

20. If an incorrect amount is posted in an account, a line should be drawn through the incorrect amount, the correct amount should be written in above the correction, and the account balance should be recalculated. (p. 111)

    20. _____

21. All corrections for posting errors should be made in a way that leaves no question as to the correct amount. (p. 111)

    21. _____

Part Three—Analyzing Posting from a Journal to a General Ledger

Directions: In the journal below, some items are identified with capital letters. In the general ledger accounts, locations to which items are posted are identified with numbers. For each number in a general ledger account, select the letter in the journal that will be posted to the account. Print the letter identifying your choice in the Answers column.

GENERAL JOURNAL   PAGE **A**

	DATE		ACCOUNT TITLE	DOC. NO.	POST. REF.	DEBIT	CREDIT	
1	Mar.	1	Cash	R1		1 5 0 0 00		1
2			R. Rosen, Capital				1 5 0 0 00	2
3		2	Supplies	M1		1 5 0 00		3
4			Accounts Payable—Casio Office Supplies				1 5 0 00	4
5		4	Prepaid Insurance	C1		7 5 0 00		5
6			Cash				7 5 0 00	6
7	**B**	**C**	**D**	**E**		**F**	**G**	7

ACCOUNT Cash   ACCOUNT NO. 110

DATE	ITEM	POST. REF.	DEBIT	CREDIT	BALANCE DEBIT	BALANCE CREDIT
1 **2**		**3**	**4**			

ACCOUNT Supplies   ACCOUNT NO. 120

DATE	ITEM	POST. REF.	DEBIT	CREDIT	BALANCE DEBIT	BALANCE CREDIT
5 **6**		**7**	**8**			

ACCOUNT Prepaid Insurance   ACCOUNT NO. 130

DATE	ITEM	POST. REF.	DEBIT	CREDIT	BALANCE DEBIT	BALANCE CREDIT
9 **10**		**11**	**12**			

ACCOUNT Accounts Payable—Casio Office Supplies   ACCOUNT NO. 210

DATE	ITEM	POST. REF.	DEBIT	CREDIT	BALANCE DEBIT	BALANCE CREDIT
13 **14**		**15**		**16**		

A through G
(pp. 98–100)

Bold Numbers in Ledger Accounts   **Answers**

1. _____
2. _____
3. _____
4. _____
5. _____
6. _____
7. _____
8. _____
9. _____
10. _____
11. _____
12. _____
13. _____
14. _____
15. _____
16. _____

Across

4. A ledger that contains all accounts needed to prepare financial statements.

5. The term for an additional journal entry when a transaction has been improperly journalized and posted to the ledger.

6. Transferring information from a journal entry to a ledger account.

7. Determining that the amount of cash agrees with the accounting records.

8. The number assigned to an account.

Down

1. A group of accounts.

2. The procedure for arranging accounts in a general ledger, assigning account numbers, and keeping records current.

3. Writing an account title and number on the heading of an account.

4-1 **WORK TOGETHER, p. 97**

Preparing a chart of accounts and opening an account

1.

(blank ruled lines)

2.

(blank ruled lines)

3.

ACCOUNT						ACCOUNT NO.		

DATE	ITEM	POST. REF.	DEBIT	CREDIT	BALANCE	
					DEBIT	CREDIT

Preparing a chart of accounts and opening an account

1.

2.

3.

ACCOUNT _____   ACCOUNT NO. _____

DATE	ITEM	POST. REF.	DEBIT	CREDIT	BALANCE	
					DEBIT	CREDIT

4-2 WORK TOGETHER, p. 108

Posting to a general ledger

GENERAL JOURNAL

PAGE 1

	DATE		ACCOUNT TITLE	DOC. NO.	POST. REF.	DEBIT	CREDIT	
1	Apr.	1	Cash	R1		2 5 0 0 00		1
2			Omar Boje, Capital				2 5 0 0 00	2
3		3	Prepaid Insurance	C1		3 3 0 00		3
4			Cash				3 3 0 00	4
5		4	Supplies	M1		1 6 0 00		5
6			Accounts Payable—Ready Supply				1 6 0 00	6
7		8	Cash	T8		3 2 5 00		7
8			Sales				3 2 5 00	8
9		9	Accounts Receivable—Dan Carroll	S1		1 2 2 00		9
10			Sales				1 2 2 00	10
11		12	Rent Expense	C2		2 6 0 00		11
12			Cash				2 6 0 00	12
13		15	Accounts Payable—Ready Supply	C3		8 0 00		13
14			Cash				8 0 00	14
15		16	Cash	R2		6 5 00		15
16			Accounts Receivable—Dan Carroll				6 5 00	16
17		25	Omar Boje, Drawing	C4		5 0 0 00		17
18			Cash				5 0 0 00	18
19								19
20								20
21								21
22								22
23								23
24								24
25								25
26								26
27								27
28								28
29								29
30								30
31								31
32								32

GENERAL LEDGER

ACCOUNT Cash   ACCOUNT NO. 110

DATE	ITEM	POST. REF.	DEBIT	CREDIT	BALANCE DEBIT	BALANCE CREDIT

ACCOUNT Accounts Receivable—Dan Carroll   ACCOUNT NO. 120

DATE	ITEM	POST. REF.	DEBIT	CREDIT	BALANCE DEBIT	BALANCE CREDIT

ACCOUNT Supplies   ACCOUNT NO. 130

DATE	ITEM	POST. REF.	DEBIT	CREDIT	BALANCE DEBIT	BALANCE CREDIT

ACCOUNT Prepaid Insurance   ACCOUNT NO. 140

DATE	ITEM	POST. REF.	DEBIT	CREDIT	BALANCE DEBIT	BALANCE CREDIT

4-2 WORK TOGETHER (concluded)

GENERAL LEDGER

ACCOUNT Accounts Payable—Ready Supply   ACCOUNT NO. 210

DATE	ITEM	POST. REF.	DEBIT	CREDIT	BALANCE DEBIT	BALANCE CREDIT

ACCOUNT Omar Boje, Capital   ACCOUNT NO. 310

DATE	ITEM	POST. REF.	DEBIT	CREDIT	BALANCE DEBIT	BALANCE CREDIT

ACCOUNT Omar Boje, Drawing   ACCOUNT NO. 320

DATE	ITEM	POST. REF.	DEBIT	CREDIT	BALANCE DEBIT	BALANCE CREDIT

ACCOUNT Sales   ACCOUNT NO. 410

DATE	ITEM	POST. REF.	DEBIT	CREDIT	BALANCE DEBIT	BALANCE CREDIT

ACCOUNT Rent Expense   ACCOUNT NO. 510

DATE	ITEM	POST. REF.	DEBIT	CREDIT	BALANCE DEBIT	BALANCE CREDIT

Posting to a general ledger

GENERAL JOURNAL

PAGE 1

	DATE		ACCOUNT TITLE	DOC. NO.	POST. REF.	DEBIT	CREDIT	
1	20-- Oct.	1	Cash	R1		2 2 5 0 00		1
2			Helen Orr, Capital				2 2 5 0 00	2
3		4	Supplies	M1		1 3 4 00		3
4			Accounts Payable—Stein Company				1 3 4 00	4
5		7	Prepaid Insurance	C1		4 1 0 00		5
6			Cash				4 1 0 00	6
7		10	Accounts Receivable—K. Green	S1		3 6 0 00		7
8			Sales				3 6 0 00	8
9		13	Cash	T13		1 5 0 0 00		9
10			Sales				1 5 0 0 00	10
11		18	Advertising Expense	C2		6 8 00		11
12			Cash				6 8 00	12
13		21	Accounts Payable—Stein Company	C3		8 0 00		13
14			Cash				8 0 00	14
15		27	Cash	R2		2 0 0 00		15
16			Accounts Receivable—K. Green				2 0 0 00	16
17		30	Helen Orr, Drawing	C4		1 0 0 0 00		17
18			Cash				1 0 0 0 00	18
19								19
20								20
21								21
22								22
23								23
24								24
25								25
26								26
27								27
28								28
29								29
30								30
31								31
32								32

4-2 **ON YOUR OWN (continued)**

GENERAL LEDGER

ACCOUNT Cash   ACCOUNT NO. 110

DATE	ITEM	POST. REF.	DEBIT	CREDIT	BALANCE DEBIT	BALANCE CREDIT

ACCOUNT Accounts Receivable—K. Green   ACCOUNT NO. 120

DATE	ITEM	POST. REF.	DEBIT	CREDIT	BALANCE DEBIT	BALANCE CREDIT

ACCOUNT Supplies   ACCOUNT NO. 130

DATE	ITEM	POST. REF.	DEBIT	CREDIT	BALANCE DEBIT	BALANCE CREDIT

ACCOUNT Prepaid Insurance   ACCOUNT NO. 140

DATE	ITEM	POST. REF.	DEBIT	CREDIT	BALANCE DEBIT	BALANCE CREDIT

GENERAL LEDGER

ACCOUNT Accounts Payable—Stein Company   ACCOUNT NO. 210

DATE	ITEM	POST. REF.	DEBIT	CREDIT	BALANCE DEBIT	BALANCE CREDIT

ACCOUNT Helen Orr, Capital   ACCOUNT NO. 310

DATE	ITEM	POST. REF.	DEBIT	CREDIT	BALANCE DEBIT	BALANCE CREDIT

ACCOUNT Helen Orr, Drawing   ACCOUNT NO. 320

DATE	ITEM	POST. REF.	DEBIT	CREDIT	BALANCE DEBIT	BALANCE CREDIT

ACCOUNT Sales   ACCOUNT NO. 410

DATE	ITEM	POST. REF.	DEBIT	CREDIT	BALANCE DEBIT	BALANCE CREDIT

ACCOUNT Advertising Expense   ACCOUNT NO. 510

DATE	ITEM	POST. REF.	DEBIT	CREDIT	BALANCE DEBIT	BALANCE CREDIT

4-3 WORK TOGETHER, p. 113

Journalizing correcting entries and correcting posting errors

1.

GENERAL JOURNAL
PAGE _____

	DATE	ACCOUNT TITLE	DOC. NO.	POST. REF.	DEBIT	CREDIT	
1							1
2							2
3							3
4							4
5							5
6							6
7							7
8							8
9							9
10							10
11							11
12							12
13							13
14							14

2.

ACCOUNT Art Stevenson, Drawing   ACCOUNT NO. 320

DATE		ITEM	POST. REF.	DEBIT	CREDIT	BALANCE DEBIT	BALANCE CREDIT
Nov.	15		G19	4 5 0 00		4 5 0 00	
	30		G20		4 0 0 00	1 5 0 00	

Journalizing correcting entries and correcting posting errors

1.

GENERAL JOURNAL

PAGE

	DATE	ACCOUNT TITLE	DOC. NO.	POST. REF.	DEBIT	CREDIT	
1							1
2							2
3							3
4							4
5							5
6							6
7							7
8							8
9							9
10							10
11							11
12							12
13							13

2.

ACCOUNT Janet Bies, Capital   ACCOUNT NO. 310

DATE		ITEM	POST. REF.	DEBIT	CREDIT	BALANCE DEBIT	BALANCE CREDIT
20-- June	1		G10		2 5 0 0 00		2 5 0 0 00
	15		G10	1 0 0 0 00			1 5 0 0 00

4-1 APPLICATION PROBLEM, p. 116

Preparing a chart of accounts and opening an account (LO1, 2, 3, 4)

1.

_____
_____
_____
_____
_____
_____
_____
_____
_____
_____
_____
_____
_____
_____
_____
_____
_____
_____

2.

_____
_____
_____
_____
_____
_____

3.

ACCOUNT   ACCOUNT NO.

DATE	ITEM	POST. REF.	DEBIT	CREDIT	BALANCE DEBIT	BALANCE CREDIT

ACCOUNT   ACCOUNT NO.

DATE	ITEM	POST. REF.	DEBIT	CREDIT	BALANCE DEBIT	BALANCE CREDIT

Posting from a general journal to a general ledger and proving cash (LO5, 6)

GENERAL JOURNAL   PAGE 1

	DATE		ACCOUNT TITLE	DOC. NO.	POST. REF.	DEBIT	CREDIT	
1	July	1	Cash	R1		4 000 00		1
2			Jing Suen, Capital				4 000 00	2
3		8	Prepaid Insurance	C1		6 00 00		3
4			Cash				6 00 00	4
5		10	Supplies	M1		1 80 00		5
6			Accounts Payable—Bayou Supply				1 80 00	6
7		12	Cash	T12		9 64 00		7
8			Sales				9 64 00	8
9		15	Accounts Receivable—M. Kadam	S1		1 50 00		9
10			Sales				1 50 00	10
11		19	Advertising Expense	C2		2 25 00		11
12			Cash				2 25 00	12
13		20	Accounts Payable—Bayou Supply	C3		1 20 00		13
14			Cash				1 20 00	14
15		27	Cash	R2		1 00 00		15
16			Accounts Receivable—M. Kadam				1 00 00	16
17		31	Jing Suen, Drawing	C4		8 00 00		17
18			Cash				8 00 00	18

4-2 **APPLICATION PROBLEM (continued)**

GENERAL LEDGER

ACCOUNT Cash   ACCOUNT NO. 110

DATE	ITEM	POST. REF.	DEBIT	CREDIT	BALANCE DEBIT	BALANCE CREDIT

ACCOUNT Accounts Receivable—M. Kadam   ACCOUNT NO. 120

DATE	ITEM	POST. REF.	DEBIT	CREDIT	BALANCE DEBIT	BALANCE CREDIT

ACCOUNT Supplies   ACCOUNT NO. 130

DATE	ITEM	POST. REF.	DEBIT	CREDIT	BALANCE DEBIT	BALANCE CREDIT

ACCOUNT Prepaid Insurance   ACCOUNT NO. 140

DATE	ITEM	POST. REF.	DEBIT	CREDIT	BALANCE DEBIT	BALANCE CREDIT

GENERAL LEDGER

ACCOUNT Accounts Payable—Bayou Supply   ACCOUNT NO. 210

DATE	ITEM	POST. REF.	DEBIT	CREDIT	BALANCE DEBIT	BALANCE CREDIT

ACCOUNT Jing Suen, Capital   ACCOUNT NO. 310

DATE	ITEM	POST. REF.	DEBIT	CREDIT	BALANCE DEBIT	BALANCE CREDIT

ACCOUNT Jing Suen, Drawing   ACCOUNT NO. 320

DATE	ITEM	POST. REF.	DEBIT	CREDIT	BALANCE DEBIT	BALANCE CREDIT

ACCOUNT Sales   ACCOUNT NO. 410

DATE	ITEM	POST. REF.	DEBIT	CREDIT	BALANCE DEBIT	BALANCE CREDIT

ACCOUNT Advertising Expense   ACCOUNT NO. 510

DATE	ITEM	POST. REF.	DEBIT	CREDIT	BALANCE DEBIT	BALANCE CREDIT

4-3 APPLICATION PROBLEM, p. 116

Journalizing correcting entries and correcting posting errors (LO7, 8)

1.

GENERAL JOURNAL   PAGE _____

	DATE	ACCOUNT TITLE	DOC. NO.	POST. REF.	DEBIT	CREDIT	
1							1
2							2
3							3
4							4
5							5
6							6
7							7
8							8
9							9
10							10
11							11
12							12
13							13
14							14

2.

ACCOUNT Supplies   ACCOUNT NO. 130

DATE	ITEM	POST. REF.	DEBIT	CREDIT	BALANCE DEBIT	BALANCE CREDIT
July 6		G13	2 6 0 00		2 6 0 00	
30		G14		1 4 0 00	1 2 0 00	

Journalizing transactions and posting to a general ledger (LO3, 4, 5)

GENERAL JOURNAL

PAGE

	DATE	ACCOUNT TITLE	DOC. NO.	POST. REF.	DEBIT	CREDIT	
1							1
2							2
3							3
4							4
5							5
6							6
7							7
8							8
9							9
10							10
11							11
12							12
13							13
14							14
15							15
16							16
17							17
18							18
19							19
20							20
21							21
22							22
23							23
24							24
25							25
26							26
27							27
28							28
29							29
30							30
31							31
32							32
33							33
34							34

4-M **MASTERY PROBLEM (continued)**

GENERAL LEDGER

ACCOUNT Cash   ACCOUNT NO. 110

DATE	ITEM	POST. REF.	DEBIT	CREDIT	BALANCE DEBIT	BALANCE CREDIT

ACCOUNT Accounts Receivable—Clara Walthers   ACCOUNT NO. 120

DATE	ITEM	POST. REF.	DEBIT	CREDIT	BALANCE DEBIT	BALANCE CREDIT

ACCOUNT Supplies   ACCOUNT NO. 130

DATE	ITEM	POST. REF.	DEBIT	CREDIT	BALANCE DEBIT	BALANCE CREDIT

GENERAL LEDGER

ACCOUNT Accounts Payable—Corner Supplies   ACCOUNT NO. 210

DATE	ITEM	POST. REF.	DEBIT	CREDIT	BALANCE DEBIT	BALANCE CREDIT

ACCOUNT Brian Ford, Capital   ACCOUNT NO. 310

DATE	ITEM	POST. REF.	DEBIT	CREDIT	BALANCE DEBIT	BALANCE CREDIT

ACCOUNT Brian Ford, Drawing   ACCOUNT NO. 320

DATE	ITEM	POST. REF.	DEBIT	CREDIT	BALANCE DEBIT	BALANCE CREDIT

ACCOUNT Sales   ACCOUNT NO. 410

DATE	ITEM	POST. REF.	DEBIT	CREDIT	BALANCE DEBIT	BALANCE CREDIT

4-M MASTERY PROBLEM (concluded)

GENERAL LEDGER

ACCOUNT Advertising Expense   ACCOUNT NO. 510

DATE	ITEM	POST. REF.	DEBIT	CREDIT	BALANCE DEBIT	BALANCE CREDIT

ACCOUNT Miscellaneous Expense   ACCOUNT NO. 520

DATE	ITEM	POST. REF.	DEBIT	CREDIT	BALANCE DEBIT	BALANCE CREDIT

ACCOUNT Rent Expense   ACCOUNT NO. 530

DATE	ITEM	POST. REF.	DEBIT	CREDIT	BALANCE DEBIT	BALANCE CREDIT

ACCOUNT   ACCOUNT NO.

DATE	ITEM	POST. REF.	DEBIT	CREDIT	BALANCE DEBIT	BALANCE CREDIT

Journalizing transactions and posting to a general ledger (LO5, 6)

Receipt No. 1	Receipt No. 1	Form __1__
Date _Sept. 2_ , 20--	Date _September 2_ 20--	
From _Darlene Steffens_	Rec'd from _Darlene Steffens_	
For _Investment_	For _Investment_	
	Thirty-five hundred and no/100 Dollars	
$ 3,500 00	Amount $ 3,500 00	
	Darlene Steffens	
	Received by	

No. 1		Form __2__
Date _Sept. 3_ 20-- $ _500.00_		
To _Ready Rental Agency_		
For _September rent_		
BALANCE BROUGHT FORWARD	0	00
AMOUNT DEPOSITED 9 2 20--	3,500	00
SUBTOTAL	3,500	00
AMOUNT THIS CHECK	500	00
BALANCE CARRIED FORWARD	3,000	00

No. 1	Form __3__
MEMORANDUM	

Bought supplies on account from Atlas Supplies, $650.00

Signed: _Darlene Steffens_   Date: _September 6, 20--_

4-S SOURCE DOCUMENTS PROBLEM (continued)

No. 2   Form _4_
Date _Sept. 7_   20-- $ _60.00_
To _Connect Telephone Company_

For _Telephone bill_

BALANCE BROUGHT FORWARD	3,000	00
AMOUNT DEPOSITED		
SUBTOTAL ᴰᵃᵗᵉ	3,000	00
AMOUNT THIS CHECK	60	00
BALANCE CARRIED FORWARD	2,940	00

Form _5_
0.00*

Sept. 7, 20--
_T1_

100.00+
300.00+
400.00*

Darlene's Music Studio   Form _6_
2356 Pacific Blvd. S.
Albany, OR 97321-7726

SOLD TO: _K. Hrbek_   No. 1
         3088 Pine Street
         Albany, OR 97321-4456   Date **9/10/--**
                                    Terms **30 days**

DESCRIPTION	Amount
Guitar lessons	$ **325.00**
Total	$ **325.00**

No. 3   Form _7_
Date _Sept. 11_   20-- $ _490.00_
To _Arneson Insurance Agency_

For _Insurance_

BALANCE BROUGHT FORWARD		2,940	00
AMOUNT DEPOSITED	9 7 20--	400	00
SUBTOTAL ᴰᵃᵗᵉ		3,340	00
AMOUNT THIS CHECK		490	00
BALANCE CARRIED FORWARD		2,850	00

Form _8_
0.00*

Sept. 14, 20--
_T14_

175.00+
375.00+
550.00*

No. 4   Form _9_
Date _Sept. 16_   20-- $ _163.00_
To _Sun Newspaper_

For _Advertising_

BALANCE BROUGHT FORWARD	2,850	00
AMOUNT DEPOSITED 9 14 20--	550	00
SUBTOTAL	3,400	00
AMOUNT THIS CHECK	163	00
BALANCE CARRIED FORWARD	3,237	00

Form _10_

    0.00*

Sept. 21, 20--
_T 21_

   215.00+
   210.00+
   425.00*

No. 5   Form _11_
Date _Sept. 23_   20-- $ _500.00_
To _Atlas Supplies_

For _On account_

BALANCE BROUGHT FORWARD	3,237	00
AMOUNT DEPOSITED 9 21 20--	425	00
SUBTOTAL	3,662	00
AMOUNT THIS CHECK	500	00
BALANCE CARRIED FORWARD	3,162	00

Receipt No. 2
Date _Sept. 24_ , 20--
From _K. Hrbek_
For _On account_

$ 213 | 00

Receipt No. 2   Form _12_
Date _September 24_   20--
Rec'd from _K. Hrbek_
For _On account_
Two hundred thirteen and no/100 Dollars
Amount $ 213 | 00
CHF
Received by

4-S SOURCE DOCUMENTS PROBLEM (continued)

No. 6   Form _13_
Date _Sept. 26_   20-- $ _300.00_
To _Atlas Supplies_

For _Supplies_

BALANCE BROUGHT FORWARD	3,162	00
AMOUNT DEPOSITED 9 24 20--	213	00
SUBTOTAL	3,375	00
AMOUNT THIS CHECK	300	00
BALANCE CARRIED FORWARD	3,075	00

Form _14_

0.00*

Sept. 28, 20--
_T 28_

250.00+

250.00*

No. 7   Form _15_
Date _Sept. 29_   20-- $ _55.00_
To _City Electric_

For _Electric bill_

BALANCE BROUGHT FORWARD	3,075	00
AMOUNT DEPOSITED 9 28 20--	250	00
SUBTOTAL	3,325	00
AMOUNT THIS CHECK	55	00
BALANCE CARRIED FORWARD	3,270	00

Darlene's Music Studio
2356 Pacific Blvd. S.
Albany, OR 97321-7726

SOLD TO: _K. Hrbek_
     3088 Pine Street
     Albany, OR 97321-4456

Form _16_

No. 2

Date _9/29/--_
Terms _30 days_

DESCRIPTION	Amount	
Guitar lessons	$	**240.00**
Total	$	**240.00**

Form _17_

0.00*

Sept. 30, 20--
T 30

125.00+
225.00+
350.00*

No. 8			Form _18_
Date _Sept. 30_ 20-- $ _500.00_			
To _Darlene Steffens_			
For _Withdrawal of equity_			
BALANCE BROUGHT FORWARD		3,270	00
AMOUNT DEPOSITED 9 30 20--		350	00
SUBTOTAL	Date	3,620	00
AMOUNT THIS CHECK		500	00
BALANCE CARRIED FORWARD		3,120	00

No. 9			Form _19_
Date _____ 20-- $ _____			
To _____			
For _____			
BALANCE BROUGHT FORWARD		3,120	00
AMOUNT DEPOSITED			
SUBTOTAL	Date		
AMOUNT THIS CHECK			
BALANCE CARRIED FORWARD			

4-S SOURCE DOCUMENTS PROBLEM (continued)

GENERAL JOURNAL

PAGE _____

	DATE	ACCOUNT TITLE	DOC. NO.	POST. REF.	DEBIT	CREDIT	
1							1
2							2
3							3
4							4
5							5
6							6
7							7
8							8
9							9
10							10
11							11
12							12
13							13
14							14
15							15
16							16
17							17
18							18
19							19
20							20
21							21
22							22
23							23
24							24
25							25
26							26
27							27
28							28
29							29
30							30
31							31
32							32
33							33

GENERAL JOURNAL

PAGE

	DATE		ACCOUNT TITLE	DOC. NO.	POST. REF.	DEBIT	CREDIT	
1								1
2								2
3								3
4								4
5								5
6								6
7								7
8								8
9								9
10								10
11								11
12								12
13								13
14								14
15								15
16								16
17								17
18								18
19								19
20								20
21								21
22								22
23								23
24								24
25								25
26								26
27								27
28								28
29								29
30								30
31								31
32								32
33								33

4-S SOURCE DOCUMENTS PROBLEM (continued)

GENERAL LEDGER

ACCOUNT Cash   ACCOUNT NO. 110

DATE	ITEM	POST. REF.	DEBIT	CREDIT	BALANCE DEBIT	BALANCE CREDIT

ACCOUNT Accounts Receivable—K. Hrbek   ACCOUNT NO. 120

DATE	ITEM	POST. REF.	DEBIT	CREDIT	BALANCE DEBIT	BALANCE CREDIT

ACCOUNT Supplies   ACCOUNT NO. 130

DATE	ITEM	POST. REF.	DEBIT	CREDIT	BALANCE DEBIT	BALANCE CREDIT

GENERAL LEDGER

ACCOUNT Prepaid Insurance   ACCOUNT NO. 140

DATE	ITEM	POST. REF.	DEBIT	CREDIT	BALANCE DEBIT	BALANCE CREDIT

ACCOUNT Accounts Payable—Atlas Supplies   ACCOUNT NO. 210

DATE	ITEM	POST. REF.	DEBIT	CREDIT	BALANCE DEBIT	BALANCE CREDIT

ACCOUNT Darlene Steffens, Capital   ACCOUNT NO. 310

DATE	ITEM	POST. REF.	DEBIT	CREDIT	BALANCE DEBIT	BALANCE CREDIT

ACCOUNT Darlene Steffens, Drawing   ACCOUNT NO. 320

DATE	ITEM	POST. REF.	DEBIT	CREDIT	BALANCE DEBIT	BALANCE CREDIT

4-S SOURCE DOCUMENTS PROBLEM (concluded)

GENERAL LEDGER

ACCOUNT Sales   ACCOUNT NO. 410

DATE	ITEM	POST. REF.	DEBIT	CREDIT	BALANCE DEBIT	BALANCE CREDIT

ACCOUNT Advertising Expense   ACCOUNT NO. 510

DATE	ITEM	POST. REF.	DEBIT	CREDIT	BALANCE DEBIT	BALANCE CREDIT

ACCOUNT Rent Expense   ACCOUNT NO. 520

DATE	ITEM	POST. REF.	DEBIT	CREDIT	BALANCE DEBIT	BALANCE CREDIT

ACCOUNT Utilities Expense   ACCOUNT NO. 530

DATE	ITEM	POST. REF.	DEBIT	CREDIT	BALANCE DEBIT	BALANCE CREDIT

Posting using a variation of the general journal (LO5, 6)

GENERAL JOURNAL　　　　　　　　　PAGE 5

	DEBIT				DATE		ACCOUNT TITLE	DOC. NO.	POST. REF.	CREDIT				
1	6 0 0 0 00				May	1	Cash	R1						1
2							Lian Liu, Capital			6 0 0 0 00				2
3	4 2 5 00					3	Rent Expense	C1						3
4							Cash			4 2 5 00				4
5	1 0 00					5	Miscellaneous Expense	C2						5
6							Cash			1 0 00				6
7	5 0 0 00					9	Accounts Receivable—Janna Spear	S1						7
8							Sales			5 0 0 00				8
9	8 0 0 00					11	Supplies	C3						9
10							Cash			8 0 0 00				10
11	9 0 0 00					13	Cash	T13						11
12							Sales			9 0 0 00				12
13	4 0 0 00					16	Supplies	M1						13
14							Accounts Payable—Dollar Smart			4 0 0 00				14
15	3 0 0 00					18	Accounts Payable—Dollar Smart	C4						15
16							Cash			3 0 0 00				16
17	1 2 0 00					19	Utilities Expense	C5						17
18							Cash			1 2 0 00				18
19	2 2 0 0 00					20	Cash	T20						19
20							Sales			2 2 0 0 00				20
21	1 0 0 00					23	Advertising Expense	C6						21
22							Cash			1 0 0 00				22
23	3 0 0 00					23	Supplies	C7						23
24							Cash			3 0 0 00				24
25	2 0 0 00					27	Supplies	C8						25
26							Cash			2 0 0 00				26
27	3 6 6 0 00					27	Cash	T27						27
28							Sales			3 6 6 0 00				28
29	2 8 0 0 00					30	Lian Liu, Drawing	C9						29
30							Cash			2 8 0 0 00				30
31	8 2 0 00					31	Cash	T31						31
32							Sales			8 2 0 00				32

4-C CHALLENGE PROBLEM (continued)

GENERAL LEDGER

ACCOUNT Cash   ACCOUNT NO. 110

DATE	ITEM	POST. REF.	DEBIT	CREDIT	BALANCE DEBIT	BALANCE CREDIT

ACCOUNT Accounts Receivable—Janna Spear   ACCOUNT NO. 120

DATE	ITEM	POST. REF.	DEBIT	CREDIT	BALANCE DEBIT	BALANCE CREDIT

ACCOUNT Supplies   ACCOUNT NO. 130

DATE	ITEM	POST. REF.	DEBIT	CREDIT	BALANCE DEBIT	BALANCE CREDIT

ACCOUNT Accounts Payable—Dollar Smart   ACCOUNT NO. 210

DATE	ITEM	POST. REF.	DEBIT	CREDIT	BALANCE DEBIT	BALANCE CREDIT

ACCOUNT Lian Liu, Capital   ACCOUNT NO. 310

DATE	ITEM	POST. REF.	DEBIT	CREDIT	BALANCE DEBIT	BALANCE CREDIT

GENERAL LEDGER

ACCOUNT Lian Liu, Drawing   ACCOUNT NO. 320

DATE	ITEM	POST. REF.	DEBIT	CREDIT	BALANCE DEBIT	BALANCE CREDIT

ACCOUNT Sales   ACCOUNT NO. 410

DATE	ITEM	POST. REF.	DEBIT	CREDIT	BALANCE DEBIT	BALANCE CREDIT

ACCOUNT Advertising Expense   ACCOUNT NO. 510

DATE	ITEM	POST. REF.	DEBIT	CREDIT	BALANCE DEBIT	BALANCE CREDIT

ACCOUNT Miscellaneous Expense   ACCOUNT NO. 520

DATE	ITEM	POST. REF.	DEBIT	CREDIT	BALANCE DEBIT	BALANCE CREDIT

ACCOUNT Rent Expense   ACCOUNT NO. 530

DATE	ITEM	POST. REF.	DEBIT	CREDIT	BALANCE DEBIT	BALANCE CREDIT

ACCOUNT Utilities Expense   ACCOUNT NO. 540

DATE	ITEM	POST. REF.	DEBIT	CREDIT	BALANCE DEBIT	BALANCE CREDIT

Study Guide 5

Name	Perfect Score	Your Score
Identifying Accounting Terms	18 Pts.	
Analyzing Transactions in a Cash Control System	12 Pts.	
Identifying Accounting Concepts and Practices	20 Pts.	
Total	50 Pts.	

Part One—Identifying Accounting Terms

Directions: Select the one term in Column I that best fits each definition in Column II. Print the letter identifying your choice in the Answers column.

Column I	Column II	Answers
A. bank statement	1. A bank account from which payments can be ordered by a depositor. (p. 123)	1. _____
B. blank endorsement	2. A bank form which lists the checks, currency, and coins an account holder is adding to the bank account. (p. 123)	2. _____
C. canceled check	3. A signature or stamp on the back of a check, transferring ownership. (p. 124)	3. _____
D. cash over	4. An endorsement consisting only of the endorser's signature. (p. 124)	4. _____
E. cash short	5. An endorsement indicating a new owner of a check. (p. 124)	5. _____
F. checking account	6. An endorsement restricting further transfer of a check's ownership. (p. 125)	6. _____
G. debit card	7. A check with a future date on it. (p. 126)	7. _____
H. deposit slip	8. A check that cannot be processed because the maker has made it invalid. (p. 127)	8. _____
I. dishonored check	9. A report of deposits, withdrawals, and bank balances sent to a depositor by a bank. (p. 129)	9. _____
J. electronic funds transfer	10. A check which has been paid by the bank. (p. 129)	10. _____
K. endorsement	11. A check that a bank refuses to pay. (p. 135)	11. _____
L. NSF check	12. A check dishonored by the bank because of insufficient funds in the account of the maker of the check. (p. 135)	12. _____
M. petty cash	13. A computerized cash payments system that transfers funds without the use of checks, currency, or other paper documents. (p. 137)	13. _____
N. petty cash slip	14. A bank card that automatically deducts the amount of a purchase from the checking account of the cardholder. (p. 138)	14. _____
O. postdated check	15. An amount of cash kept on hand and used for making small payments. (p. 140)	15. _____
P. restrictive endorsement	16. A form showing proof of a petty cash payment. (p. 141)	16. _____
Q. special endorsement	17. A petty cash on hand amount that is less than a recorded amount. (p. 143)	17. _____
R. voided check	18. A petty cash on hand amount that is more than a recorded amount. (p. 143)	18. _____

Part Two—Analyzing Transactions in a Cash Control System

Directions: Analyze each of the following transactions into debit and credit parts. Print the letter identifying your choice in the proper Answers columns.

Account Titles

A. Cash
B. Petty Cash
C. Accounts Receivable—
   J. Erlandson

D. Supplies
E. Accounts Payable—Fargo
   Supplies

F. Cash Short and Over
G. Miscellaneous Expense

		Answers	
		Debit	**Credit**
1–2.	Received bank statement showing bank service charge. (p. 133)	1. _____	2. _____
3–4.	Received notice from the bank of a dishonored check from J. Erlandson. (p. 136)	3. _____	4. _____
5–6.	Paid cash on account to Fargo Supplies using EFT. (p. 137)	5. _____	6. _____
7–8.	Purchased supplies using a debit card. (p. 138)	7. _____	8. _____
9–10.	Paid cash to establish a petty cash fund. (p. 140)	9. _____	10. _____
11–12.	Paid cash to replenish a petty cash fund: $50.00; supplies, $35.00; miscellaneous expense, $14.00; cash short, $1.00. (p. 144)	11. _____	12. _____

Part Three—Identifying Accounting Concepts and Practices

Directions: Place a *T* for True or *F* for False in the Answers column to show whether each of the following statements is true or false.

Answers

1. Because cash transactions occur more frequently than other transactions, there is more chance for making recording errors affecting cash. (p. 122)

1. _____

2. When a deposit is made in a bank account, the bank issues a check. (p. 123)

2. _____

3. There are three types of endorsements commonly used: blank, special, and restrictive. (p. 124)

3. _____

4. A check with a blank endorsement can be cashed by anyone who has possession of the check. (p. 124)

4. _____

5. When writing a check, the first step is to prepare the check. (p. 126)

5. _____

6. Most banks do not look at the date the check is written and will withdraw money from the depositor's account anytime. (p. 126)

6. _____

7. The amount of a check is written twice on each check. (p. 126)

7. _____

8. A check that contains minor errors can be corrected neatly and initialed. (p. 127)

8. _____

9. An important aspect of cash control is verifying that the information on a bank statement and a checkbook are in agreement. (p. 130)

9. _____

10. An outstanding check is one that has not yet been issued. (p. 130)

10. _____

11. Banks deduct service charges from customers' checking accounts without requiring customers to write a check for the amount. (p. 132)

11. _____

12. Not only do banks charge a fee for handling a dishonored check, but they also deduct the amount of the check from the account as well. (p. 135)

12. _____

13. The journal entry for a payment on account using electronic funds transfer is exactly the same as when the payment is made by debit card. (p. 137)

13. _____

14. The source document for an electronic funds transfer is a check number. (p. 137)

14. _____

15. The source document for a debit card purchase is a memorandum. (p. 138)

15. _____

16. The purpose of a petty cash fund is to make small cash payments without writing checks. (p. 140)

16. _____

17. Businesses use petty cash when writing a check is not time or cost effective. (p. 140)

17. _____

18. A petty cash report is completed at the end of each business day. (p. 143)

18. _____

19. A memorandum is the source document for the entry to record replenishing the petty cash fund. (p. 144)

19. _____

20. When the petty cash fund is replenished, the balance of the petty cash account increases. (p. 145)

20. _____

Across

1. A report of deposits, withdrawals, and bank balances sent to a depositor by a bank.

4. A bank card that automatically deducts the amount of a purchase from the checking account of the cardholder.

7. A petty cash on hand amount that is less than the recorded amount.

10. A check that cannot be processed because the maker has made it invalid.

12. A check with a future date on it.

14. A petty cash on hand amount that is more than the recorded amount.

15. A bank account from which payments can be ordered by a depositor.

Down

2. A signature or stamp on the back of a check transferring ownership.

3. A form showing proof of a petty cash payment.

5. An accounting worker who processes routine details about accounting transactions.

6. A bank form which lists the checks, currency, and coins an account holder is adding to a bank account.

8. An endorsement indicating a new owner of a check.

9. An endorsement consisting only of the endorser's signature.

11. A check that a bank refuses to pay.

12. An amount of cash kept on hand and used for making small payments.

13. A check which has been paid by the bank.

5-1 WORK TOGETHER, p. 128

Endorsing and writing checks

1. a.

```
ENDORSE HERE
X

_____

_____

_____

DO NOT WRITE, STAMP, OR SIGN BELOW THIS LINE
RESERVED FOR FINANCIAL INSTITUTION USE
```

b.

```
ENDORSE HERE
X

_____

_____

_____

DO NOT WRITE, STAMP, OR SIGN BELOW THIS LINE
RESERVED FOR FINANCIAL INSTITUTION USE
```

c.

```
ENDORSE HERE
X

_____

_____

_____

DO NOT WRITE, STAMP, OR SIGN BELOW THIS LINE
RESERVED FOR FINANCIAL INSTITUTION USE
```

2., 3., 4a.

NO. **151** $ _____	
Date: _____ 20 __	**GRANTSBURG ACCOUNTING** NO. **151** 93-552/920
To: _____	1198 Rose Lane
For: _____	New Brighton, MN 55112
	_____ 20 _____
	PAY TO THE
	ORDER OF _____ $ _____
BALANCE BROUGHT FORWARD	
AMOUNT DEPOSITED	_____ DOLLARS
SUBTOTAL Date	
OTHER:	**Northstar Federal Bank**
_____	Minneapolis, MN
_____	FOR _____ _____
SUBTOTAL	
AMOUNT THIS CHECK	⑈09200552⑈: 7079666312781⑈ 151
BALANCE CARRIED FORWARD	

4b.

NO. **152** $ _____	
Date: _____ 20 __	**GRANTSBURG ACCOUNTING** NO. **152** 93-552/920
To: _____	1198 Rose Lane
For: _____	New Brighton, MN 55112
	_____ 20 _____
	PAY TO THE
	ORDER OF _____ $ _____
BALANCE BROUGHT FORWARD	
AMOUNT DEPOSITED	_____ DOLLARS
SUBTOTAL Date	
OTHER:	**Northstar Federal Bank**
_____	Minneapolis, MN
_____	FOR _____ _____
SUBTOTAL	
AMOUNT THIS CHECK	⑈09200552⑈: 7079666312781⑈ 152
BALANCE CARRIED FORWARD	

Endorsing and writing checks

1. a.

ENDORSE HERE
X
DO NOT WRITE, STAMP, OR SIGN BELOW THIS LINE
RESERVED FOR FINANCIAL INSTITUTION USE

b.

ENDORSE HERE
X
DO NOT WRITE, STAMP, OR SIGN BELOW THIS LINE
RESERVED FOR FINANCIAL INSTITUTION USE

2., 3., 4a.

NO. **317** $ _____
Date: _____ 20__
To: _____
For: _____

BALANCE BROUGHT FORWARD		
AMOUNT DEPOSITED		
SUBTOTAL	Date	
OTHER:		
SUBTOTAL		
AMOUNT THIS CHECK		
BALANCE CARRIED FORWARD		

MILLTOWN HAIR CARE   NO. **317**   93-109/730
7921 Main Street
Milltown, WI 54825   _____ 20 _____
PAY TO THE
ORDER OF _____ $ _____
_____ DOLLARS

Wisconsin National Bank
Milltown, WI 54825

FOR _____   _____

⑆073008219⑆ 60796451127811⁰ 317

4b.

NO. **318** $ _____
Date: _____ 20__
To: _____
For: _____

BALANCE BROUGHT FORWARD		
AMOUNT DEPOSITED		
SUBTOTAL	Date	
OTHER:		
SUBTOTAL		
AMOUNT THIS CHECK		
BALANCE CARRIED FORWARD		

MILLTOWN HAIR CARE   NO. **318**   93-109/730
7921 Main Street
Milltown, WI 54825   _____ 20 _____
PAY TO THE
ORDER OF _____ $ _____
_____ DOLLARS

Wisconsin National Bank
Milltown, WI 54825

FOR _____   _____

⑆073008219⑆ 60796451127811⁰ 318

5-2 WORK TOGETHER, p. 134

Reconciling a bank statement and recording a bank service charge

1.

RECONCILIATION OF BANK STATEMENT

_____
(Date)

Balance On Check Stub No. ____ .... $ |

DEDUCT BANK CHARGES:

Description	Amount
	$

Total bank charges ▶

Adjusted Check Stub Balance .... $ |

Balance On Bank Statement .... $ |

ADD OUTSTANDING DEPOSITS:

Date	Amount
	$

Total outstanding deposits ▶

SUBTOTAL .... $ |

DEDUCT OUTSTANDING CHECKS:

Ck. No.	Amount	Ck. No.	Amount

Total outstanding checks ▶

Adjusted Bank Balance .... $ |

2.

NO. **309** $ _____

Date: _____ 20 __

To: _____

For: _____

_____

BALANCE BROUGHT FORWARD		
AMOUNT DEPOSITED	Date	
SUBTOTAL		
OTHER:		
_____		
_____		
SUBTOTAL		
AMOUNT THIS CHECK		
BALANCE CARRIED FORWARD		

3.

GENERAL JOURNAL

PAGE ____

	DATE	ACCOUNT TITLE	DOC. NO.	POST. REF.	DEBIT	CREDIT	
1							1
2							2
3							3

Reconciling a bank statement and recording a bank service charge

1.

RECONCILIATION OF BANK STATEMENT

_____
(Date)

Balance On Check Stub No. ___ . . . . $ _____

DEDUCT BANK CHARGES:

Description	Amount	
	$	

Total bank charges ▶

Balance On Bank Statement . . . . $ _____

ADD OUTSTANDING DEPOSITS:

Date	Amount	
	$	

Total outstanding deposits ▶

SUBTOTAL . . . . $ _____

DEDUCT OUTSTANDING CHECKS:

Ck. No.	Amount	Ck. No.	Amount

Total outstanding checks ▶

Adjusted Check Stub Balance . . . . $ _____

Adjusted Bank Balance . . . . $ _____

2.

NO. **224**	$ _____

Date: _____ 20 __

To: _____

For: _____

BALANCE BROUGHT FORWARD		
AMOUNT DEPOSITED		
SUBTOTAL	Date	
OTHER:		
_____		
_____		
SUBTOTAL		
AMOUNT THIS CHECK		
BALANCE CARRIED FORWARD		

3.

GENERAL JOURNAL   PAGE

	DATE	ACCOUNT TITLE	DOC. NO.	POST. REF.	DEBIT	CREDIT	
1							1
2							2
3							3

5-3 WORK TOGETHER, p. 139

Recording dishonored checks, electronic funds transfers, and debit card purchases

GENERAL JOURNAL

PAGE _____

	DATE		ACCOUNT TITLE	DOC. NO.	POST. REF.	DEBIT	CREDIT	
1								1
2								2
3								3
4								4
5								5
6								6
7								7

Recording dishonored checks, electronic funds transfers, and debit card purchases

GENERAL JOURNAL   PAGE

	DATE	ACCOUNT TITLE	DOC. NO.	POST. REF.	DEBIT	CREDIT	
1							1
2							2
3							3
4							4
5							5
6							6
7							7

5-4 WORK TOGETHER, p. 146

Establishing and replenishing a petty cash fund

1.

PETTY CASH REPORT			
Date: _____		Custodian: _____	
	Explanation	Reconciliation	Replenish Amount
Fund Total Payments: _____			
_____			
_____			
Less:	Total payments	→	
Equals:	Recorded amount on hand	_____	
Less:	Actual amount on hand	_____	
Equals:	Cash short (over)	→	
Amount to Replenish			

2.

GENERAL JOURNAL   PAGE

	DATE	ACCOUNT TITLE	DOC. NO.	POST. REF.	DEBIT	CREDIT	
1							1
2							2
29							29
30							30
31							31
32							32

Establishing and replenishing a petty cash fund

1.

PETTY CASH REPORT			
Date: _____		Custodian: _____	
	Explanation	Reconciliation	Replenish Amount
Fund Total Payments: _____ _____ _____			
Less:	Total payments	→	
Equals:	Recorded amount on hand		
Less:	Actual amount on hand		
Equals:	Cash short (over)	→	
Amount to Replenish			

2.

GENERAL JOURNAL

PAGE

	DATE	ACCOUNT TITLE	DOC. NO.	POST. REF.	DEBIT	CREDIT	
1							1
2							2
29							29
30							30
31							31
32							32

5-1 APPLICATION PROBLEM, p. 149

Endorsing and writing checks (LO1, 2, 3)

1. a.

```
ENDORSE HERE

X

_____

_____

_____

DO NOT WRITE, STAMP, OR SIGN BELOW THIS LINE
RESERVED FOR FINANCIAL INSTITUTION USE
```

b.

```
ENDORSE HERE

X

_____

_____

_____

DO NOT WRITE, STAMP, OR SIGN BELOW THIS LINE
RESERVED FOR FINANCIAL INSTITUTION USE
```

c.

```
ENDORSE HERE

X

_____

_____

_____

DO NOT WRITE, STAMP, OR SIGN BELOW THIS LINE
RESERVED FOR FINANCIAL INSTITUTION USE
```

2., 3., 4a.

NO. **410**	$ _____
Date: _____ 20__
To: _____
_____
For: _____

BALANCE BROUGHT FORWARD		
AMOUNT DEPOSITED [Date]		
SUBTOTAL		
OTHER:		
_____		
_____		
SUBTOTAL		
AMOUNT THIS CHECK		
BALANCE CARRIED FORWARD		

Wash N' Dry
2525 Niles Lane
Centuria, WI 54824

NO. **410** $\frac{17\text{-}432}{965}$

_____ 20 ____

PAY TO THE
ORDER OF _____ $ _____

_____ DOLLARS

Barron County Bank
Balsam Lake, WI

FOR _____   _____

⑈096575527⑈ 70159663⑊726⑊⑊ 410

4b.

NO. **411**	$ _____
Date: _____ 20__
To: _____
_____
For: _____

BALANCE BROUGHT FORWARD		
AMOUNT DEPOSITED [Date]		
SUBTOTAL		
OTHER:		
_____		
_____		
SUBTOTAL		
AMOUNT THIS CHECK		
BALANCE CARRIED FORWARD		

Wash N' Dry
2525 Niles Lane
Centuria, WI 54824

NO. **411** $\frac{17\text{-}432}{965}$

_____ 20 ____

PAY TO THE
ORDER OF _____ $ _____

_____ DOLLARS

Barron County Bank
Balsam Lake, WI

FOR _____   _____

⑈096575527⑈ 70159663⑊726⑊⑊ 411

4c.

NO. **412**	$ _____
Date: _____ 20__
To: _____
_____
For: _____

BALANCE BROUGHT FORWARD		
AMOUNT DEPOSITED [Date]		
SUBTOTAL		
OTHER:		
_____		
_____		
SUBTOTAL		
AMOUNT THIS CHECK		
BALANCE CARRIED FORWARD		

Wash N' Dry
2525 Niles Lane
Centuria, WI 54824

NO. **412** $\frac{17\text{-}432}{965}$

_____ 20 ____

PAY TO THE
ORDER OF _____ $ _____

_____ DOLLARS

Barron County Bank
Balsam Lake, WI

FOR _____   _____

⑈096575527⑈ 70159663⑊726⑊⑊ 412

5-2 APPLICATION PROBLEM, p. 149

Reconciling a bank statement and recording a bank service charge (LO4, 5)

1.

RECONCILIATION OF BANK STATEMENT

_____
(Date)

Balance On Check Stub No. ____ .... $ | |

DEDUCT BANK CHARGES:

Description	Amount	
	$	

Total bank charges ▶

Balance On Bank Statement .... $ | |

ADD OUTSTANDING DEPOSITS:

Date	Amount	
	$	

Total outstanding deposits ▶

SUBTOTAL .... $ | |

DEDUCT OUTSTANDING CHECKS:

Ck. No.	Amount	Ck. No.	Amount	

Total outstanding checks ▶

Adjusted Check Stub Balance .... $ | |

Adjusted Bank Balance .... $ | |

2.

NO. **477**	$ _____
Date: _____ 20 ___	
To: _____	
_____	
For: _____	
_____	

BALANCE BROUGHT FORWARD		
AMOUNT DEPOSITED	Date	
SUBTOTAL		
OTHER:		
_____		
_____		
SUBTOTAL		
AMOUNT THIS CHECK		
BALANCE CARRIED FORWARD		

3.

GENERAL JOURNAL

PAGE

	DATE	ACCOUNT TITLE	DOC. NO.	POST. REF.	DEBIT	CREDIT	
1							1
2							2
3							3

Recording dishonored checks, electronic funds transfers, and debit card purchases (LO6, 7, 8)

GENERAL JOURNAL
PAGE

	DATE		ACCOUNT TITLE	DOC. NO.	POST. REF.	DEBIT	CREDIT	
1								1
2								2
3								3
4								4
5								5
6								6
7								7

5-4 APPLICATION PROBLEM, p. 150

Establishing and replenishing a petty cash fund (LO9, 10, 11)

1.

PETTY CASH REPORT			
Date: _____		Custodian: _____	
	Explanation	Reconciliation	Replenish Amount
Fund Total			
Payments:	_____		
	_____		
	_____		
Less:	Total payments		→
Equals:	Recorded amount on hand		
Less:	Actual amount on hand		
Equals:	Cash short (over)		→
Amount to Replenish			

2.

GENERAL JOURNAL   PAGE _____

	DATE	ACCOUNT TITLE	DOC. NO.	POST. REF.	DEBIT	CREDIT	
1							1
2							2
26							26
27							27
28							28
29							29

Reconciling a bank statement; journalizing a bank service charge, a dishonored check, and petty cash transactions (LO4, 5, 6, 9, 10, 11)

1., 3., 5.

GENERAL JOURNAL   PAGE

	DATE	ACCOUNT TITLE	DOC. NO.	POST. REF.	DEBIT	CREDIT	
1							1
2							2
3							3
4							4
5							5
6							6
7							7
8							8
9							9
10							10
11							11
12							12
13							13
14							14
15							15
16							16
17							17
18							18
19							19
20							20
21							21
22							22
23							23
24							24
25							25

5-M   **MASTERY PROBLEM (concluded)**

2.

PETTY CASH REPORT

Date: _____   Custodian: _____

Explanation		Reconciliation	Replenish Amount
Fund Total Payments:			
	_____		
	_____		
	_____		
Less:	Total payments	→	
Equals:	Recorded amount on hand		
Less:	Actual amount on hand		
Equals:	Cash short (over)	→	
Amount to Replenish			

4.

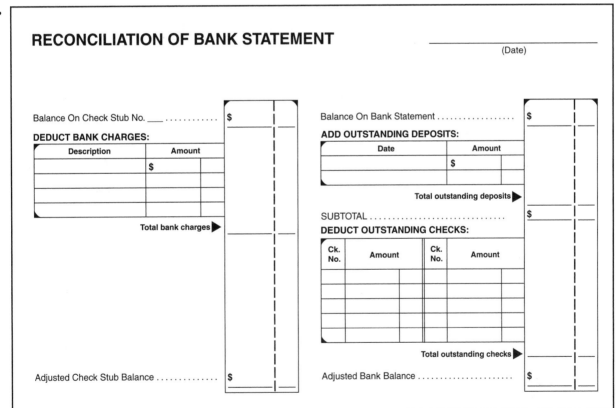

RECONCILIATION OF BANK STATEMENT   _____
(Date)

Balance On Check Stub No. ____ . . . . $

DEDUCT BANK CHARGES:

Description	Amount	
	$	

Total bank charges ▶

Adjusted Check Stub Balance . . . . $

Balance On Bank Statement . . . . $

ADD OUTSTANDING DEPOSITS:

Date	Amount	
	$	

Total outstanding deposits ▶

SUBTOTAL . . . . $

DEDUCT OUTSTANDING CHECKS:

Ck. No.	Amount	Ck. No.	Amount

Total outstanding checks ▶

Adjusted Bank Balance . . . . $

Reconciling a bank statement and recording a bank service charge and a dishonored check (LO4, 5, 6)

1., 2.

Fidelity NATIONAL BANK
Bonita Springs, FL 34135

STATEMENT OF ACCOUNT FOR
POOL CLEAN
75214 Bonita Beach Road
Bonita Springs, FL 34135

ACCOUNT NUMBER
8524655

STATEMENT DATE
July 28, 20 – –

BALANCE FROM PREVIOUS STATEMENT	NO. OF CHECKS	AMOUNT OF CHECKS	NO. OF DEPOSITS	AMOUNT OF DEPOSITS	SERVICE CHARGES	STATEMENT BALANCE
0.00	11	9,350.00	4	25,910.00	10.00	16,550.00

DATE	CHECK	AMOUNT	CHECK	AMOUNT	DEPOSITS	BALANCE
07/01/– –						0.00
07/01/– –					24,000.00	24,000.00
07/05/– –	251	3,154.00				20,846.00
07/08/– –	252	400.00			250.00	20,696.00
07/15/– –	254	500.00	256	270.00		19,926.00
07/15/– –	253	3,120.00	258	150.00	520.00	17,176.00
07/18/– –	255	410.00	259	196.00		16,570.00
07/18/– –	260	280.00				16,290.00
07/19/– –	257	500.00				15,790.00
07/25/– –					1,140.00	16,930.00
07/25/– –	262	370.00				16,560.00
07/27/– –	SC	10.00				16,550.00

PLEASE EXAMINE AT ONCE • IF NO ERRORS ARE REPORTED WITHIN 10 DAYS, THE ACCOUNT WILL BE CONSIDERED CORRECT. REFER ANY DISCREPANCY TO OUR ACCOUNTING DEPARTMENT IMMEDIATELY.

Pool Clean
75214 Bonita Beach Road
Bonita Springs, FL 34135
NO. 251   13-7552/965
July 1 20 – –
PAY TO THE ORDER OF *Industrial Supplies* $ 3,154.00

Pool Clean
75214 Bonita Beach Road
Bonita Springs, FL 34135
NO. 252   13-7552/965
July 5 20 – –
PAY TO THE ORDER OF *LMC Property Management* $ 400.00

Pool Clean
75214 Bonita Beach Road
Bonita Springs, FL 34135
NO. 253   13-7552/965
July 8 20 – –
PAY TO THE ORDER OF *Aqua Supplies* $ 3,120.00

Pool Clean
75214 Bonita Beach Road
Bonita Springs, FL 34135
NO. 254   13-7552/965
July 8 20 – –
PAY TO THE ORDER OF *American Insurance Company* $ 500.00

Pool Clean
75214 Bonita Beach Road
Bonita Springs, FL 34135
NO. 255   13-7552/965
July 10 20 – –
PAY TO THE ORDER OF *Bonita Springs Electric Company* $ 410.00

Pool Clean
75214 Bonita Beach Road
Bonita Springs, FL 34135
NO. 256   13-7552/965
July 10 20 – –
PAY TO THE ORDER OF *Fort Myers Supplies* $ 270.00
Two hundred seventy dollars and no/100 ———————— DOLLARS
Fidelity National Bank
Bonita Springs, FL
FOR *Payment on account*   John Warner
⑆096575527⑆ 8524655⑈ 256

Pool Clean
75214 Bonita Beach Road
Bonita Springs, FL 34135
NO. 257   13-7552/965
July 11 20 – –
PAY TO THE ORDER OF *Eduardo Gomez* $ 500.00

Pool Clean
75214 Bonita Beach Road
Bonita Springs, FL 34135
NO. 258   13-7552/965
July 11 20 – –
PAY TO THE ORDER OF *Century Telephone Company* $ 150.00

Pool Clean
75214 Bonita Beach Road
Bonita Springs, FL 34135
NO. 259   13-7552/965
July 15 20 – –
PAY TO THE ORDER OF *Sunshine Cleaning Company* $ 196.00

Pool Clean
75214 Bonita Beach Road
Bonita Springs, FL 34135
NO. 260   13-7552/965
July 15 20 – –
PAY TO THE ORDER OF *Tri-State Agency* $ 280.00

Pool Clean
75214 Bonita Beach Road
Bonita Springs, FL 34135
NO. 262   13-7552/965
July 23 20 – –
PAY TO THE ORDER OF *Harned Company* $ 370.00
Three hundred seventy dollars and no/100 ———————— DOLLARS
Fidelity National Bank
Bonita Springs, FL
FOR *Payment on account*   John Warner
⑆096575527⑆ 8524655⑈ 262

5-C   CHALLENGE PROBLEM (continued)

1., 2., 3.

NO. **251**	$ *3,154.00*		
Date: *July 1*		20 --	
To: *Industrial Supplies*			
For: *Supplies*			
BALANCE BROUGHT FORWARD		0	00
AMOUNT DEPOSITED *07* *01* -- Date		24,000	00
SUBTOTAL		24,000	00
OTHER:			
SUBTOTAL		24,000	00
AMOUNT THIS CHECK		3,154	00
BALANCE CARRIED FORWARD		20,846	00

NO. **252**	$ *400.00*		
Date: *July 5*		20 --	
To: *LMC Property Management*			
For: *Rent*			
BALANCE BROUGHT FORWARD		20,846	00
AMOUNT DEPOSITED			
SUBTOTAL Date		20,846	00
OTHER:			
SUBTOTAL		20,846	00
AMOUNT THIS CHECK		400	00
BALANCE CARRIED FORWARD		20,446	00

NO. **253**	$ *3,120.00*		
Date: *July 8*		20 --	
To: *Aqua Supplies*			
For: *Supplies*			
BALANCE BROUGHT FORWARD		20,446	00
AMOUNT DEPOSITED *07* *08* -- Date		250	00
SUBTOTAL		20,696	00
OTHER:			
SUBTOTAL		20,696	00
AMOUNT THIS CHECK		3,120	00
BALANCE CARRIED FORWARD		17,576	00

NO. **254**	$ *500.00*		
Date: *July 8*		20 --	
To: *American Insurance Company*			
For: *Insurance*			
BALANCE BROUGHT FORWARD		17,576	00
AMOUNT DEPOSITED			
SUBTOTAL Date		17,576	00
OTHER:			
SUBTOTAL		17,576	00
AMOUNT THIS CHECK		500	00
BALANCE CARRIED FORWARD		17,076	00

NO. **255**	$ *410.00*		
Date: *July 10*		20 --	
To: *Bonita Springs Electric Company*			
For: *Utilities*			
BALANCE BROUGHT FORWARD		17,076	00
AMOUNT DEPOSITED			
SUBTOTAL Date		17,076	00
OTHER:			
SUBTOTAL		17,076	00
AMOUNT THIS CHECK		410	00
BALANCE CARRIED FORWARD		16,666	00

NO. **256**	$ *270.00*		
Date: *July 10*		20 --	
To: *Fort Myers Supplies*			
For: *Payment on account*			
BALANCE BROUGHT FORWARD		16,666	00
AMOUNT DEPOSITED			
SUBTOTAL Date		16,666	00
OTHER:			
SUBTOTAL		16,666	00
AMOUNT THIS CHECK		270	00
BALANCE CARRIED FORWARD		16,396	00

NO. **257**	$ *500.00*		
Date: *July 11*		20 --	
To: *Eduardo Gomez*			
For: *Owner's withdrawal*			
BALANCE BROUGHT FORWARD		16,396	00
AMOUNT DEPOSITED			
SUBTOTAL Date		16,396	00
OTHER:			
SUBTOTAL		16,396	00
AMOUNT THIS CHECK		500	00
BALANCE CARRIED FORWARD		15,896	00

NO. **258**	$ *150.00*		
Date: *July 11*		20 --	
To: *Century Telephone Company*			
For: *Utilities*			
BALANCE BROUGHT FORWARD		15,896	00
AMOUNT DEPOSITED			
SUBTOTAL Date		15,896	00
OTHER:			
SUBTOTAL		15,896	00
AMOUNT THIS CHECK		150	00
BALANCE CARRIED FORWARD		15,746	00

NO. **259**	$ *196.00*		
Date: *July 15*		20 --	
To: *Sunshine Cleaning Company*			
For: *Cleaning*			
BALANCE BROUGHT FORWARD		15,746	00
AMOUNT DEPOSITED			
SUBTOTAL Date		15,746	00
OTHER:			
SUBTOTAL		15,746	00
AMOUNT THIS CHECK		196	00
BALANCE CARRIED FORWARD		15,550	00

1., 2., 3.

NO. **260**	$ 280.00		
Date: July 15			20 --
To: Tri-State Agency			
For: Miscellaneous			
BALANCE BROUGHT FORWARD		15,550	00
AMOUNT DEPOSITED 07 15 --		520	00
SUBTOTAL	Date	16,070	00
OTHER:			
SUBTOTAL		16,070	00
AMOUNT THIS CHECK		280	00
BALANCE CARRIED FORWARD		15,790	00

NO. **261**	$ 750.00		
Date: July 22			20 --
To: Naples Press			
For: Advertising			
BALANCE BROUGHT FORWARD		15,790	00
AMOUNT DEPOSITED			
SUBTOTAL	Date	15,790	00
OTHER:			
SUBTOTAL		15,790	00
AMOUNT THIS CHECK		750	00
BALANCE CARRIED FORWARD		15,040	00

NO. **262**	$ 370.00		
Date: July 23			20 --
To: Harned Company			
For: Payment on account			
BALANCE BROUGHT FORWARD		15,040	00
AMOUNT DEPOSITED 07 25 --		1,140	00
SUBTOTAL	Date	16,180	00
OTHER:			
SUBTOTAL		16,180	00
AMOUNT THIS CHECK		370	00
BALANCE CARRIED FORWARD		15,810	00

4.

NO. **263**	$ 34.00		
Date: July 23			20 --
To: Amy West			
For: Miscellaneous			
BALANCE BROUGHT FORWARD		15,810	00
AMOUNT DEPOSITED			
SUBTOTAL	Date	15,810	00
OTHER:			
SUBTOTAL		15,810	00
AMOUNT THIS CHECK		34	00
BALANCE CARRIED FORWARD		15,776	00

NO. **264**	$ 500.00		
Date: July 28			20 --
To: Eduardo Gomez			
For: Owner's withdrawal			
BALANCE BROUGHT FORWARD		15,776	00
AMOUNT DEPOSITED 07 28 --		860	00
SUBTOTAL	Date	16,636	00
OTHER:			
SUBTOTAL		16,636	00
AMOUNT THIS CHECK		500	00
BALANCE CARRIED FORWARD		16,136	00

NO. **265**	$		
Date:			20 __
To:			
For:			
BALANCE BROUGHT FORWARD		16,136	00
AMOUNT DEPOSITED			
SUBTOTAL	Date	16,136	00
OTHER:			
SUBTOTAL			
AMOUNT THIS CHECK			
BALANCE CARRIED FORWARD			

5-C **CHALLENGE PROBLEM (concluded)**

2.

RECONCILIATION OF BANK STATEMENT _____
(Date)

Balance On Check Stub No. ____ . . . . $ |

DEDUCT BANK CHARGES:

Description	Amount	
	$	

Total bank charges ▶ |

Adjusted Check Stub Balance . . . . $ |

Balance On Bank Statement . . . . $ |

ADD OUTSTANDING DEPOSITS:

Date	Amount	
	$	

Total outstanding deposits ▶

SUBTOTAL . . . . $ |

DEDUCT OUTSTANDING CHECKS:

Ck. No.	Amount	Ck. No.	Amount

Total outstanding checks ▶ |

Adjusted Bank Balance . . . . $ |

3.

GENERAL JOURNAL   PAGE

	DATE	ACCOUNT TITLE	DOC. NO.	POST. REF.	DEBIT	CREDIT	
1							1
2							2
3							3
4							4
5							5
6							6
7							7

REINFORCEMENT ACTIVITY 1, Part A, p. 153

An Accounting Cycle for a Proprietorship: Journalizing and Posting Transactions

1., 2.

GENERAL JOURNAL PAGE _____

	DATE	ACCOUNT TITLE	DOC. NO.	POST. REF.	DEBIT	CREDIT	
1							1
2							2
3							3
4							4
5							5
6							6
7							7
8							8
9							9
10							10
11							11
12							12
13							13
14							14
15							15
16							16
17							17
18							18
19							19
20							20
21							21
22							22
23							23
24							24
25							25
26							26
27							27
28							28
29							29
30							30
31							31
32							32
33							33
34							34

3., 5., 6.

GENERAL JOURNAL   PAGE

	DATE		ACCOUNT TITLE	DOC. NO.	POST. REF.	DEBIT	CREDIT	
1								1
2								2
3								3
4								4
5								5
6								6
7								7
8								8
9								9
10								10
11								11
12								12
13								13
14								14
15								15
16								16
17								17
18								18
19								19
20								20
21								21
22								22
23								23
24								24
25								25
26								26
27								27
28								28
29								29
30								30
31								31
32								32
33								33

REINFORCEMENT ACTIVITY 1, Part A (continued)

4.

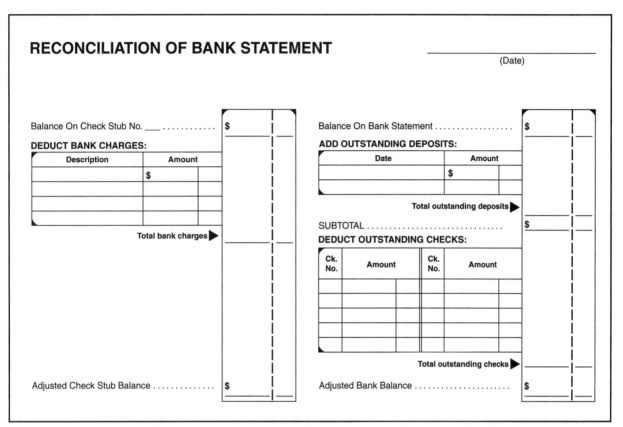

RECONCILIATION OF BANK STATEMENT

_____
(Date)

Balance On Check Stub No. ____ . . . . $ |

DEDUCT BANK CHARGES:

Description	Amount	
	$	

Total bank charges ▶

Balance On Bank Statement . . . . $ |

ADD OUTSTANDING DEPOSITS:

Date	Amount	
	$	

Total outstanding deposits ▶

SUBTOTAL . . . . $ |

DEDUCT OUTSTANDING CHECKS:

Ck. No.	Amount	Ck. No.	Amount

Total outstanding checks ▶

Adjusted Check Stub Balance . . . . $

Adjusted Bank Balance . . . . $

REINFORCEMENT ACTIVITY 1, Part A (continued)

The general ledger prepared in Reinforcement Activity 1, Part A, is needed to complete Reinforcement Activity 1, Part B.

2., 6., 7., 13., 16.

NOTE: August 31 postings from page 3 of the journal are part of the solution to Part B.

ACCOUNT _____   ACCOUNT NO. _____

DATE	ITEM	POST. REF.	DEBIT	CREDIT	BALANCE DEBIT	BALANCE CREDIT

REINFORCEMENT ACTIVITY 1, Part A (continued)

2., 6., 13., 16.

NOTE: August 31 postings from page 3 of the journal are part of the solution to Part B.

ACCOUNT _____ ACCOUNT NO. _____

DATE	ITEM	POST. REF.	DEBIT	CREDIT	BALANCE DEBIT	BALANCE CREDIT

ACCOUNT _____ ACCOUNT NO. _____

DATE	ITEM	POST. REF.	DEBIT	CREDIT	BALANCE DEBIT	BALANCE CREDIT

ACCOUNT _____ ACCOUNT NO. _____

DATE	ITEM	POST. REF.	DEBIT	CREDIT	BALANCE DEBIT	BALANCE CREDIT

ACCOUNT _____ ACCOUNT NO. _____

DATE	ITEM	POST. REF.	DEBIT	CREDIT	BALANCE DEBIT	BALANCE CREDIT

REINFORCEMENT ACTIVITY 1, Part A (continued)

ACCOUNT							ACCOUNT NO.	
							BALANCE	
DATE		ITEM	POST. REF.	DEBIT	CREDIT	DEBIT		CREDIT

ACCOUNT							ACCOUNT NO.	
							BALANCE	
DATE		ITEM	POST. REF.	DEBIT	CREDIT	DEBIT		CREDIT

ACCOUNT							ACCOUNT NO.	
							BALANCE	
DATE		ITEM	POST. REF.	DEBIT	CREDIT	DEBIT		CREDIT

ACCOUNT							ACCOUNT NO.	
							BALANCE	
DATE		ITEM	POST. REF.	DEBIT	CREDIT	DEBIT		CREDIT

ACCOUNT							ACCOUNT NO.	
							BALANCE	
DATE		ITEM	POST. REF.	DEBIT	CREDIT	DEBIT		CREDIT

REINFORCEMENT ACTIVITY 1, Part A (continued)

ACCOUNT _____ ACCOUNT NO. _____

DATE	ITEM	POST. REF.	DEBIT	CREDIT	BALANCE DEBIT	BALANCE CREDIT

ACCOUNT _____ ACCOUNT NO. _____

DATE	ITEM	POST. REF.	DEBIT	CREDIT	BALANCE DEBIT	BALANCE CREDIT

ACCOUNT _____ ACCOUNT NO. _____

DATE	ITEM	POST. REF.	DEBIT	CREDIT	BALANCE DEBIT	BALANCE CREDIT

REINFORCEMENT ACTIVITY 1, Part A (continued)

ACCOUNT _____ ACCOUNT NO. _____

DATE	ITEM	POST. REF.	DEBIT	CREDIT	BALANCE DEBIT	BALANCE CREDIT

ACCOUNT _____ ACCOUNT NO. _____

DATE	ITEM	POST. REF.	DEBIT	CREDIT	BALANCE DEBIT	BALANCE CREDIT

ACCOUNT _____ ACCOUNT NO. _____

DATE	ITEM	POST. REF.	DEBIT	CREDIT	BALANCE DEBIT	BALANCE CREDIT

ACCOUNT _____ ACCOUNT NO. _____

DATE	ITEM	POST. REF.	DEBIT	CREDIT	BALANCE DEBIT	BALANCE CREDIT

REINFORCEMENT ACTIVITY 1, Part A (concluded)

ACCOUNT _____ ACCOUNT NO. _____

DATE	ITEM	POST. REF.	DEBIT	CREDIT	BALANCE DEBIT	BALANCE CREDIT

ACCOUNT _____ ACCOUNT NO. _____

DATE	ITEM	POST. REF.	DEBIT	CREDIT	BALANCE DEBIT	BALANCE CREDIT

ACCOUNT _____ ACCOUNT NO. _____

DATE	ITEM	POST. REF.	DEBIT	CREDIT	BALANCE DEBIT	BALANCE CREDIT

Name	Perfect Score	Your Score
Identifying Accounting Terms	13 Pts.	
Analyzing Accounting Practices Related to a Work Sheet and Adjusting Entries	20 Pts.	
Analyzing Adjustments and Extending Account Balances on a Work Sheet	17 Pts.	
Total	50 Pts.	

Part One—Identifying Accounting Terms

Directions: Select the one term in Column I that best fits each definition in Column II. Print the letter identifying your choice in the Answers column.

Column I	Column II	Answers
A. accrual basis of accounting	**1.** The length of time for which a business summarizes its financial information and reports its financial performance. (p. 159)	**1.** _____
B. adjusting entries	**2.** A fiscal period consisting of 12 consecutive months. (p. 159)	**2.** _____
C. adjustments	**3.** A columnar accounting form used to summarize the general ledger information needed to prepare financial statements. (p. 159)	**3.** _____
D. balance sheet	**4.** A proof of equality of debits and credits in a general ledger. (p. 160)	**4.** _____
E. cash basis of accounting	**5.** Cash paid for an expense in one fiscal period that is not used until a later period. (p. 163)	**5.** _____
F. fiscal period	**6.** Reporting income when it is earned and expenses when they are incurred. (p. 163)	**6.** _____
G. fiscal year	**7.** Reporting income when the cash is received and expenses when the cash is paid. (p. 163)	**7.** _____
H. income statement	**8.** Changes recorded on a work sheet to update general ledger accounts at the end of a fiscal period. (p. 163)	**8.** _____
I. net income	**9.** A financial statement that reports assets, liabilities, and owner's equity on a specific date. (p. 169)	**9.** _____
J. net loss	**10.** A financial statement showing the revenue and expenses for a fiscal period. (p. 170)	**10.** _____
K. prepaid expense	**11.** The difference between total revenue and total expenses when total revenue is greater. (p. 171)	**11.** _____
L. trial balance	**12.** The difference between total revenue and total expenses when total expenses are greater. (p. 172)	**12.** _____
M. work sheet	**13.** Journal entries recorded to update general ledger accounts at the end of a fiscal period. (p. 176)	**13.** _____

Part Two—Analyzing Accounting Practices Related to a Work Sheet and Adjusting Entries

Directions: Place a *T* for True or an *F* for False in the Answers column to show whether each of the following statements is true or false.

Answers

1. The accounting concept Consistent Reporting is being applied when a delivery business reports revenue for the number of deliveries made one year and the amount of revenue received for the deliveries made the next year. (p. 158)

1. _____

2. A fiscal period must be 12 months in length. (p. 159)

2. _____

3. Journals, ledgers, and work sheets are considered permanent records. (p. 159)

3. _____

4. The heading on a work sheet contains the name of the business, the name of the report, and the date of the report. (p. 159)

4. _____

5. Only accounts with a balance are listed on a trial balance. (p. 160)

5. _____

6. The four questions asked when analyzing an adjustment are: Why? Where? When? and How? (p. 164)

6. _____

7. The two accounts affected by the adjustment for supplies are Supplies and Supplies Expense. (p. 164)

7. _____

8. The two accounts affected by the adjustment for insurance are Prepaid Insurance Expense and Insurance. (p. 165)

8. _____

9. The balance in Prepaid Insurance after adjusting entries are recorded represents the amount of insurance premium still remaining. (p. 165)

9. _____

10. Totaling and ruling the Adjustments columns of a work sheet are necessary to prove the equality of debits and credits. (p. 166)

10. _____

11. The income statement and balance sheet are prepared from the Trial Balance columns on the work sheet. (p. 169)

11. _____

12. Net income on a work sheet is calculated by subtracting the Income Statement Debit column total from the Income Statement Credit column total. (p. 171)

12. _____

13. If errors are found on a work sheet, they must be erased and corrected before any further work is completed. (p. 173)

13. _____

14. When two column totals are not in balance on the work sheet, the difference between the two totals is calculated and checked. (p. 173)

14. _____

15. If the difference between the totals of Debit and Credit columns on a work sheet can be evenly divided by 9, then the error is most likely a transposed number. (p. 173)

15. _____

16. If there are errors in the work sheet's Trial Balance columns, it might be because a general ledger account balance was recorded in the wrong Trial Balance column. (p. 174)

16. _____

17. Most errors occur in doing arithmetic. (p. 174)

17. _____

18. The best way to prevent errors is to use a calculator. (p. 174)

18. _____

19. Adjusting entries must be posted to the general ledger accounts. (p. 176)

19. _____

20. The balance in Supplies Expense after adjusting entries are recorded represents the amount of supplies used during the fiscal period. (p. 176)

20. _____

Part Three—Analyzing Adjustments and Extending Account Balances on a Work Sheet

Directions: For each account listed below, determine in which work sheet column(s) an amount typically will be written. Place a check mark in the proper Answers column to show your answer.

	Adjustments Debit Credit (pp. 164–166)		Income Statement Debit Credit (p. 170)		Balance Sheet Debit Credit (p. 169)	
1. Cash	____	____	____	____	____	____
2. Petty Cash	____	____	____	____	____	____
3. Accounts Receivable—Corner Bakery	____	____	____	____	____	____
4. Supplies	____	____	____	____	____	____
5. Prepaid Insurance	____	____	____	____	____	____
6. Accounts Payable—Suburban Office Supplies	____	____	____	____	____	____
7. K. Strand, Capital	____	____	____	____	____	____
8. K. Strand, Drawing	____	____	____	____	____	____
9. Income Summary	____	____	____	____	____	____
10. Sales	____	____	____	____	____	____
11. Advertising Expense	____	____	____	____	____	____
12. Cash Short and Over (Debit Balance)	____	____	____	____	____	____
13. Insurance Expense	____	____	____	____	____	____
14. Miscellaneous Expense	____	____	____	____	____	____
15. Rent Expense	____	____	____	____	____	____
16. Supplies Expense	____	____	____	____	____	____
17. Utilities Expense	____	____	____	____	____	____

Across

1. The difference between total revenue and total expenses when total expenses are greater.

4. Journal entries recorded to update general ledger accounts at the end of a fiscal period.

5. A columnar accounting form used to summarize the general ledger information needed to prepare financial statements.

6. Cash paid for an expense in one fiscal period that is not used until a later period.

7. A fiscal period consisting of 12 consecutive months.

9. A proof of the equality of debits and credits in a general ledger.

10. A financial statement that reports assets, liabilities, and owner's equity on a specific date.

11. Changes recorded on a work sheet to update general ledger accounts at the end of a fiscal period.

12. The length of time for which a business summarizes its financial information and reports its financial performance.

Down

1. The difference between total revenue and total expenses when total revenue is greater.

2. A trial balance prepared after adjusting entries are posted.

3. A financial statement showing the revenue and expenses for a fiscal period.

8. An accountant who has passed the uniform certified public accounting exam and met the licensing requirement for a state. (Note: Please enter into the puzzle as an acronym.)

6-1, 6-2, and 6-3 WORK TOGETHER, pp. 162, 168, and 175

6-1 Recording the trial balance on a work sheet
6-2 Planning adjustments on a work sheet
6-3 Completing a work sheet

ACCOUNT TITLE	TRIAL BALANCE		ADJUSTMENTS		INCOME STATEMENT		BALANCE SHEET	
	DEBIT	CREDIT	DEBIT	CREDIT	DEBIT	CREDIT	DEBIT	CREDIT
1								
2								
3								
4								
5								
6								
7								
8								
9								
10								
11								
12								
13								
14								
15								
16								
17								
18								
19								
20								

6-1 Recording the trial balance on a work sheet
6-2 Planning adjustments on a work sheet
6-3 Completing a work sheet

ACCOUNT TITLE	TRIAL BALANCE		ADJUSTMENTS		INCOME STATEMENT		BALANCE SHEET	
	DEBIT	CREDIT	DEBIT	CREDIT	DEBIT	CREDIT	DEBIT	CREDIT
1								
2								
3								
4								
5								
6								
7								
8								
9								
10								
11								
12								
13								
14								
15								
16								
17								
18								
19								
20								

Name _____ Date _____ Class _____

6-4 **WORK TOGETHER, p. 179**

Journalizing and posting adjusting entries

GENERAL JOURNAL   PAGE _____

	DATE	ACCOUNT TITLE	DOC. NO.	POST. REF.	DEBIT	CREDIT	
1							1
2							2
3							3
4							4
5							5
6							6
7							7
8							8
9							9
10							10
11							11
12							12
13							13
14							14
15							15
16							16
17							17
18							18
19							19
20							20
21							21
22							22
23							23
24							24
25							25
26							26
27							27
28							28
29							29
30							30
31							31
32							32

GENERAL LEDGER

ACCOUNT Supplies   ACCOUNT NO. 140

DATE		ITEM	POST. REF.	DEBIT	CREDIT	BALANCE	
						DEBIT	CREDIT
Apr. 20--	30	Balance	✔			2 2 8 00	

ACCOUNT Prepaid Insurance   ACCOUNT NO. 150

DATE		ITEM	POST. REF.	DEBIT	CREDIT	BALANCE	
						DEBIT	CREDIT
Apr. 20--	30	Balance	✔			3 7 5 00	

ACCOUNT Insurance Expense   ACCOUNT NO. 530

DATE	ITEM	POST. REF.	DEBIT	CREDIT	BALANCE	
					DEBIT	CREDIT

ACCOUNT Supplies Expense   ACCOUNT NO. 550

DATE	ITEM	POST. REF.	DEBIT	CREDIT	BALANCE	
					DEBIT	CREDIT

6-4 **ON YOUR OWN, p. 179**

Journalizing and posting adjusting entries

GENERAL JOURNAL

PAGE _____

	DATE	ACCOUNT TITLE	DOC. NO.	POST. REF.	DEBIT	CREDIT	
1							1
2							2
3							3
4							4
5							5
6							6
7							7
8							8
9							9
10							10
11							11
12							12
13							13
14							14
15							15
16							16
17							17
18							18
19							19
20							20
21							21
22							22
23							23
24							24
25							25
26							26
27							27
28							28
29							29
30							30
31							31
32							32

GENERAL LEDGER

ACCOUNT Supplies   ACCOUNT NO. 140

DATE	ITEM	POST. REF.	DEBIT	CREDIT	BALANCE DEBIT	BALANCE CREDIT
Dec. 20-- 31	Balance	✔			4 7 6 00	

ACCOUNT Prepaid Insurance   ACCOUNT NO. 150

DATE	ITEM	POST. REF.	DEBIT	CREDIT	BALANCE DEBIT	BALANCE CREDIT
Dec. 20-- 31	Balance	✔			6 5 0 00	

ACCOUNT Insurance Expense   ACCOUNT NO. 530

DATE	ITEM	POST. REF.	DEBIT	CREDIT	BALANCE DEBIT	BALANCE CREDIT

ACCOUNT Supplies Expense   ACCOUNT NO. 550

DATE	ITEM	POST. REF.	DEBIT	CREDIT	BALANCE DEBIT	BALANCE CREDIT

6-1, 6-2, and 6-3   APPLICATION PROBLEM (LO1, 2, 3, 4, 5, 6), p. 183

6-1 Recording the trial balance on a work sheet
6-2 Planning adjustments on a work sheet
6-3 Completing a work sheet

ACCOUNT TITLE	TRIAL BALANCE		ADJUSTMENTS		INCOME STATEMENT		BALANCE SHEET	
	DEBIT	CREDIT	DEBIT	CREDIT	DEBIT	CREDIT	DEBIT	CREDIT
	1	2	3	4	5	6	7	8

Journalizing and posting adjusting entries

1.

GENERAL JOURNAL

	DATE	ACCOUNT TITLE	DOC. NO.	POST. REF.	DEBIT	CREDIT	
1							1
2							2
3							3
4							4
5							5
6							6
7							7
8							8
9							9
10							10
11							11
12							12
13							13
14							14
15							15
16							16
17							17
18							18
19							19
20							20
21							21
22							22
23							23
24							24
25							25
26							26
27							27
28							28
29							29
30							30
31							31

6-4 **APPLICATION PROBLEM (concluded)**

GENERAL LEDGER

ACCOUNT Supplies   ACCOUNT NO. 140

DATE	ITEM	POST. REF.	DEBIT	CREDIT	BALANCE DEBIT	BALANCE CREDIT
June 30	Balance	✔			5 1 8 00	

ACCOUNT Prepaid Insurance   ACCOUNT NO. 150

DATE	ITEM	POST. REF.	DEBIT	CREDIT	BALANCE DEBIT	BALANCE CREDIT
June 30	Balance	✔			6 7 5 00	

ACCOUNT Insurance Expense   ACCOUNT NO. 530

DATE	ITEM	POST. REF.	DEBIT	CREDIT	BALANCE DEBIT	BALANCE CREDIT

ACCOUNT Supplies Expense   ACCOUNT NO. 550

DATE	ITEM	POST. REF.	DEBIT	CREDIT	BALANCE DEBIT	BALANCE CREDIT

Completing a work sheet; journalizing and posting adjusting entries

1., 2., 3., 4., 5., 6.

ACCOUNT TITLE	TRIAL BALANCE		ADJUSTMENTS		INCOME STATEMENT		BALANCE SHEET	
	1 DEBIT	2 CREDIT	3 DEBIT	4 CREDIT	5 DEBIT	6 CREDIT	7 DEBIT	8 CREDIT

6-M   MASTERY PROBLEM (continued)

7.

GENERAL JOURNAL   PAGE _____

	DATE		ACCOUNT TITLE	DOC. NO.	POST. REF.	DEBIT	CREDIT	
1								1
2								2
3								3
4								4
5								5
6								6
7								7
8								8
9								9
10								10
11								11
12								12
13								13
14								14
15								15
16								16
17								17
18								18
19								19
20								20
21								21
22								22
23								23
24								24
25								25
26								26
27								27
28								28
29								29
30								30
31								31
32								32

GENERAL LEDGER

ACCOUNT Supplies   ACCOUNT NO. 140

DATE	ITEM	POST. REF.	DEBIT	CREDIT	BALANCE DEBIT	BALANCE CREDIT
Apr. 30	Balance	✔			1 7 1 0 00	

ACCOUNT Prepaid Insurance   ACCOUNT NO. 150

DATE	ITEM	POST. REF.	DEBIT	CREDIT	BALANCE DEBIT	BALANCE CREDIT
Apr. 30	Balance	✔			2 2 0 0 00	

ACCOUNT Insurance Expense   ACCOUNT NO. 530

DATE	ITEM	POST. REF.	DEBIT	CREDIT	BALANCE DEBIT	BALANCE CREDIT

ACCOUNT Supplies Expense   ACCOUNT NO. 560

DATE	ITEM	POST. REF.	DEBIT	CREDIT	BALANCE DEBIT	BALANCE CREDIT

6-C CHALLENGE PROBLEM (LO1, 2, 3, 4, 5, 6), p. 185

Completing a work sheet

1., 2.

ACCOUNT TITLE	TRIAL BALANCE		ADJUSTMENTS		INCOME STATEMENT		BALANCE SHEET	
	DEBIT	CREDIT	DEBIT	CREDIT	DEBIT	CREDIT	DEBIT	CREDIT
1								
2								
3								
4								
5								
6								
7								
8								
9								
10								
11								
12								
13								
14								
15								
16								
17								
18								
19								
20								

Study Guide 7

Name		Perfect Score	Your Score
	Identifying Accounting Concepts and Practices	20 Pts.	
	Analyzing an Income Statement	15 Pts.	
	Analyzing Statement of Owner's Equity and Balance Sheet Procedures	6 Pts.	
	Total	41 Pts.	

Part One—Identifying Accounting Concepts and Practices

Directions: Place a *T* for True or an *F* for False in the Answers column to show whether each of the following statements is true or false.

Answers

1. The Full Disclosure accounting concept is applied when a company always prepares financial statements at the end of each monthly fiscal period. (p. 190)

   1. _____

2. Internal users of accounting information include company managers, officers, and creditors. (p. 190)

   2. _____

3. The statement of owner's equity reports changes in the capital account for a period of time. (p. 190).

   3. _____

4. Information needed to prepare a statement of owner's equity is obtained from the balance sheet. (p. 190)

   4. _____

5. When a business has a net loss, the current capital amount will be less than the capital account balance. (p. 192)

   5. _____

6. On the balance sheet, the current capital amount is taken from the work sheet. (p. 192)

   6. _____

7. An income statement reports information on a specific date indicating the financial condition of a business. (p. 192)

   7. _____

8. The Matching Expenses with Revenue accounting concept is applied when the revenue earned and the expenses incurred to earn that revenue are reported in the same fiscal period. (p. 192)

   8. _____

9. Information needed to prepare an income statement comes from the Account Title column and the Income Statement columns of a work sheet. (p. 192)

   9. _____

10. The income statement for a service business has five sections: heading, Revenue, Expenses, Net Income or Net Loss, and Capital. (p. 192)

    10. _____

11. The income statement's account balances are obtained from the work sheet's Income Statement columns. (p. 192)

    11. _____

12. The net income on an income statement is verified by checking the balance sheet. (p. 194)

    12. _____

13. Double lines ruled across both amount columns of an income statement indicate that the amount has been verified. (p. 194)

    13. _____

14. A financial ratio is a comparison between two components of financial information. (p. 195)

    14. _____

15. Financial ratios on an income statement are calculated by dividing sales and total expenses by net income. (p. 195)

    15. _____

16. When a business has two different sources of revenue, both revenue accounts are listed on the income statement. (p. 197)

    16. _____

17. An amount written in parentheses on a financial statement indicates a negative amount. (p. 197)

    17. _____

18. A balance sheet reports financial information on a specific date and includes the assets, liabilities, and owner's equity. (p. 199)

    18. _____

19. The position of the total asset line on the balance sheet is determined after the Equities section is prepared. (p. 202)

    19. _____

20. Double lines are ruled across the Balance Sheet columns to show that the column totals have been verified as correct. (p. 202)

    20. _____

Part Two—Analyzing an Income Statement

Directions: The parts of the income statement below are identified with capital letters. Decide the location of each of the following items. Print the letter identifying your choice in the Answers column.

				% OF SALES
A				
B				
C				
D				
E		**F**		
G				
H		**I**		
J		**K**	**N**	
L		**M**	**O**	

(pp. 192–195)

Answers

1. Date of the income statement.   1. _____

2. Heading of Expenses section.   2. _____

3. Statement name.   3. _____

4. Expense account titles.   4. _____

5. Expense account balances.   5. _____

6. The amount of net income or loss.   6. _____

7. Heading of Revenue section.   7. _____

8. Net income ratio (or return on sales).   8. _____

9. Revenue account title.   9. _____

10. Words *Total Expenses*.   10. _____

11. Business name.   11. _____

12. Total amount of revenue.   12. _____

13. Total amount of expenses.   13. _____

14. Words *Net Income* or *Net Loss*.   14. _____

15. Total expenses ratio.   15. _____

Part Three—Analyzing Statement of Owner's Equity and Balance Sheet Procedures

Directions: For each of the following items, select the choice that best completes the statement. Print the letter identifying your choice in the Answers column.

Answers

1. The date on a monthly statement of owner's equity prepared on May 31 is written as (A) For Month Ended May 31, 20-- (B) May 31, 20-- (C) 20--, May 31 (D) none of the above. (p. 199)

   1. _____

2. Information needed to prepare a statement of owner's equity is obtained from a work sheet's Account Title column and (A) Income Statement columns (B) Balance Sheet columns (C) Adjustment columns (D) none of the above. (p. 199)

   2. _____

3. The amount of capital reported on a statement of owner's equity when there is a net loss is calculated as (A) Capital Account Balance + Net Loss – Drawing Account Balance (B) Capital Account Balance – Net Loss – Drawing Account Balance (C) Capital Account Balance + Net Loss + Drawing Account Balance (D) Capital Account Balance – Net Loss + Drawing Account Balance. (p. 200)

   3. _____

4. The date on a monthly balance sheet prepared on July 31 is written as (A) For Month Ended July 31, 20-- (B) July 31, 20-- (C) 20--, July 31 (D) none of the above. (p. 201)

   4. _____

5. Information needed to prepare a balance sheet's Assets section is obtained from a work sheet's Account Title column and (A) Income Statement Debit column (B) Income Statement Credit column (C) Balance Sheet Debit column (D) Balance Sheet Credit column. (p. 201)

   5. _____

6. Information needed to prepare a balance sheet's Liabilities section is obtained from a work sheet's Account Title column and (A) Income Statement Debit column (B) Income Statement Credit column (C) Balance Sheet Debit column (D) Balance Sheet Credit column. (p. 201)

   6. _____

Across

6. A negative balance that remains after total expenses are subtracted from total income.

8. The ratio of net income to total sales.

9. Reporting an amount on a financial statement as a percentage of another item on the same financial statement.

10. Any persons or groups who will be affected by an action.

11. The area of accounting which focuses on reporting information to internal users.

Down

1. The calculation and interpretation of a financial ratio.

2. The area of accounting which focuses on reporting information to external users.

3. A budgeting strategy of setting aside at least 10% of after-tax income for saving and investing.

4. A financial road map used by individuals and companies as a guide for spending and saving.

5. A comparison between two components of financial information.

7. A positive balance that remains after total expenses are subtracted from total income.

7-1 WORK TOGETHER, p. 198

Preparing an income statement

		INCOME STATEMENT		BALANCE SHEET			
ACCOUNT TITLE		5 DEBIT	6 CREDIT	7 DEBIT	8 CREDIT		
12	Sales		5 8 0 0 00			12
13	Advertising Expense	7 5 0 00				13
14	Cash Short and Over	3 00				14
15	Insurance Expense	6 1 0 00				15
16	Miscellaneous Expense	1 6 7 00				16
17	Supplies Expense	5 4 0 00				17
18	Utilities Expense	3 0 0 00				18
19		2 3 7 0 00	5 8 0 0 00	7 5 5 4 00	4 1 2 4 00	19
20	Net Income	3 4 3 0 00			3 4 3 0 00	20
21		5 8 0 0 00	5 8 0 0 00	7 5 5 4 00	7 5 5 4 00	21
22						22
23						23

		% OF SALES

Preparing an income statement

	ACCOUNT TITLE		INCOME STATEMENT		BALANCE SHEET		
			5 DEBIT	6 CREDIT	7 DEBIT	8 CREDIT	
12	Sales			3 4 0 0 00			12
13	Advertising Expense		2 2 5 00				13
14	Cash Short and Over		1 00				14
15	Insurance Expense		3 4 0 00				15
16	Miscellaneous Expense		2 1 0 00				16
17	Supplies Expense		9 8 00				17
18	Utilities Expense		1 4 0 00				18
19			1 0 1 4 00	3 4 0 0 00	3 6 2 0 00	1 2 3 4 00	19
20	Net Income		2 3 8 6 00			2 3 8 6 00	20
21			3 4 0 0 00	3 4 0 0 00	3 6 2 0 00	3 6 2 0 00	21
22							22
23							23

						% OF SALES

7-2 WORK TOGETHER, p. 205

Preparing a statement of owner's equity and a balance sheet

	ACCOUNT TITLE	BALANCE SHEET	
		DEBIT	CREDIT
1	Cash	4 7 5 0 00	
2	Petty Cash	7 5 00	
3	Accounts Receivable—G. Mackermann	8 2 5 00	
4	Accounts Receivable—R. Whu	7 1 5 00	
5	Supplies	1 1 0 00	
6	Prepaid Insurance	3 2 0 00	
7	Accounts Payable—Belmont Supplies		2 7 5 00
8	Accounts Payable—Lurgert Paints		4 9 0 00
9	Dwight Sundeen, Capital		3 5 0 0 00
10	Dwight Sundeen, Drawing	1 2 0 0 00	
20		7 9 9 5 00	4 2 6 5 00
21	Net Income		3 7 3 0 00
22		7 9 9 5 00	7 9 9 5 00
23			

1.

Preparing a statement of owner's equity and a balance sheet

2.

7-2 ON YOUR OWN, p. 205

Preparing a statement of owner's equity and a balance sheet

	ACCOUNT TITLE	BALANCE SHEET	
		DEBIT	CREDIT
1	Cash	2 6 5 0 00		1
2	Petty Cash	2 0 0 00		2
3	Accounts Receivable—Sunshine Café	2 5 0 00		3
4	Accounts Receivable—Dependable Cleaners	1 3 0 00		4
5	Supplies	3 5 0 00		5
6	Prepaid Insurance	2 9 0 00		6
7	Accounts Payable—Computer Supplies Co.		3 4 0 00	7
8	Accounts Payable—Westside Supplies		1 2 0 00	8
9	Eva Nelsen, Capital		3 9 5 0 00	9
10	Eva Nelsen, Drawing	1 5 0 0 00		10
20		5 3 7 0 00	4 4 1 0 00	20
21	Net Income		9 6 0 00	21
22		5 3 7 0 00	5 3 7 0 00	22
23				23

1.

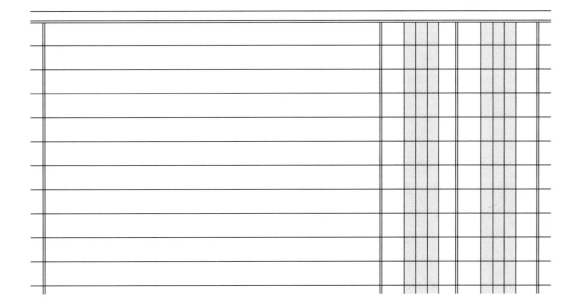

Preparing a statement of owner's equity and a balance sheet

2.

7-1   APPLICATION PROBLEM (LO1, 2), p. 208

Preparing an income statement

1., 2.

				% OF SALES

APPLICATION PROBLEM (LO3), p. 208

Preparing a statement of owner's equity and a balance sheet

1.

2.

7-M MASTERY PROBLEM (LO1, 2, 3), p. 209

Preparing financial statements with a net loss

1., 2.

				% OF SALES

3.

Preparing financial statements with a net loss

4.

7-C CHALLENGE PROBLEM (LO1, 2, 3), p. 210

Preparing financial statements with two sources of revenue and a net loss

1., 2.

					% OF SALES

3.

Preparing financial statements with two sources of revenue and a net loss

4.

Name	Perfect Score	Your Score
Identifying Accounting Terms	5 Pts.	
Analyzing Accounts Affected by Adjusting and Closing Entries	10 Pts.	
Analyzing Closing Entries	10 Pts.	
Identifying the Accounting Cycle for a Service Business	8 Pts.	
Total	33 Pts.	

Study Guide 8

Part One—Identifying Accounting Terms

Directions: Select the one term in Column I that best fits each definition in Column II. Print the letter identifying your choice in the Answers column.

Column I	Column II	Answers
A. accounting cycle	**1.** Accounts used to accumulate information from one fiscal period to the next. (p. 214)	1. _____
B. closing entries	**2.** Accounts used to accumulate information until it is transferred to the owner's capital account. (p. 214)	2. _____
C. permanent accounts	**3.** Journal entries used to prepare temporary accounts for a new fiscal period. (p. 214)	3. _____
D. post-closing trial balance	**4.** A trial balance prepared after the closing entries are posted. (p. 227)	4. _____
E. temporary accounts	**5.** The series of accounting activities included in recording financial information for a fiscal period. (p. 228)	5. _____

Part Two—Analyzing Accounts Affected by Adjusting and Closing Entries

Directions: Use the partial chart of accounts given below. For each closing entry described, decide which accounts are debited and credited. Write the account numbers identifying your choice in the proper Answers column.

Account Titles	Acct. No.
K. Schenk, Capital	310
K. Schenk, Drawing	320
Income Summary	330
Sales	410
Advertising Expense	510
Insurance Expense	520
Supplies Expense	550

	Accounts to Be	
	Debited	Credited
1–2. Closing entry for Sales. (p. 217)	1. _____	2. _____
3–4. Closing entry for all expense accounts. (p. 219)	3. _____	4. _____
5–6. Closing entry for Income Summary with a net income. (p. 220)	5. _____	6. _____
7–8. Closing entry for Income Summary with a net loss. (p. 220)	7. _____	8. _____
9–10. Closing entry for owner's drawing account. (p. 221)	9. _____	10. _____

Part Three—Analyzing Closing Entries

Directions: For each of the following items, select the choice that best completes the statement. Print the letter identifying your choice in the Answers column.

Answers

1. Which accounting concept applies when a work sheet is prepared at the end of each fiscal cycle to summarize the general ledger information needed to prepare financial statements? (A) Business Entity (B) Accounting Period Cycle (C) Going Concern (D) Full Disclosure. (p. 214)

1. _____

2. The ending account balances of permanent accounts for one fiscal period are (A) the same as the prior period's ending balance (B) equal to the capital account balance (C) all equal to zero (D) the beginning account balances for the next fiscal period. (p. 214)

2. _____

3. Which of the following accounts is a temporary account? (A) Cash (B) Accounts Payable (C) Clyde Sullivan, Capital (D) Rent Expense. (p. 214)

3. _____

4. Which accounting concept applies when expenses are reported in the same fiscal period that they are used to produce revenue? (A) Business Entity (B) Going Concern (C) Matching Expenses with Revenue (D) Full Disclosure. (p. 214)

4. _____

5. When revenue is greater than total expenses, resulting in a net income, the Income Summary account has a (A) debit balance (B) credit balance (C) normal debit balance (D) normal credit balance. (p. 216)

5. _____

6. Information needed for recording the closing entries is obtained from the (A) general ledger accounts' Debit Balance columns (B) work sheet's Income Statement and Balance Sheet columns (C) balance sheet (D) income statement. (p. 216)

6. _____

7. Income Summary is (A) an asset account (B) a liability account (C) a temporary account (D) a permanent account. (p. 216)

7. _____

8. After the closing entries are posted, the Sales account balance should be (A) equal to the Sales account balance on the unadjusted trial balance (B) equal to the Sales account balance on the adjusted trial balance (C) zero (D) the same as the beginning balance for that same fiscal period. (p. 218)

8. _____

9. After the closing entries are posted, the owner's capital account balances should be the same as shown (A) on the balance sheet for the fiscal period (B) in the work sheet's Balance Sheet Debit column (C) in the work sheet's Balance Sheet Credit column (D) in the work sheet's Income Statement Debit column. (p. 221)

9. _____

10. The accounts listed on a post-closing trial balance are (A) general ledger accounts with balances after the closing entries are posted (B) all general ledger accounts (C) those that have no balances after adjusting and closing entries (D) those that appear in the work sheet's Trial Balance columns. (p. 227)

10. _____

Part Four—Identifying the Accounting Cycle for a Service Business

Directions: Arrange the series of accounting activities listed below for the accounting cycle for a service business. Indicate the sequence of the steps by writing a number from 1 to 8 to the left of each activity. (p. 228)

Answers

1. _____ A work sheet, including a trial balance, is prepared from the general ledger.

2. _____ Transactions, from information on source documents, are recorded in a journal.

3. _____ Source documents are checked for accuracy, and transactions are analyzed into debit and credit parts.

4. _____ Adjusting entries are journalized and posted to the general ledger.

5. _____ Financial statements are prepared from the work sheet.

6. _____ Closing entries are journalized and posted to the general ledger.

7. _____ A post-closing trial balance of the general ledger is prepared.

8. _____ Journal entries are posted to the general ledger.

8-1 WORK TOGETHER, p. 222

Journalizing and posting closing entries

ACCOUNT TITLE	INCOME STATEMENT		BALANCE SHEET		
	DEBIT (5)	CREDIT (6)	DEBIT (7)	CREDIT (8)	
1 Cash			4 9 0 0 00		1
2 Petty Cash			7 5 00		2
3 Accounts Receivable—B. Widell			1 3 8 7 00		3
4 Supplies			7 5 00		4
5 Prepaid Insurance			2 5 0 00		5
6 Accounts Payable—Southside Supplies				2 6 7 00	6
7 Connor Whitney, Capital				7 4 4 3 00	7
8 Connor Whitney, Drawing			1 7 0 0 00		8
9 Income Summary					9
10 Sales		2 1 6 0 00			10
11 Advertising Expense	4 6 0 00				11
12 Cash Short and Over	6 00				12
13 Insurance Expense	1 2 5 00				13
14 Miscellaneous Expense	1 8 9 00				14
15 Supplies Expense	1 5 3 00				15
16 Utilities Expense	5 5 0 00				16
17	1 4 8 3 00	2 1 6 0 00	8 3 8 7 00	7 7 1 0 00	17
18 Net Income	6 7 7 00			6 7 7 00	18
19	2 1 6 0 00	2 1 6 0 00	8 3 8 7 00	8 3 8 7 00	19
20					20
21					21
22					22
23					23
24					24
25					25
26					26
27					27
28					28
29					29
30					30
31					31
32					32

GENERAL JOURNAL

PAGE

	DATE	ACCOUNT TITLE	DOC. NO.	POST. REF.	GENERAL DEBIT	GENERAL CREDIT	
6							6
7							7
8							8
9							9
10							10
11							11
12							12
13							13
14							14
15							15
16							16
17							17
18							18
19							19
20							20
21							21
22							22
23							23
24							24
25							25
26							26
27							27
28							28

GENERAL LEDGER

ACCOUNT Cash   ACCOUNT NO. 110

DATE	ITEM	POST. REF.	DEBIT	CREDIT	BALANCE DEBIT	BALANCE CREDIT
20-- Apr. 30	Balance	✔			4 9 0 0 00	

ACCOUNT Petty Cash   ACCOUNT NO. 120

DATE	ITEM	POST. REF.	DEBIT	CREDIT	BALANCE DEBIT	BALANCE CREDIT
20-- Apr. 30	Balance	✔			7 5 00	

ACCOUNT Accounts Receivable—B. Widell   ACCOUNT NO. 130

DATE	ITEM	POST. REF.	DEBIT	CREDIT	BALANCE DEBIT	BALANCE CREDIT
20-- Apr. 30	Balance	✔			1 3 8 7 00	

ACCOUNT Supplies   ACCOUNT NO. 140

DATE	ITEM	POST. REF.	DEBIT	CREDIT	BALANCE DEBIT	BALANCE CREDIT
20-- Apr. 30	Balance	✔			7 5 00	

ACCOUNT Prepaid Insurance   ACCOUNT NO. 150

DATE	ITEM	POST. REF.	DEBIT	CREDIT	BALANCE DEBIT	BALANCE CREDIT
20-- Apr. 30	Balance	✔			2 5 0 00	

ACCOUNT Accounts Payable—Southside Supplies   ACCOUNT NO. 210

DATE	ITEM	POST. REF.	DEBIT	CREDIT	BALANCE DEBIT	BALANCE CREDIT
20-- Apr. 30	Balance	✔				2 6 7 00

ACCOUNT Connor Whitney, Capital   ACCOUNT NO. 310

DATE	ITEM	POST. REF.	DEBIT	CREDIT	BALANCE DEBIT	BALANCE CREDIT
20-- Apr. 30	Balance	✔				7 4 4 3 00

ACCOUNT Connor Whitney, Drawing   ACCOUNT NO. 320

DATE	ITEM	POST. REF.	DEBIT	CREDIT	BALANCE DEBIT	BALANCE CREDIT
20-- Apr. 30	Balance	✔			1 7 0 0 00	

ACCOUNT Income Summary   ACCOUNT NO. 330

DATE	ITEM	POST. REF.	DEBIT	CREDIT	BALANCE DEBIT	BALANCE CREDIT

ACCOUNT Sales   ACCOUNT NO. 410

DATE	ITEM	POST. REF.	DEBIT	CREDIT	BALANCE DEBIT	BALANCE CREDIT
20-- Apr. 30	Balance	✔				2 1 6 0 00

8-1 WORK TOGETHER (concluded)

ACCOUNT Advertising Expense   ACCOUNT NO. 510

DATE	ITEM	POST. REF.	DEBIT	CREDIT	BALANCE DEBIT	BALANCE CREDIT
20-- Apr. 30	Balance	✔			4 6 0 00	

ACCOUNT Cash Short and Over   ACCOUNT NO. 520

DATE	ITEM	POST. REF.	DEBIT	CREDIT	BALANCE DEBIT	BALANCE CREDIT
20-- Apr. 30	Balance	✔			6 00	

ACCOUNT Insurance Expense   ACCOUNT NO. 530

DATE	ITEM	POST. REF.	DEBIT	CREDIT	BALANCE DEBIT	BALANCE CREDIT
20-- Apr. 30	Balance	✔			1 2 5 00	

ACCOUNT Miscellaneous Expense   ACCOUNT NO. 540

DATE	ITEM	POST. REF.	DEBIT	CREDIT	BALANCE DEBIT	BALANCE CREDIT
20-- Apr. 30	Balance	✔			1 8 9 00	

ACCOUNT Supplies Expense   ACCOUNT NO. 550

DATE	ITEM	POST. REF.	DEBIT	CREDIT	BALANCE DEBIT	BALANCE CREDIT
20-- Apr. 30	Balance	✔			1 5 3 00	

ACCOUNT Utilities Expense   ACCOUNT NO. 560

DATE	ITEM	POST. REF.	DEBIT	CREDIT	BALANCE DEBIT	BALANCE CREDIT
20-- Apr. 30	Balance	✔			5 5 0 00	

Journalizing and posting closing entries

	ACCOUNT TITLE	5 INCOME STATEMENT DEBIT	6 INCOME STATEMENT CREDIT	7 BALANCE SHEET DEBIT	8 BALANCE SHEET CREDIT	
1	Cash			13 6 0 0 00		1
2	Petty Cash			1 5 0 00		2
3	Accounts Receivable—Eat Right Eatery			2 9 9 6 00		3
4	Supplies			2 4 0 00		4
5	Prepaid Insurance			5 2 0 00		5
6	Accounts Payable—Lakeville Supplies				5 9 6 00	6
7	Sawyer Parker, Capital				14 8 8 6 00	7
8	Sawyer Parker, Drawing			3 4 0 0 00		8
9	Income Summary					9
10	Sales		8 2 8 0 00			10
11	Advertising Expense	9 1 0 00				11
12	Cash Short and Over	2 00				12
13	Insurance Expense	1 3 0 00				13
14	Miscellaneous Expense	3 7 8 00				14
15	Supplies Expense	2 3 6 00				15
16	Utilities Expense	1 2 0 0 00				16
17		2 8 5 6 00	8 2 8 0 00	20 9 0 6 00	15 4 8 2 00	17
18	Net Income	5 4 2 4 00			5 4 2 4 00	18
19		8 2 8 0 00	8 2 8 0 00	20 9 0 6 00	20 9 0 6 00	19
20						20
21						21
22						22
23						23
24						24
25						25
26						26
27						27
28						28
29						29
30						30
31						31
32						32

8-1 **ON YOUR OWN (continued)**

GENERAL JOURNAL

PAGE ___

	DATE		ACCOUNT TITLE	DOC. NO.	POST. REF.	GENERAL		
						DEBIT	CREDIT	
6								6
7								7
8								8
9								9
10								10
11								11
12								12
13								13
14								14
15								15
16								16
17								17
18								18
19								19
20								20
21								21
22								22
23								23
24								24
25								25
26								26
27								27
28								28

GENERAL LEDGER

ACCOUNT Cash   ACCOUNT NO. 110

DATE	ITEM	POST. REF.	DEBIT	CREDIT	BALANCE DEBIT	BALANCE CREDIT
20-- Dec. 31	Balance	✔			13 6 0 0 00	

ACCOUNT Petty Cash   ACCOUNT NO. 120

DATE	ITEM	POST. REF.	DEBIT	CREDIT	BALANCE DEBIT	BALANCE CREDIT
20-- Dec. 31	Balance	✔			1 5 0 00	

ACCOUNT Accounts Receivable—Eat Right Eatery   ACCOUNT NO. 130

DATE	ITEM	POST. REF.	DEBIT	CREDIT	BALANCE DEBIT	BALANCE CREDIT
20-- Dec. 31	Balance	✔			2 9 9 6 00	

ACCOUNT Supplies   ACCOUNT NO. 140

DATE	ITEM	POST. REF.	DEBIT	CREDIT	BALANCE DEBIT	BALANCE CREDIT
20-- Dec. 31	Balance	✔			2 4 0 00	

ACCOUNT Prepaid Insurance   ACCOUNT NO. 150

DATE	ITEM	POST. REF.	DEBIT	CREDIT	BALANCE DEBIT	BALANCE CREDIT
20-- Dec. 31	Balance	✔			5 2 0 00	

ACCOUNT Accounts Payable—Lakeville Supplies   ACCOUNT NO. 210

DATE	ITEM	POST. REF.	DEBIT	CREDIT	BALANCE DEBIT	BALANCE CREDIT
20-- Dec. 31	Balance	✔				5 9 6 00

8-1 ON YOUR OWN (continued)

ACCOUNT Sawyer Parker, Capital   ACCOUNT NO. 310

DATE	ITEM	POST. REF.	DEBIT	CREDIT	BALANCE DEBIT	BALANCE CREDIT
20-- Dec. 31	Balance	✔				14 8 8 6 00

ACCOUNT Sawyer Parker, Drawing   ACCOUNT NO. 320

DATE	ITEM	POST. REF.	DEBIT	CREDIT	BALANCE DEBIT	BALANCE CREDIT
20-- Dec. 31	Balance	✔			3 4 0 0 00	

ACCOUNT Income Summary   ACCOUNT NO. 330

DATE	ITEM	POST. REF.	DEBIT	CREDIT	BALANCE DEBIT	BALANCE CREDIT

ACCOUNT Sales   ACCOUNT NO. 410

DATE	ITEM	POST. REF.	DEBIT	CREDIT	BALANCE DEBIT	BALANCE CREDIT
20-- Dec. 31	Balance	✔				8 2 8 0 00

ACCOUNT Advertising Expense   ACCOUNT NO. 510

DATE	ITEM	POST. REF.	DEBIT	CREDIT	BALANCE DEBIT	BALANCE CREDIT
20-- Dec. 31	Balance	✔			9 1 0 00	

ACCOUNT Cash Short and Over ACCOUNT NO. 520

DATE		ITEM	POST. REF.	DEBIT	CREDIT	BALANCE	
						DEBIT	CREDIT
20-- Dec.	31	Balance	✔			2 00	

ACCOUNT Insurance Expense ACCOUNT NO. 530

DATE		ITEM	POST. REF.	DEBIT	CREDIT	BALANCE	
						DEBIT	CREDIT
20-- Dec.	31	Balance	✔			1 3 0 00	

ACCOUNT Miscellaneous Expense ACCOUNT NO. 540

DATE		ITEM	POST. REF.	DEBIT	CREDIT	BALANCE	
						DEBIT	CREDIT
20-- Dec.	31	Balance	✔			3 7 8 00	

ACCOUNT Supplies Expense ACCOUNT NO. 550

DATE		ITEM	POST. REF.	DEBIT	CREDIT	BALANCE	
						DEBIT	CREDIT
20-- Dec.	31	Balance	✔			2 3 6 00	

ACCOUNT Utilities Expense ACCOUNT NO. 560

DATE		ITEM	POST. REF.	DEBIT	CREDIT	BALANCE	
						DEBIT	CREDIT
20-- Dec.	31	Balance	✔			1 2 0 0 00	

8-2 **WORK TOGETHER, p. 230**

Preparing a post-closing trial balance

ACCOUNT TITLE	DEBIT	CREDIT

Preparing a post-closing trial balance

ACCOUNT TITLE	DEBIT	CREDIT

8-1 APPLICATION PROBLEM, p. 233

Journalizing and posting closing entries (LO1)

GENERAL JOURNAL   PAGE

	DATE	ACCOUNT TITLE	DOC. NO.	POST. REF.	GENERAL DEBIT	GENERAL CREDIT	
6							6
7							7
8							8
9							9
10							10
11							11
12							12
13							13
14							14
15							15
16							16
17							17
18							18
19							19
20							20
21							21
22							22
23							23
24							24
25							25
26							26
27							27
28							28

GENERAL LEDGER

ACCOUNT Cash   ACCOUNT NO. 110

DATE		ITEM	POST. REF.	DEBIT	CREDIT	BALANCE	
						DEBIT	CREDIT
20-- June	30	Balance	✔			8 7 1 5 00	

ACCOUNT Petty Cash   ACCOUNT NO. 120

DATE		ITEM	POST. REF.	DEBIT	CREDIT	BALANCE	
						DEBIT	CREDIT
20-- June	30	Balance	✔			7 5 00	

ACCOUNT Accounts Receivable—Raymond O'Neil   ACCOUNT NO. 130

DATE		ITEM	POST. REF.	DEBIT	CREDIT	BALANCE	
						DEBIT	CREDIT
20-- June	30	Balance	✔			6 4 2 00	

ACCOUNT Supplies   ACCOUNT NO. 140

DATE		ITEM	POST. REF.	DEBIT	CREDIT	BALANCE	
						DEBIT	CREDIT
20-- June	30	Balance	✔			1 8 8 00	

ACCOUNT Prepaid Insurance   ACCOUNT NO. 150

DATE		ITEM	POST. REF.	DEBIT	CREDIT	BALANCE	
						DEBIT	CREDIT
20-- June	30	Balance	✔			5 4 0 00	

8-1 APPLICATION PROBLEM (continued)

ACCOUNT Accounts Payable—Western Supplies · ACCOUNT NO. 210

DATE	ITEM	POST. REF.	DEBIT	CREDIT	BALANCE DEBIT	BALANCE CREDIT
20-- June 30	Balance	✔				2 6 8 00

ACCOUNT Akbar Sharma, Capital · ACCOUNT NO. 310

DATE	ITEM	POST. REF.	DEBIT	CREDIT	BALANCE DEBIT	BALANCE CREDIT
20-- June 30	Balance	✔				9 6 9 5 00

ACCOUNT Akbar Sharma, Drawing · ACCOUNT NO. 320

DATE	ITEM	POST. REF.	DEBIT	CREDIT	BALANCE DEBIT	BALANCE CREDIT
20-- June 30	Balance	✔			3 7 5 00	

ACCOUNT Income Summary · ACCOUNT NO. 330

DATE	ITEM	POST. REF.	DEBIT	CREDIT	BALANCE DEBIT	BALANCE CREDIT

ACCOUNT Sales · ACCOUNT NO. 410

DATE	ITEM	POST. REF.	DEBIT	CREDIT	BALANCE DEBIT	BALANCE CREDIT
20-- June 30	Balance	✔				1 7 0 4 00

ACCOUNT Advertising Expense   ACCOUNT NO. 510

DATE		ITEM	POST. REF.	DEBIT	CREDIT	BALANCE	
						DEBIT	CREDIT
20-- June	30	Balance	✔			2 5 5 00	

ACCOUNT Cash Short and Over   ACCOUNT NO. 520

DATE		ITEM	POST. REF.	DEBIT	CREDIT	BALANCE	
						DEBIT	CREDIT
20-- June	30	Balance	✔			2 00	

ACCOUNT Insurance Expense   ACCOUNT NO. 530

DATE		ITEM	POST. REF.	DEBIT	CREDIT	BALANCE	
						DEBIT	CREDIT
20-- June	30	Balance	✔			1 3 5 00	

ACCOUNT Miscellaneous Expense   ACCOUNT NO. 540

DATE		ITEM	POST. REF.	DEBIT	CREDIT	BALANCE	
						DEBIT	CREDIT
20-- June	30	Balance	✔			1 3 8 00	

ACCOUNT Supplies Expense   ACCOUNT NO. 550

DATE		ITEM	POST. REF.	DEBIT	CREDIT	BALANCE	
						DEBIT	CREDIT
20-- June	30	Balance	✔			3 3 0 00	

ACCOUNT Utilities Expense   ACCOUNT NO. 560

DATE		ITEM	POST. REF.	DEBIT	CREDIT	BALANCE	
						DEBIT	CREDIT
20-- June	30	Balance	✔			2 7 2 00	

8-2 APPLICATION PROBLEM, p. 233

Preparing a post-closing trial balance (LO2)

ACCOUNT TITLE	DEBIT	CREDIT

8-M **MASTERY PROBLEM, p. 234**

Journalizing and posting closing entries with a net loss; preparing a post-closing trial balance (LO1, 2)

1.

GENERAL JOURNAL

PAGE

	DATE	ACCOUNT TITLE	DOC. NO.	POST. REF.	GENERAL DEBIT	GENERAL CREDIT	
6							6
7							7
8							8
9							9
10							10
11							11
12							12
13							13
14							14
15							15
16							16
17							17
18							18
19							19
20							20
21							21
22							22
23							23
24							24
25							25
26							26
27							27

8-M MASTERY PROBLEM (continued)

GENERAL LEDGER

1.

ACCOUNT Cash   ACCOUNT NO. 110

DATE	ITEM	POST. REF.	DEBIT	CREDIT	BALANCE DEBIT	BALANCE CREDIT
20-- May 31	Balance	✔			3 4 7 5 00	

ACCOUNT Petty Cash   ACCOUNT NO. 120

DATE	ITEM	POST. REF.	DEBIT	CREDIT	BALANCE DEBIT	BALANCE CREDIT
20-- May 31	Balance	✔			2 0 0 00	

ACCOUNT Accounts Receivable—M. Monesrud   ACCOUNT NO. 130

DATE	ITEM	POST. REF.	DEBIT	CREDIT	BALANCE DEBIT	BALANCE CREDIT
20-- May 31	Balance	✔			3 7 5 00	

ACCOUNT Supplies   ACCOUNT NO. 140

DATE	ITEM	POST. REF.	DEBIT	CREDIT	BALANCE DEBIT	BALANCE CREDIT
20-- May 31	Balance	✔			3 9 0 00	

ACCOUNT Prepaid Insurance   ACCOUNT NO. 150

DATE	ITEM	POST. REF.	DEBIT	CREDIT	BALANCE DEBIT	BALANCE CREDIT
20-- May 31	Balance	✔			4 0 0 00	

ACCOUNT **Accounts Payable—Lexington Supply**   ACCOUNT NO. 210

DATE		ITEM	POST. REF.	DEBIT	CREDIT	BALANCE	
						DEBIT	CREDIT
20-- May	31	Balance	✔				3 0 0 00

ACCOUNT **Rhonda Rausch, Capital**   ACCOUNT NO. 310

DATE		ITEM	POST. REF.	DEBIT	CREDIT	BALANCE	
						DEBIT	CREDIT
20-- May	31	Balance	✔				5 0 1 2 00

ACCOUNT **Rhonda Rausch, Drawing**   ACCOUNT NO. 320

DATE		ITEM	POST. REF.	DEBIT	CREDIT	BALANCE	
						DEBIT	CREDIT
20-- May	31	Balance	✔			3 0 0 00	

ACCOUNT **Income Summary**   ACCOUNT NO. 330

DATE		ITEM	POST. REF.	DEBIT	CREDIT	BALANCE	
						DEBIT	CREDIT

ACCOUNT **Sales**   ACCOUNT NO. 410

DATE		ITEM	POST. REF.	DEBIT	CREDIT	BALANCE	
						DEBIT	CREDIT
20-- May	31	Balance	✔				1 7 9 0 00

8-M MASTERY PROBLEM (continued)

ACCOUNT Advertising Expense   ACCOUNT NO. 510

DATE	ITEM	POST. REF.	DEBIT	CREDIT	BALANCE DEBIT	BALANCE CREDIT
20-- May 31	Balance	✔			2 2 5 00	

ACCOUNT Cash Short and Over   ACCOUNT NO. 520

DATE	ITEM	POST. REF.	DEBIT	CREDIT	BALANCE DEBIT	BALANCE CREDIT
20-- May 31	Balance	✔			2 00	

ACCOUNT Insurance Expense   ACCOUNT NO. 530

DATE	ITEM	POST. REF.	DEBIT	CREDIT	BALANCE DEBIT	BALANCE CREDIT
20-- May 31	Balance	✔			1 7 5 00	

ACCOUNT Miscellaneous Expense   ACCOUNT NO. 540

DATE	ITEM	POST. REF.	DEBIT	CREDIT	BALANCE DEBIT	BALANCE CREDIT
20-- May 31	Balance	✔			4 0 00	

ACCOUNT Supplies Expense   ACCOUNT NO. 550

DATE	ITEM	POST. REF.	DEBIT	CREDIT	BALANCE DEBIT	BALANCE CREDIT
20-- May 31	Balance	✔			7 0 0 00	

ACCOUNT Utilities Expense   ACCOUNT NO. 560

DATE	ITEM	POST. REF.	DEBIT	CREDIT	BALANCE DEBIT	BALANCE CREDIT
20-- May 31	Balance	✔			8 2 0 00	

2.

ACCOUNT TITLE	DEBIT	CREDIT

8-C CHALLENGE PROBLEM, p. 235

Journalizing and posting closing entries with two revenue accounts and a net loss; preparing a post-closing trial balance (LO1, 2)

1.

GENERAL JOURNAL

PAGE _____

	DATE	ACCOUNT TITLE	DOC. NO.	POST. REF.	GENERAL DEBIT	GENERAL CREDIT	
6							6
7							7
8							8
9							9
10							10
11							11
12							12
13							13
14							14
15							15
16							16
17							17
18							18
19							19
20							20
21							21
22							22
23							23
24							24
25							25
26							26
27							27

GENERAL LEDGER

1.

ACCOUNT Cash   ACCOUNT NO. 110

DATE		ITEM	POST. REF.	DEBIT	CREDIT	BALANCE	
						DEBIT	CREDIT
20-- June	30	Balance	✔			3 7 9 6 00	

ACCOUNT Accounts Receivable—V. Mathaney   ACCOUNT NO. 120

DATE		ITEM	POST. REF.	DEBIT	CREDIT	BALANCE	
						DEBIT	CREDIT
20-- June	30	Balance	✔			1 9 0 00	

ACCOUNT Supplies   ACCOUNT NO. 130

DATE		ITEM	POST. REF.	DEBIT	CREDIT	BALANCE	
						DEBIT	CREDIT
20-- June	30	Balance	✔			1 3 0 0 00	

ACCOUNT Prepaid Insurance   ACCOUNT NO. 140

DATE		ITEM	POST. REF.	DEBIT	CREDIT	BALANCE	
						DEBIT	CREDIT
20-- June	30	Balance	✔			2 4 0 0 00	

ACCOUNT Accounts Payable—Eveleth Repair   ACCOUNT NO. 210

DATE		ITEM	POST. REF.	DEBIT	CREDIT	BALANCE	
						DEBIT	CREDIT
20-- June	30	Balance	✔				1 1 6 00

8-C CHALLENGE PROBLEM (continued)

ACCOUNT Accounts Payable—Fremont Supplies   ACCOUNT NO. 220

DATE		ITEM	POST. REF.	DEBIT	CREDIT	BALANCE DEBIT	BALANCE CREDIT
20-- June	30	Balance	✔				2 2 0 00

ACCOUNT Accounts Payable—Olmstad Company   ACCOUNT NO. 230

DATE		ITEM	POST. REF.	DEBIT	CREDIT	BALANCE DEBIT	BALANCE CREDIT
20-- June	30	Balance	✔				4 3 0 00

ACCOUNT Jon Yanta, Capital   ACCOUNT NO. 310

DATE		ITEM	POST. REF.	DEBIT	CREDIT	BALANCE DEBIT	BALANCE CREDIT
20-- June	30	Balance	✔				8 0 0 0 00

ACCOUNT Jon Yanta, Drawing   ACCOUNT NO. 320

DATE		ITEM	POST. REF.	DEBIT	CREDIT	BALANCE DEBIT	BALANCE CREDIT
20-- June	30	Balance	✔			2 0 0 00	

ACCOUNT Income Summary   ACCOUNT NO. 330

DATE		ITEM	POST. REF.	DEBIT	CREDIT	BALANCE DEBIT	BALANCE CREDIT

ACCOUNT Sales—Lawn Care   ACCOUNT NO. 410

DATE		ITEM	POST. REF.	DEBIT	CREDIT	BALANCE DEBIT	BALANCE CREDIT
20-- June	30	Balance	✔				9 8 0 0 00

ACCOUNT Sales—Shrub Care   ACCOUNT NO. 420

DATE		ITEM	POST. REF.	DEBIT	CREDIT	BALANCE	
						DEBIT	CREDIT
20-- June	30	Balance	✔				5 0 0 0 00

ACCOUNT Advertising Expense   ACCOUNT NO. 510

DATE		ITEM	POST. REF.	DEBIT	CREDIT	BALANCE	
						DEBIT	CREDIT
20-- June	30	Balance	✔			7 8 0 00	

ACCOUNT Insurance Expense   ACCOUNT NO. 520

DATE		ITEM	POST. REF.	DEBIT	CREDIT	BALANCE	
						DEBIT	CREDIT
20-- June	30	Balance	✔			8 0 0 00	

ACCOUNT Miscellaneous Expense   ACCOUNT NO. 530

DATE		ITEM	POST. REF.	DEBIT	CREDIT	BALANCE	
						DEBIT	CREDIT
20-- June	30	Balance	✔			1 1 0 0 00	

ACCOUNT Rent Expense   ACCOUNT NO. 540

DATE		ITEM	POST. REF.	DEBIT	CREDIT	BALANCE	
						DEBIT	CREDIT
20-- June	30	Balance	✔			6 6 0 0 00	

ACCOUNT Supplies Expense   ACCOUNT NO. 550

DATE		ITEM	POST. REF.	DEBIT	CREDIT	BALANCE	
						DEBIT	CREDIT
20-- June	30	Balance	✔			6 4 0 0 00	

8-C CHALLENGE PROBLEM (continued)

2.

ACCOUNT TITLE	DEBIT	CREDIT

Chapter 8 Recording Closing Entries and Preparing a Post-Closing Trial Balance for a Service Business • **189**

3.

_____

_____

_____

_____

_____

_____

_____

_____

_____

_____

_____

_____

_____

REINFORCEMENT ACTIVITY 1, Part B, p. 238

An Accounting Cycle for a Proprietorship: End-of-Fiscal-Period Work

The general ledger prepared in Reinforcement Activity 1, Part A, is needed to complete Reinforcement Activity 1, Part B.

8., 9., 10., 11., 12.

ACCOUNT TITLE	TRIAL BALANCE		ADJUSTMENTS		INCOME STATEMENT		BALANCE SHEET	
	DEBIT	CREDIT	DEBIT	CREDIT	DEBIT	CREDIT	DEBIT	CREDIT
	1	2	3	4	5	6	7	8

REINFORCEMENT ACTIVITY 1, Part B (continued)

13., 17.

GENERAL JOURNAL

PAGE

	DATE		ACCOUNT TITLE	DOC. NO.	POST. REF.	DEBIT	CREDIT	
1								1
2								2
3								3
4								4
5								5
6								6
7								7
8								8
9								9
10								10
11								11
12								12
13								13
14								14
15								15
16								16
17								17
18								18
19								19
20								20
21								21
22								22
23								23
24								24

REINFORCEMENT ACTIVITY 1, Part B (continued)

14.

_____

_____

			% OF SALES

15.

_____

_____

16.

REINFORCEMENT ACTIVITY 1, Part B (concluded)

18.

_____

_____

_____

ACCOUNT TITLE	DEBIT	CREDIT

Name	Perfect Score	Your Score
Identifying Accounting Terms	41 Pts.	
Analyzing Accounting Concepts and Practices	20 Pts.	
Analyzing Transactions Recorded in Special Journals	24 Pts.	
Total	85 Pts.	

Part One—Identifying Accounting Terms

Directions: Select the one term in Column I that best fits each definition in Column II. Print the letter identifying your choice in the Answers column.

Contains accounting terms for Lessons 9-1.

Column I	Column II	Answers
A. accounts payable ledger	**1.** Goods that a business purchases in order to sell. (p. 244)	1._____
B. articles of incorporation	**2.** A business that purchases and resells goods. (p. 244)	2._____
C. capital	**3.** A merchandising business that sells to those who use or consume the goods. (p. 244)	3._____
D. capital stock	**4.** A business that buys and resells merchandise primarily to other merchandising businesses. (p. 244)	4._____
E. charter	**5.** An organization with the legal rights of a person which many persons or other corporations may own. (p. 244)	5._____
F. controlling account	**6.** The assets or other financial resources available to a business. (p. 244)	6._____
G. corporation	**7.** Each unit of ownership in a corporation. (p. 244)	7._____
H. merchandise	**8.** The owner of one or more shares of stock. (p. 244)	8._____
I. merchandising business	**9.** The total shares of ownership in a corporation. (p. 244)	9._____
J. retail merchandising business	**10.** A legal document that identifies basic characteristics of a corporation. (p. 244)	10._____
K. share of stock	**11.** The legal right for a business to conduct operations as a corporation. (p. 244)	11._____
L. stockholder	**12.** A business from which merchandise, supplies, or other assets are purchased. (p. 246)	12._____
M. subsidiary ledger	**13.** A ledger that is summarized in a single general ledger account. (p. 246)	13._____
N. vendor	**14.** The subsidiary ledger containing vendor accounts. (p. 246)	14._____
O. wholesale merchandising business	**15.** An account in a general ledger that summarizes all accounts in a subsidiary ledger. (p. 246)	15._____

Accounting terms for Lessons 9-2 through 9-5 are presented on the following page.

Directions: Select the one term in Column I that best fits each definition in Column II. Print the letter identifying your choice in the Answers column.

Contains accounting terms for Lessons 9-2 through 9-5.

Column I	Column II	Answers
A. cash discount	1. A list of assets, usually containing the value of individual items. (p. 249)	1. _____
B. cash payments journal	2. The goods a business has on hand for sale to customers. (p. 249)	2. _____
C. contra account	3. An inventory determined by keeping a continuous record of increases, decreases, and the balance on hand of each item of merchandise. (p. 249)	3. _____
D. cost of merchandise	4. A merchandise inventory evaluated at the end of a fiscal period. (p. 249)	4. _____
E. credit limit	5. When a periodic inventory is conducted by counting, weighing, or measuring items of merchandise on hand. (p. 249)	5. _____
F. discount period	6. The amount a business pays for goods it purchases to sell. (p. 250)	6. _____
G. due date	7. A form requesting the purchase of merchandise. (p. 251)	7. _____
H. general amount column	8. A form requesting that a vendor sell merchandise to a business. (p. 251)	8. _____
I. inventory	9. A journal used to record only one kind of transaction. (p. 251)	9. _____
J. list price	10. A transaction in which the items purchased are to be paid for later. (p. 252)	10. _____
K. merchandise inventory	11. A special journal used to record only purchases of merchandise on account. (p. 252)	11. _____
L. net price	12. A journal amount column headed with an account title. (p. 252)	12. _____
M. periodic inventory	13. An invoice used as a source document for recording a purchase on account transaction. (p. 252)	13. _____
N. perpetual inventory	14. An agreement between a buyer and a seller about payment for merchandise. (p. 252)	14. _____
O. physical inventory	15. The date by which an invoice must be paid. (p. 252)	15. _____
P. purchase invoice	16. A special journal used to record only cash payment transactions. (p. 260)	16. _____
Q. purchase on account	17. The retail price listed in a catalog or on an Internet site. (p. 260)	17. _____
R. purchase order	18. A reduction in the list price granted to a merchandising business. (p. 260)	18. _____
S. purchases discount	19. The price after the trade discount has been deducted from the list price. (p. 260)	19. _____
T. purchases journal	20. A deduction that a vendor allows on an invoice amount to encourage prompt payment. (p. 260)	20. _____
U. requisition	21. A journal amount column that is not headed with an account title. (p. 260)	21. _____
V. schedule of accounts payable	22. The period of time during which a customer may take a cash discount. (p. 263)	22. _____
W. special amount column	23. When a company that has purchased merchandise on account takes a cash discount. (p. 263)	23. _____
X. special journal	24. An account that reduces a related account on a financial statement. (p. 263)	24. _____
Y. terms of sale	25. The maximum outstanding balance allowed to a customer by a vendor. (p. 267)	25. _____
Z. trade discount	26. A listing of vendor accounts, account balances, and the total amount due to all vendors. (p. 272)	26. _____

Part Two—Analyzing Accounting Concepts and Practices

Directions: Place a *T* for True or an *F* for False in the Answers column to show whether each of the following statements is true or false.

Answers

1. A corporation can incur liabilities but cannot own property. (p. 244)

   1. _____

2. The articles of incorporation typically include the name and address of the business, its purpose for operating, any limitations on its activities and rules for dissolving the corporation. (p. 244)

   2. _____

3. Unlike a proprietorship, a corporation exists independent of its owners. (p. 245)

   3. _____

4. The total of accounts in the accounts payable ledger equals the balance of the controlling account, Accounts Payable. (p. 246)

   4. _____

5. The accounts payable ledger form contains the same columns as the general ledger except that it lacks a Credit Balance column. (p. 247)

   5. _____

6. When a perpetual inventory system is used, purchases of merchandise are accounted for directly to Merchandise Inventory. (p. 249)

   6. _____

7. The perpetual inventory method is easier to maintain than the periodic method. The perpetual method does not require records of the quantity and cost of individual goods. (p. 249)

   7. _____

8. When a periodic inventory system is used, the cost of merchandise is recorded to Purchases. (p. 250)

   8. _____

9. The income statement of a merchandising business places Purchases in a section titled Cost of Goods Sold, separate from other expenses. (p. 250)

   9. _____

10. A purchase invoice lists the quantity, the description, and the price of each item and shows the total amount of the purchase. (p. 253)

    10. _____

11. A transaction to record merchandise purchased with a trade discount would include a credit to Merchandise Discount. (p. 260)

    11. _____

12. When journalizing a cash payment for advertising, the vendor's name is written in the Account Title column of the cash payments journal. (p. 261)

    12. _____

13. When supplies are purchased for use in the business, the amount is recorded as a debit to Purchases. (p. 262)

    13. _____

14. The terms of sale 2/15, n/30 mean that 2% of the invoice amount may be deducted if paid within 15 days of the invoice date or the total invoice amount must be paid within 30 days. (p. 263)

    14. _____

15. The contra account Purchases Discount has a normal credit balance. (p. 263)

    15. _____

16. The source document for journalizing the direct withdrawal of credit card fees from a checking account is a memorandum. (p. 264)

    16. _____

17. Exceeding a vendor's credit limit can cause a disruption in the company's ability to purchase merchandise. (p. 267)

    17. _____

18. A journal is proved and ruled whenever a journal page is filled, and always at the end of a month. (p. 269)

    18. _____

19. The totals of the General amount columns of a cash payments journal are posted to the general ledger. (p. 270)

    19. _____

20. The total of an accounts payable trial balance should equal the total of Accounts Payable. (p. 272)

    20. _____

Part Three—Analyzing Transactions Recorded in Special Journals

Directions: In Answers Column l, print the abbreviation for the journal in which each transaction is to be recorded. In Answers Columns 2 and 3, print the letters identifying the accounts to be debited and credited for each transaction.

PJ—Purchases journal; **CPJ**—Cash payments journal

Account Titles	Transactions	Answers Journal	Debit	Credit
A. Accounts Payable	1-2-3. Purchased merchandise on account from Walner Electric. (p. 253)	1. ____	2. ____	3. ____
B. Cash	4-5-6. Paid cash for rent. (p. 261)	4. ____	5. ____	6. ____
C. Cash Short and Over	7-8-9. Paid cash to Triangle Suppliers for supplies. (pp. 261 and 262)	7. ____	8. ____	9. ____
D. Credit Card Fee Expense	10-11-12. Purchased merchandise from Zaben Corp. for cash. (p. 262)	10. ____	11. ____	12. ____
E. Miscellaneous Expense	13-14-15. Paid cash on account to Walner Electric, less purchases discount. (p. 263)	13. ____	14. ____	15. ____
F. Petty Cash	16-17-18. Paid cash on account to Triangle Suppliers. (p. 264)	16. ____	17. ____	18. ____
G. Purchases	19-20-21. Analyzed the bank statement showing recent credit card fees, $54.23. (p. 264)	19. ____	20. ____	21. ____
H. Purchases Discount	22-23-24. Paid cash to replenish the petty cash fund: supplies, miscellaneous, cash over. (p. 265)	22. ____	23. ____	24. ____
I. Purchases Returns and Allowances				
J. Rent Expense				
K. Supplies				
L. Triangle Suppliers				
M. Walner Electric				
N. Zaben Corp.				

9-1 WORK TOGETHER, p. 248

Starting an accounts payable ledger form

1.

VENDOR											VENDOR NO.							

DATE	ITEM	POST. REF.	DEBIT	CREDIT	CREDIT BALANCE

2.

VENDOR											VENDOR NO.							

DATE	ITEM	POST. REF.	DEBIT	CREDIT	CREDIT BALANCE

Starting an accounts payable ledger form

1.

	DATE		ITEM	POST. REF.	DEBIT	CREDIT	CREDIT BALANCE
VENDOR							VENDOR NO.

2.

	DATE		ITEM	POST. REF.	DEBIT	CREDIT	CREDIT BALANCE
VENDOR							VENDOR NO.

9-2, 9-3, 9-4, and 9-5   WORK TOGETHER, pp. 254, 259, 266, and 273

9-2 Journalizing purchases using a purchases journal
9-3 Posting from a purchases journal
9-4 Journalizing cash payments using a cash payments journal
9-5 Posting from a cash payments journal

1., 2., 3.

PURCHASES JOURNAL

PAGE

DATE	ACCOUNT CREDITED	PURCH. NO.	POST. REF.	PURCHASES DR. ACCTS. PAY. CR.	
1					1
2					2
3					3
4					4
5					5
6					6
7					7

CASH PAYMENTS JOURNAL

PAGE

				GENERAL		ACCOUNTS PAYABLE DEBIT	PURCHASES DISCOUNT CREDIT	CASH CREDIT	
DATE	ACCOUNT TITLE	CK. NO.	POST. REF.	DEBIT	CREDIT				
				1	2	3	4	5	
1									1
2									2
3									3
4									4
5									5
6									6
7									7
8									8
9									9
10									10
11									11
12									12

1.

VENDOR Coastal Company   VENDOR NO. 210

	DATE		ITEM	POST. REF.	DEBIT	CREDIT	CREDIT BALANCE
	Oct. 20--	1	Balance	✔			1 6 9 8 88

VENDOR Grey Manufacturing, Inc.   VENDOR NO. 220

	DATE		ITEM	POST. REF.	DEBIT	CREDIT	CREDIT BALANCE
	Oct. 20--	1	Balance	✔			1 6 4 0 00

VENDOR Pacific Supply   VENDOR NO. 230

	DATE		ITEM	POST. REF.	DEBIT	CREDIT	CREDIT BALANCE
	Oct. 20--	1	Balance	✔			9 2 5 65

VENDOR Westland Supply   VENDOR NO. 240

	DATE		ITEM	POST. REF.	DEBIT	CREDIT	CREDIT BALANCE
	Oct. 20--	1	Balance	✔			9 9 2 00

VENDOR Yeatman Designs   VENDOR NO. 250

	DATE		ITEM	POST. REF.	DEBIT	CREDIT	CREDIT BALANCE
	Oct. 20--	1	Balance	✔			8 7 7 00

9-2, 9-3, 9-4, and 9-5   WORK TOGETHER (continued)

3.

ACCOUNT Cash   ACCOUNT NO. 1110

DATE		ITEM	POST. REF.	DEBIT	CREDIT	BALANCE DEBIT	BALANCE CREDIT
20-- Oct.	1	Balance	✔			16 4 5 5 19	

ACCOUNT Supplies—Office   ACCOUNT NO. 1145

DATE		ITEM	POST. REF.	DEBIT	CREDIT	BALANCE DEBIT	BALANCE CREDIT
20-- Oct.	1	Balance	✔			3 1 8 4 17	

ACCOUNT Supplies—Store   ACCOUNT NO. 1150

DATE		ITEM	POST. REF.	DEBIT	CREDIT	BALANCE DEBIT	BALANCE CREDIT
20-- Oct.	1	Balance	✔			4 1 8 0 18	

ACCOUNT Accounts Payable   ACCOUNT NO. 2110

DATE		ITEM	POST. REF.	DEBIT	CREDIT	BALANCE DEBIT	BALANCE CREDIT
20-- Oct.	1	Balance	✔				6 1 3 3 53

ACCOUNT Purchases   ACCOUNT NO. 5110

DATE		ITEM	POST. REF.	DEBIT	CREDIT	BALANCE DEBIT	BALANCE CREDIT
20-- Oct.	1	Balance	✔			89 4 7 8 25	

ACCOUNT Purchases Discount   ACCOUNT NO. 5120

DATE		ITEM	POST. REF.	DEBIT	CREDIT	BALANCE DEBIT	BALANCE CREDIT
20-- Oct.	1	Balance	✔				6 2 1 48

ACCOUNT Cash Short and Over   ACCOUNT NO. 6110

DATE		ITEM	POST. REF.	DEBIT	CREDIT	BALANCE DEBIT	BALANCE CREDIT
20-- Oct.	1	Balance	✔			1 9 95	

ACCOUNT Credit Card Fee Expense   ACCOUNT NO. 6115

DATE		ITEM	POST. REF.	DEBIT	CREDIT	BALANCE DEBIT	BALANCE CREDIT
20-- Oct.	1	Balance	✔			4 8 1 15	

ACCOUNT Miscellaneous Expense   ACCOUNT NO. 6135

DATE		ITEM	POST. REF.	DEBIT	CREDIT	BALANCE DEBIT	BALANCE CREDIT
20-- Oct.	1	Balance	✔			2 4 8 9 97	

ACCOUNT Utilities Expense   ACCOUNT NO. 6170

DATE		ITEM	POST. REF.	DEBIT	CREDIT	BALANCE DEBIT	BALANCE CREDIT
20-- Oct.	1	Balance	✔			9 4 8 59	

9-2, 9-3, 9-4, and 9-5   **WORK TOGETHER (concluded)**

PETTY CASH REPORT				
Date: October 31, 20--			Custodian: John Sandersen	
	Explanation		Reconciliation	Replenish Amount
Fund Total			200.00	
Payments:	Supplies—Office	48.15		
	Supplies—Store	57.18		
	Miscellaneous	47.64		
Less:	Total payments		152.97	⟶ 152.97
Equals:	Recorded amount on hand		47.03	
Less:	Actual amount on hand		45.98	
Equals:	Cash short (over)		1.05	⟶ 1.05
Amount to Replenish				154.02

4.

9-2 Journalizing purchases using a purchases journal

9-3 Posting from a purchases journal

9-4 Journalizing cash payments using a cash payments journal

9-5 Posting from a cash payments journal

1., 2., 3.

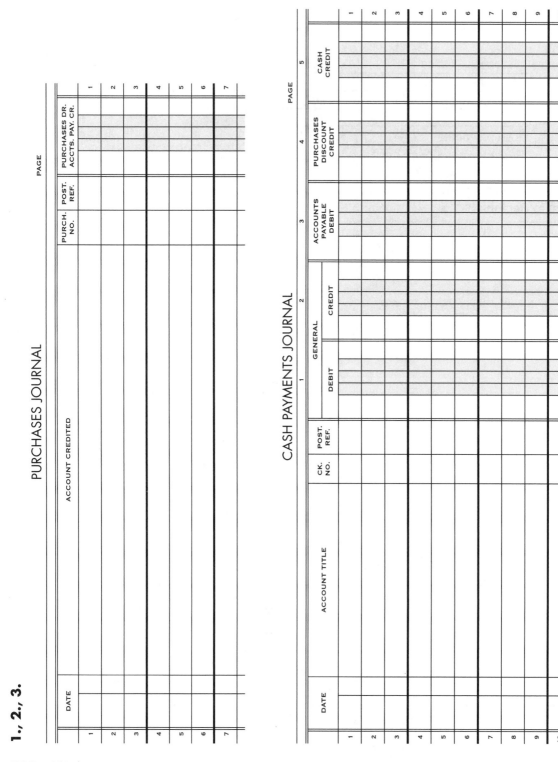

PURCHASES JOURNAL

CASH PAYMENTS JOURNAL

9-2, 9-3, 9-4, and 9-5   ON YOUR OWN (continued)

1.

VENDOR Gillis Glass Co.   VENDOR NO. 210

DATE		ITEM	POST. REF.	DEBIT	CREDIT	CREDIT BALANCE
20-- Nov.	1	Balance	✔			2 1 2 0 00

VENDOR Lawes Imports   VENDOR NO. 220

DATE		ITEM	POST. REF.	DEBIT	CREDIT	CREDIT BALANCE
20-- Nov.	1	Balance	✔			1 9 0 8 35

VENDOR McKell Supply, Inc.   VENDOR NO. 230

DATE		ITEM	POST. REF.	DEBIT	CREDIT	CREDIT BALANCE
20-- Nov.	1	Balance	✔			6 4 8 50

VENDOR Sheng Industries   VENDOR NO. 240

DATE		ITEM	POST. REF.	DEBIT	CREDIT	CREDIT BALANCE
20-- Nov.	1	Balance	✔			2 1 6 9 00

VENDOR Tresler Corporation   VENDOR NO. 250

DATE		ITEM	POST. REF.	DEBIT	CREDIT	CREDIT BALANCE
20-- Nov.	1	Balance	✔			2 9 1 3 00

3.

ACCOUNT Cash   ACCOUNT NO. 1110

DATE		ITEM	POST. REF.	DEBIT	CREDIT	BALANCE	
						DEBIT	CREDIT
20-- Nov.	1	Balance	✔			9 1 8 3 10	

ACCOUNT Supplies—Office   ACCOUNT NO. 1145

DATE		ITEM	POST. REF.	DEBIT	CREDIT	BALANCE	
						DEBIT	CREDIT
20-- Nov.	1	Balance	✔			2 4 9 8 21	

ACCOUNT Accounts Payable   ACCOUNT NO. 2110

DATE		ITEM	POST. REF.	DEBIT	CREDIT	BALANCE	
						DEBIT	CREDIT
20-- Nov.	1	Balance	✔				9 7 5 8 85

ACCOUNT Purchases   ACCOUNT NO. 5110

DATE		ITEM	POST. REF.	DEBIT	CREDIT	BALANCE	
						DEBIT	CREDIT
20-- Nov.	1	Balance	✔			92 1 8 4 11	

ACCOUNT Purchases Discount   ACCOUNT NO. 5120

DATE		ITEM	POST. REF.	DEBIT	CREDIT	BALANCE	
						DEBIT	CREDIT
20-- Nov.	1	Balance	✔				7 0 1 57

9-2, 9-3, 9-4, and 9-5   ON YOUR OWN (continued)

ACCOUNT Advertising Expense   ACCOUNT NO. 6105

DATE	ITEM	POST. REF.	DEBIT	CREDIT	BALANCE DEBIT	BALANCE CREDIT
20-- Nov. 1	Balance	✔			16 5 5 4 69	

ACCOUNT Cash Short and Over   ACCOUNT NO. 6110

DATE	ITEM	POST. REF.	DEBIT	CREDIT	BALANCE DEBIT	BALANCE CREDIT
20-- Nov. 1	Balance	✔			1 6 99	

ACCOUNT Credit Card Fee Expense   ACCOUNT NO. 6115

DATE	ITEM	POST. REF.	DEBIT	CREDIT	BALANCE DEBIT	BALANCE CREDIT
20-- Nov. 1	Balance	✔			6 2 5 05	

ACCOUNT Miscellaneous Expense   ACCOUNT NO. 6135

DATE	ITEM	POST. REF.	DEBIT	CREDIT	BALANCE DEBIT	BALANCE CREDIT
20-- Nov. 1	Balance	✔			1 0 9 2 05	

ACCOUNT Utilities Expense   ACCOUNT NO. 6170

DATE	ITEM	POST. REF.	DEBIT	CREDIT	BALANCE DEBIT	BALANCE CREDIT
20-- Nov. 1	Balance	✔			9 1 0 5 40	

PETTY CASH REPORT

Date: November 30, 20--   Custodian: Aimee Smith

Explanation			Reconciliation		Replenish Amount
Fund Total			250.00		
Payments:	Supplies—Office	56.21			
	Advertising	82.25			
	Miscellaneous	36.17			
Less:	Total payments		174.63	⟶	174.63
Equals:	Recorded amount on hand		75.37		
Less:	Actual amount on hand		76.82		
Equals:	Cash short (over)		(1.45)	⟶	(1.45)
Amount to Replenish					173.18

4.

9-1 APPLICATION PROBLEM (LO3), p. 277

Starting an accounts payable ledger form

1., 2.

VENDOR _____   VENDOR NO. _____

	DATE	ITEM	POST. REF.	DEBIT	CREDIT	CREDIT BALANCE	

VENDOR _____   VENDOR NO. _____

	DATE	ITEM	POST. REF.	DEBIT	CREDIT	CREDIT BALANCE	

9-2 Journalizing purchases using a purchases journal

9-3 Posting from a purchases journal

9-4 Journalizing cash payments using a cash payments journal

9-5 Posting from a cash payments journal

9-2, 9-3, 9-4, and 9-5   APPLICATION PROBLEMS (continued)

VENDOR **Atlanta Systems**   VENDOR NO. 210

DATE		ITEM	POST. REF.	DEBIT	CREDIT	CREDIT BALANCE
20-- Sept.	1	Balance	✔			2 6 2 1 48

VENDOR **Henson Audio**   VENDOR NO. 220

DATE		ITEM	POST. REF.	DEBIT	CREDIT	CREDIT BALANCE
20-- Sept.	1	Balance	✔			2 4 8 9 00

VENDOR **Lester Corporation**   VENDOR NO. 230

DATE		ITEM	POST. REF.	DEBIT	CREDIT	CREDIT BALANCE
20-- Sept.	1	Balance	✔			6 3 8 00

VENDOR **Masonville Music**   VENDOR NO. 240

DATE		ITEM	POST. REF.	DEBIT	CREDIT	CREDIT BALANCE
20-- Sept.	1	Balance	✔			1 1 8 9 00

VENDOR **Peterson Electronics**   VENDOR NO. 250

DATE		ITEM	POST. REF.	DEBIT	CREDIT	CREDIT BALANCE
20-- Sept.	1	Balance	✔			3 4 8 4 00

3.

ACCOUNT Cash   ACCOUNT NO. 1110

DATE	ITEM	POST. REF.	DEBIT	CREDIT	BALANCE DEBIT	BALANCE CREDIT
Sept. 1	Balance	✔			22 1 8 9 18	

ACCOUNT Supplies—Office   ACCOUNT NO. 1145

DATE	ITEM	POST. REF.	DEBIT	CREDIT	BALANCE DEBIT	BALANCE CREDIT
Sept. 1	Balance	✔			4 2 2 4 18	

ACCOUNT Supplies—Store   ACCOUNT NO. 1150

DATE	ITEM	POST. REF.	DEBIT	CREDIT	BALANCE DEBIT	BALANCE CREDIT
Sept. 1	Balance	✔			3 9 1 4 11	

ACCOUNT Accounts Payable   ACCOUNT NO. 2110

DATE	ITEM	POST. REF.	DEBIT	CREDIT	BALANCE DEBIT	BALANCE CREDIT
Sept. 1	Balance	✔				10 4 2 1 48

ACCOUNT Purchases   ACCOUNT NO. 5110

DATE	ITEM	POST. REF.	DEBIT	CREDIT	BALANCE DEBIT	BALANCE CREDIT
Sept. 1	Balance	✔			241 9 4 7 18	

9-2, 9-3, 9-4, and 9-5   APPLICATION PROBLEMS (continued)

ACCOUNT Purchases Discount   ACCOUNT NO. 5120

DATE		ITEM	POST. REF.	DEBIT	CREDIT	BALANCE	
						DEBIT	CREDIT
20-- Sept.	1	Balance	✔				1 4 8 7 17

ACCOUNT Advertising Expense   ACCOUNT NO. 6105

DATE		ITEM	POST. REF.	DEBIT	CREDIT	BALANCE	
						DEBIT	CREDIT
20-- Sept.	1	Balance	✔			9 2 0 9 61	

ACCOUNT Cash Short and Over   ACCOUNT NO. 6110

DATE		ITEM	POST. REF.	DEBIT	CREDIT	BALANCE	
						DEBIT	CREDIT
20-- Sept.	1	Balance	✔			2 2 04	

ACCOUNT Credit Card Fee Expense   ACCOUNT NO. 6115

DATE		ITEM	POST. REF.	DEBIT	CREDIT	BALANCE	
						DEBIT	CREDIT
20-- Sept.	1	Balance	✔			2 1 4 8 00	

ACCOUNT Miscellaneous Expense   ACCOUNT NO. 6135

DATE		ITEM	POST. REF.	DEBIT	CREDIT	BALANCE	
						DEBIT	CREDIT
20-- Sept.	1	Balance	✔			8 6 4 9 31	

ACCOUNT Utilities Expense   ACCOUNT NO. 6170

DATE		ITEM	POST. REF.	DEBIT	CREDIT	BALANCE	
						DEBIT	CREDIT
20-- Sept.	1	Balance	✔			6 7 4 9 89	

PETTY CASH REPORT

Date: September 30, 20--   Custodian: Eddie Henderson

	Explanation		Reconciliation		Replenish Amount
Fund Total			200.00		
Payments:	Advertising	60.00			
	Miscellaneous	26.50			
	Supplies—Store	35.00			
	Supplies—Office	23.24			
Less:	Total payments		144.74	⟶	144.74
Equals:	Recorded amount on hand		55.26		
Less:	Actual amount on hand		55.14		
Equals:	Cash short (over)		0.12	⟶	0.12
Amount to Replenish					144.86

4.

9-M MASTERY PROBLEM (LO6, 7, 8, 10), p. 279

Journalizing purchases, cash payments, and other transactions
1., 2., 3.

PURCHASES JOURNAL

PAGE

	DATE		ACCOUNT CREDITED	PURCH. NO.	POST. REF.	PURCHASES DR. ACCTS. PAY. CR.	
1							1
2							2
3							3
4							4
5							5
6							6
7							7
8							8
9							9
10							10
11							11
12							12
13							13
14							14
15							15
16							16
17							17
18							18
19							19
20							20
21							21
22							22
23							23
24							24
25							25
26							26
27							27
28							28
29							29
30							30
31							31
32							32

1., 4., 5.

CASH PAYMENTS JOURNAL

PAGE

					GENERAL		ACCOUNTS PAYABLE DEBIT	PURCHASES DISCOUNT CREDIT	CASH CREDIT
DATE	ACCOUNT TITLE	CK. NO.	POST. REF.	DEBIT	CREDIT				
				1	2	3	4	5	

9-M MASTERY PROBLEM (continued)

1.

VENDOR Delmar, Inc.   VENDOR NO. 210

DATE		ITEM	POST. REF.	DEBIT	CREDIT	CREDIT BALANCE
July	1	Balance	✔			3 0 4 9 00

VENDOR Helms Supply   VENDOR NO. 220

DATE		ITEM	POST. REF.	DEBIT	CREDIT	CREDIT BALANCE
July	1	Balance	✔			1 2 8 0 00

VENDOR Kelsay Parts   VENDOR NO. 230

DATE		ITEM	POST. REF.	DEBIT	CREDIT	CREDIT BALANCE
July	1	Balance	✔			3 9 4 0 00

VENDOR Rackley Industries   VENDOR NO. 240

DATE		ITEM	POST. REF.	DEBIT	CREDIT	CREDIT BALANCE
July	1	Balance	✔			2 1 1 9 00

1., 3., 5.

ACCOUNT Cash   ACCOUNT NO. 1110

DATE		ITEM	POST. REF.	DEBIT	CREDIT	BALANCE	
						DEBIT	CREDIT
July	1	Balance	✔			18 4 9 9 17	

ACCOUNT Supplies—Office   ACCOUNT NO. 1145

DATE		ITEM	POST. REF.	DEBIT	CREDIT	BALANCE	
						DEBIT	CREDIT
July	1	Balance	✔			3 4 1 8 07	

ACCOUNT Supplies—Store   ACCOUNT NO. 1150

DATE		ITEM	POST. REF.	DEBIT	CREDIT	BALANCE	
						DEBIT	CREDIT
July	1	Balance	✔			4 1 8 4 17	

ACCOUNT Accounts Payable   ACCOUNT NO. 2110

DATE		ITEM	POST. REF.	DEBIT	CREDIT	BALANCE	
						DEBIT	CREDIT
July	1	Balance	✔				10 3 8 8 00

ACCOUNT Purchases   ACCOUNT NO. 5110

DATE		ITEM	POST. REF.	DEBIT	CREDIT	BALANCE	
						DEBIT	CREDIT
July	1	Balance	✔			294 1 8 4 14	

ACCOUNT Purchases Discount   ACCOUNT NO. 5120

DATE		ITEM	POST. REF.	DEBIT	CREDIT	BALANCE	
						DEBIT	CREDIT
July 1	1	Balance	✔				3 1 4 8 14

ACCOUNT Advertising Expense   ACCOUNT NO. 6105

DATE		ITEM	POST. REF.	DEBIT	CREDIT	BALANCE	
						DEBIT	CREDIT
July 1	1	Balance	✔			12 4 9 5 16	

ACCOUNT Cash Short and Over   ACCOUNT NO. 6110

DATE		ITEM	POST. REF.	DEBIT	CREDIT	BALANCE	
						DEBIT	CREDIT
July 1	1	Balance	✔			3 4 18	

ACCOUNT Credit Card Fee Expense   ACCOUNT NO. 6115

DATE		ITEM	POST. REF.	DEBIT	CREDIT	BALANCE	
						DEBIT	CREDIT
July 1	1	Balance	✔			5 4 8 00	

ACCOUNT Miscellaneous Expense   ACCOUNT NO. 6135

DATE		ITEM	POST. REF.	DEBIT	CREDIT	BALANCE	
						DEBIT	CREDIT
July 1	1	Balance	✔			14 0 8 8 63	

ACCOUNT Utilities Expense   ACCOUNT NO. 6170

DATE		ITEM	POST. REF.	DEBIT	CREDIT	BALANCE	
						DEBIT	CREDIT
July 1	1	Balance	✔			7 6 3 3 69	

PETTY CASH REPORT				
Date: July 31, 20--			Custodian: Sean Williams	
	Explanation		Reconciliation	Replenish Amount
Fund Total			200.00	
Payments:	Supplies—Office	45.60		
	Supplies—Store	67.30		
	Miscellaneous	23.89		
Less:	Total payments		136.79 →	136.79
Equals:	Recorded amount on hand		63.21	
Less:	Actual amount on hand		61.98	
Equals:	Cash short (over)		1.23 →	1.23
Amount to Replenish				138.02

6.

9-S SOURCE DOCUMENTS PROBLEM (LO6, 8), p. 280

Journalizing purchases, cash payments, and other transactions from source documents

Coastal Sailing, Inc. 1423 Commerical Road Bell City, LA 70630		INVOICE		REC'D 10/04/-- P324	
		TO: Messler Sailing 142 River Street Naperville, IL 60540	DATE: 9/30/-- INV. NO. 6234 TERMS: 30 days ACCT. NO. 2450		

QUANTITY	CAT. NO.	DESCRIPTION	UNIT PRICE	TOTAL
25	4323	jib sheet	$ 45.00	$ 1,125.00
20	4233	jib halyard	165.00	3,300.00
		TOTAL		$ 4,425.00

Aquatic Manufacturing 42 Industrial Road Stratford, CA 93266		INVOICE		REC'D 10/11/-- P325	
		TO: Messler Sailing 142 River Street Naperville, IL 60540	DATE: 10/08/-- INV. NO. 15484 TERMS: 2/10,n/30 ACCT. NO. 1420		

QUANTITY	CAT. NO.	DESCRIPTION	UNIT PRICE	TOTAL
10	532	Fiberglass repair kit	$ 83.00	$ 830.00
35	6346	U-bolts, 1"	16.00	560.00
40	6347	U-bolts, 2"	23.00	920.00
		TOTAL		$ 2,310.00

Northern Sail Company 253 Beach Blvd. Boston, MA 02169		INVOICE		REC'D 10/20/-- P326	
		TO: Messler Sailing 142 River Street Naperville, IL 60540	DATE: 10/18/-- INV. NO. 895 TERMS: 30 days ACCT. NO. 1820		

QUANTITY	CAT. NO.	DESCRIPTION	UNIT PRICE	TOTAL
2	B-23	Viking-16 mainsail	$ 1,599.00	$ 3,198.00
4	B-44	Sunset-13 mainsail	459.00	1,836.00
		TOTAL		$ 5,034.00

NO. **621** $ _1,725.00_

Date: _October 4_   20 _--_

To: _Seaside Manufacturing_

For: _On account_

BALANCE BROUGHT FORWARD	12,485	25
AMOUNT DEPOSITED		
SUBTOTAL Date	12,485	25
OTHER:		
SUBTOTAL	12,485	25
AMOUNT THIS CHECK	1,725	00
BALANCE CARRIED FORWARD	10,760	25

NO. **623** $ _321.15_

Date: _October 15_   20 _--_

To: _Northern Electric_

For: _Utilities_

BALANCE BROUGHT FORWARD	11,355	50
AMOUNT DEPOSITED		
SUBTOTAL Date	11,355	50
OTHER:		
SUBTOTAL	11,355	50
AMOUNT THIS CHECK	321	15
BALANCE CARRIED FORWARD	11,034	35

NO. **622** $ _668.75_

Date: _October 10_   20 _--_

To: _Willcutt & Bishop_

For: _Supplies-Office_

BALANCE BROUGHT FORWARD			10,760	25
AMOUNT DEPOSITED	10	9	20-- 1,264	00
SUBTOTAL Date			12,024	25
OTHER:				
SUBTOTAL			12,024	25
AMOUNT THIS CHECK			668	75
BALANCE CARRIED FORWARD			11,355	50

NO. **624** $ _2,263.80_

Date: _October 19_   20 _--_

To: _Aquatic Manufacturing_

For: _On account payment for P325_

BALANCE BROUGHT FORWARD			11,034	35
AMOUNT DEPOSITED	10	18	20-- 546	50
SUBTOTAL Date			11,580	85
OTHER:				
SUBTOTAL			11,580	85
AMOUNT THIS CHECK			2,263	80
BALANCE CARRIED FORWARD			9,317	05

9-S SOURCE DOCUMENTS PROBLEM (continued)

NO. **625**	$ 2,560.00		
Date: October 20		20 --	
To: WRRX Radio			
For: Advertising			
BALANCE BROUGHT FORWARD		9,317	05
AMOUNT DEPOSITED			
SUBTOTAL Date		9,317	05
OTHER:			
SUBTOTAL		9,317	05
AMOUNT THIS CHECK		2,560	00
BALANCE CARRIED FORWARD		6,757	05

NO. **627**	$ 4,425.00		
Date: October 29		20 --	
To: Coastal Sailing, Inc.			
For: On account			
BALANCE BROUGHT FORWARD		7,954	13
AMOUNT DEPOSITED			
SUBTOTAL Date		7,954	13
OTHER:			
SUBTOTAL		7,954	13
AMOUNT THIS CHECK		4,425	00
BALANCE CARRIED FORWARD		3,529	13

NO. **626**	$ 224.00		
Date: October 22		20 --	
To: Michigan Sail Co.			
For: Purchases			
BALANCE BROUGHT FORWARD		6,757	05
AMOUNT DEPOSITED 10 21 20--		1,421	08
SUBTOTAL Date		8,178	13
OTHER:			
SUBTOTAL		8,178	13
AMOUNT THIS CHECK		224	00
BALANCE CARRIED FORWARD		7,954	13

NO. **628**	$ 112.94		
Date: October 31		20 --	
To: Mary Donovan, Petty Cash			
For: Petty cash			
BALANCE BROUGHT FORWARD		3,529	13
AMOUNT DEPOSITED 10 18 20--		648	22
SUBTOTAL Date		4,177	35
OTHER:			
SUBTOTAL		4,177	35
AMOUNT THIS CHECK		112	94
BALANCE CARRIED FORWARD		4,064	41

Willcutt & Bishop
132 Washington Street
Naperville, IL 60540

INVOICE

TO: Messler Sailing
142 River Street
Naperville, IL 60540

DATE: 10/10/20--

INV. NO. 1548

QUANTITY	CAT. NO.	DESCRIPTION	UNIT PRICE		TOTAL	
6	4818	computer paper	$	25.00	$	150.00
5	5518	pen packs		5.00		25.00
3	1548	jump drive		50.00		150.00
1	n/a	custom document print job #126		300.00		300.00
		SUBTOTAL			$	625.00
		TAX				43.75
		TOTAL			$	668.75

Northern Electric
125 Burlington Drive
Aurora, IL 60507-1523

October 13, 20-- 43643

Messler Sailing
142 River Street
Naperville, IL 60540

	This Month	Last Month		
Kilowatts	1548	1613	Paid this amount ⟶	$ 321.15
per Day	50	52		

Serving Your Energy Needs Since 1897

9-S **SOURCE DOCUMENTS PROBLEM (continued)**

WRRX Radio

The Voice of the Fox River Valley
P.O. Box 1223
Aurora, IL 60507-1223

TO: Messler Sailing
142 River Street
Naperville, IL 60540

October 20, 20--
Invoice No. 2355

Advertising spots for October, 60 30-second spots at various times during prime-time commuting periods	$ 2,160.00
Recording of radio spot by Kenneth Black	400.00
	$ 2,560.00

Thank you for your business!

Michigan Sail Company	**INVOICE**	**48448**
1442 Lakefront Avenue		
Evanston, IL 60204		

TO: Messler Sailing
142 River Street
Naperville, IL 60540

DATE: *10/22/20--*

QUANTITY	CAT. NO.	DESCRIPTION	UNIT PRICE	TOTAL
1	18–235	*Sunlight 13' mainsail*	$224.00	$ 224.00
		TOTAL		$ 224.00

PETTY CASH REPORT

Date: October 31, 20--   Custodian: Mary Donovan

Explanation		Reconciliation		Replenish Amount
Fund Total		250.00		
Payments:	Supplies—Office	23.45		
	Supplies—Store	65.25		
	Miscellaneous	26.14		
Less:	Total payments	114.84	⟶	114.84
Equals:	Recorded amount on hand	135.16		
Less:	Actual amount on hand	137.06		
Equals:	Cash short (over)	(1.90)	⟶	(1.90)
Amount to Replenish				112.94

9-S SOURCE DOCUMENTS PROBLEM (continued)

1., 2.

PURCHASES JOURNAL   PAGE _____

	DATE		ACCOUNT CREDITED	PURCH. NO.	POST. REF.	PURCHASES DR. ACCTS. PAY. CR.		
1								1
2								2
3								3
4								4
5								5
6								6
7								7
8								8
9								9
10								10
11								11
12								12
13								13
14								14
15								15
16								16
17								17
18								18
19								19
20								20
21								21
22								22
23								23
24								24
25								25
26								26
27								27
28								28
29								29
30								30
31								31
32								32

1., 3.

CASH PAYMENTS JOURNAL

PAGE 5

	ACCOUNT TITLE	CK. NO.	POST. REF.	GENERAL DEBIT	GENERAL CREDIT	ACCOUNTS PAYABLE DEBIT	PURCHASES DISCOUNT CREDIT	CASH CREDIT	
DATE				1	2	3	4	5	
1									1
2									2
3									3
4									4
5									5
6									6
7									7
8									8
9									9
10									10
11									11
12									12
13									13
14									14
15									15
16									16
17									17
18									18
19									19
20									20
21									21
22									22

9-C **CHALLENGE PROBLEM (LO6, 8), p. 280**

Journalizing purchases and cash payments

1.

PURCHASES JOURNAL   PAGE

	DATE		ACCOUNT CREDITED	PURCH. NO.	POST. REF.	PURCHASES DR. ACCTS. PAY. CR.	
1							1
2							2
3							3
4							4
5							5
6							6
7							7
8							8
9							9
10							10
11							11
12							12
13							13
14							14
15							15
16							16
17							17
18							18
19							19
20							20
21							21
22							22
23							23
24							24
25							25
26							26
27							27
28							28
29							29
30							30
31							31

1.

CASH PAYMENTS JOURNAL

PAGE 5

DATE		ACCOUNT TITLE	CK. NO.	POST. REF.	GENERAL DEBIT	GENERAL CREDIT	ACCOUNTS PAYABLE DEBIT	PURCHASES DISCOUNT CREDIT	CASH CREDIT	
					1	2	3	4	5	
Dec. 20‑	1	Pacific Guitar	82	230			5 4 8 6 00	1 0 9 72	5 3 7 6 28	1
										2
										3
										4
										5
										6
										7
										8
										9
										10
										11
										12
	31	Totals					32 5 0 5 00	3 9 8 12	32 1 0 6 88	13
										14
										15
										16
										17
										18
										19
										20
										21
										22

9-C CHALLENGE PROBLEM (continued)

1.

VENDOR Abraham Instruments   VENDOR NO. 210

DATE		ITEM	POST. REF.	DEBIT	CREDIT	CREDIT BALANCE
20-- Nov.	13		P11		1 4 8 5 00	1 4 8 5 00

VENDOR Brassworks   VENDOR NO. 220

DATE		ITEM	POST. REF.	DEBIT	CREDIT	CREDIT BALANCE
20-- Nov.	15		P11		6 2 8 00	6 2 8 00
	24		P11		2 4 8 00	8 7 6 00

VENDOR Pacific Guitar   VENDOR NO. 230

DATE		ITEM	POST. REF.	DEBIT	CREDIT	CREDIT BALANCE
20-- Nov.	24		P11		5 4 8 6 00	5 4 8 6 00
	29		P11		3 6 9 0 00	9 1 7 6 00
Dec.	1		CP12	5 4 8 6 00		3 6 9 0 00

VENDOR Pratt Publishing   VENDOR NO. 240

DATE	ITEM	POST. REF.	DEBIT	CREDIT	CREDIT BALANCE
20-- Nov. 16		P11		2 4 7 8 00	2 4 7 8 00

VENDOR Southern Music Supply   VENDOR NO. 250

DATE	ITEM	POST. REF.	DEBIT	CREDIT	CREDIT BALANCE
20-- Nov. 5		P11		4 8 1 0 00	4 8 1 0 00
30		P11		2 4 9 0 00	7 3 0 0 00

9-C **CHALLENGE PROBLEM (concluded)**

2.

Name	Perfect Score	Your Score
Identifying Accounting Terms	13 Pts.	
Analyzing Accounting Concepts and Practices	20 Pts.	
Analyzing Transactions Recorded in Special Journals	12 Pts.	
Total	45 Pts.	

Part One—Identifying Accounting Terms

Directions: Select the one term in Column I that best fits each definition in Column II. Print the letter identifying your choice in the Answers column.

Column I	Column II	Answers
A. accounts receivable ledger	**1.** The amount a business receives from the sale of an item of merchandise. (p. 284)	1. _____
B. batch report	**2.** The amount a business adds to the cost of merchandise to arrive at the selling price. (p. 284)	2. _____
C. batching out	**3.** A subsidiary ledger containing all accounts for charge customers. (p. 284)	3. _____
D. cash receipts journal	**4.** A tax on a sale of merchandise or services. (p. 286)	4. _____
E. cash sale	**5.** A special journal used to record only sales of merchandise on account. (p. 287)	5. _____
F. markup	**6.** A sale in which the customer pays for the total amount of the sale at the time of the transaction. (p. 294)	6. _____
G. point-of-sale (POS) terminal	**7.** A specialized computer used to collect, store, and report all the information about a sales transaction. (p. 294)	7. _____
H. sales discount	**8.** The report that summarizes the cash and credit card sales of a point-of-sale terminal. (p. 294)	8. _____
I. sales journal	**9.** A report of credit card sales produced by a point-of-sale terminal. (p. 295)	9. _____
J. sales tax	**10.** The process of preparing a batch report from a point-of-sale terminal. (p. 295)	10. _____
K. schedule of accounts receivable	**11.** A special journal used to record only cash receipt transactions. (p. 296)	11. _____
L. selling price	**12.** A cash discount on a sale taken by the customer. (p. 296)	12. _____
M. terminal summary	**13.** A listing of customer accounts, account balances, and total amount due from all customers. (p. 308)	13. _____

Part Two—Analyzing Accounting Concepts and Practices

Directions: Place a *T* for True or an *F* for False in the Answers column to show whether each of the following statements is true or false.

1. Regardless of when payment is received, the revenue should be recorded when a sale is made, not on the date cash is received. (p. 284)

2. The accounts receivable ledger form is based on the general ledger form and contains the same columns, except the Credit balance amount column. (p. 286)

3. Most states do not require a business to collect sales tax from customers. (p. 286)

4. Sales tax rates are usually stated as a percentage of sales. (p. 286)

5. The amount of sales tax collected is an expense of operating a business. (p. 286)

6. Only the federal government can exempt from sales taxes some types of merchandise or sales to certain types of customers. (p. 286)

7. An invoice is a form that describes the goods or services sold, the quantity and the price, and the terms of the sale. (p. 287)

8. The invoice used as a source document for recording a sale on account is often referred to as a sales invoice, a sales ticket, or a sales slip. (p. 287)

9. While the seller considers an invoice for a sale on account to be a sales invoice, the same invoice is considered by the customer to be a purchase invoice. (p. 287)

10. Credit card and debit card sales are treated as cash sales because the business receives its cash in a very short time. (p. 294)

11. A terminal summary is also known as a *T tape*. (p. 294)

12. A batch report can be detailed, showing every credit card sale. Or, the batch report can be a summary, showing only the number and total of sales by credit card type. (p. 295)

13. Separate transactions are recorded for cash, credit card, and debit card totals listed on a terminal summary. (p. 297)

14. Sales Tax Payable has a normal debit balance. (p. 297)

15. When a sales discount is taken, a customer pays less cash than the invoice amount previously recorded in the sales account. (p. 299)

16. Maintaining a separate account for sales discounts provides business managers with information to evaluate whether a sales discount is a cost-effective method. (p. 300)

17. The posting references on the accounts receivable ledger form enable the company to locate the sales invoices and receipts supporting each transaction. (p. 302)

18. The total of each general amount column of a cash receipts journal is posted to the corresponding general ledger account. (p. 302)

19. A schedule of accounts receivable contains a complete listing of each sales invoice owed by customers. (p. 308)

20. Some businesses call the schedule of accounts receivable the *accounts receivable trial balance*. (p. 308)

Answers
1. _____
2. _____
3. _____
4. _____
5. _____
6. _____
7. _____
8. _____
9. _____
10. _____
11. _____
12. _____
13. _____
14. _____
15. _____
16. _____
17. _____
18. _____
19. _____
20. _____

Part Three—Analyzing Transactions Recorded in Special Journals

Directions: In Answers Column 1, print the abbreviation for the journal in which each transaction is to be recorded. In Answers Columns 2 and 3, print the letters identifying the accounts to be debited and credited for each transaction. For transactions affecting accounts receivable, be sure to also include the subsidiary ledger account affected.

SJ—Sales journal; **CRJ**—Cash receipts journal

			Answers		
			1	**2**	**3**
Account Titles	**Transactions**		**Journal**	**Debit**	**Credit**
A. Accounts Receivable	1-2-3. Sold merchandise on account to Doris Edwards, plus sales tax. (p. 288)		1. ____	2. ____	3. ____
B. Cash	4-5-6. Recorded cash and credit card sales, plus sales tax. (p. 297)		4. ____	5. ____	6. ____
C. Doris Edwards	7-8-9. Received cash on account from Jim North. (p. 298)		7. ____	8. ____	9. ____
D. Jim North	10-11-12. Received cash on account from Doris Edwards, less sales discount. (p. 300)		10. ____	11. ____	12. ____
E. Sales					
F. Sales Discount					
G. Sales Returns and Allowances					
H. Sales Tax Payable					

Across

2. A report of credit card sales produced by a point-of-sale terminal.

3. A special journal used to record only cash receipt transactions.

6. A special journal used to record only sales of merchandise on account.

7. The amount a business receives from the sale of an item of merchandise.

8. A tax on a sale of merchandise or services.

9. A cash discount on a sale taken by the customer.

Down

1. The amount a business adds to the cost of merchandise to establish the selling price.

2. The process of preparing a batch report from a point-of-sale terminal.

4. A sale in which the customer pays for the total amount of the sale at the time of the transaction.

5. The report that summarizes the cash and credit card sales of a point-of-sale terminal. This is also known as a Z tape.

Name _____ Date _____ Class _____

10-1 Accounting for sales on account

10-2 Posting from a sales journal

10-4 Posting from a cash receipts journal

ACCOUNTS RECEIVABLE LEDGER

CUSTOMER Lenny Stanford   CUSTOMER NO. 110

DATE		ITEM	POST. REF.	DEBIT	CREDIT	DEBIT BALANCE
Sept.	1	Balance	✔			2 1 8 9 36

CUSTOMER   CUSTOMER NO.

DATE	ITEM	POST. REF.	DEBIT	CREDIT	DEBIT BALANCE

CUSTOMER Washington City Schools   CUSTOMER NO. 130

DATE		ITEM	POST. REF.	DEBIT	CREDIT	DEBIT BALANCE
Sept.	1	Balance	✔			1 5 0 9 45

SALES JOURNAL   PAGE

	DATE	ACCOUNT DEBITED	SALE. NO.	POST. REF.	1 ACCOUNTS RECEIVABLE DEBIT	2 SALES CREDIT	3 SALES TAX PAYABLE CREDIT	
1								1
2								2
3								3
4								4
5								5
6								6

Column Title	Debit Totals	Credit Totals
Accounts Receivable Debit	_____	
Sales Credit		_____
Sales Tax Payable Credit		_____
Totals	=========	=========

ACCOUNT Cash   **ACCOUNT NO.** 1110

DATE		ITEM	POST. REF.	DEBIT	CREDIT	BALANCE DEBIT	BALANCE CREDIT
Sept.²⁰⁻⁻	1	Balance	✔			11 4 8 6 16	
	30		CP9		9 4 8 4 24	2 0 0 1 92	

ACCOUNT Accounts Receivable   **ACCOUNT NO.** 1130

DATE		ITEM	POST. REF.	DEBIT	CREDIT	BALANCE DEBIT	BALANCE CREDIT
Sept.²⁰⁻⁻	1	Balance	✔			4 0 8 9 15	

ACCOUNT Sales Tax Payable   **ACCOUNT NO.** 2120

DATE		ITEM	POST. REF.	DEBIT	CREDIT	BALANCE DEBIT	BALANCE CREDIT
Sept.²⁰⁻⁻	1	Balance	✔				2 4 8 4 18

ACCOUNT Sales   **ACCOUNT NO.** 4110

DATE		ITEM	POST. REF.	DEBIT	CREDIT	BALANCE DEBIT	BALANCE CREDIT
Sept.²⁰⁻⁻	1	Balance	✔				185 1 9 6 31

ACCOUNT Sales Discount   **ACCOUNT NO.** 4120

DATE		ITEM	POST. REF.	DEBIT	CREDIT	BALANCE DEBIT	BALANCE CREDIT
Sept.²⁰⁻⁻	1	Balance	✔			7 2 1 06	

10-3 and 10-4 **WORK TOGETHER, p. 301, and 309**

10-3 Accounting for cash and credit card sales
10-4 Posting from a cash receipts journal

CASH RECEIPTS JOURNAL

PAGE ___

DATE	ACCOUNT TITLE	DOC. NO.	POST. REF.	GENERAL DEBIT	GENERAL CREDIT	ACCOUNTS RECEIVABLE CREDIT	SALES CREDIT	SALES TAX PAYABLE CREDIT	SALES DISCOUNT DEBIT	CASH DEBIT	
											1
											2
											3
											4
											5
											6
											7
											8
											9

2.

Column Title	Debit Totals	Credit Totals
General Debit	_____	
General Credit		_____
Accounts Receivable Credit		_____
Sales Credit		_____
Sales Tax Payable Credit		_____
Sales Discount Debit	_____	
Cash Debit	_____	
Totals	═════════	═════════

3.

Cash on hand at the beginning of the month
(Sept. 1 balance of general ledger Cash account) . . . .

Plus total cash received during the month
(Cash Debit column total, cash receipts journal) . . . .   _____

Equal total. . . . .

Less total cash paid during the month
(General ledger posting in Cash account) . . . .   _____

Equals cash balance on hand at the end of the month. . . . .   ═════════

Checkbook balance on the next unused check stub. . . . .   ═════════

6.

10-1, 10-2, and 10-4 ON YOUR OWN, pp. 289, 293, and 309

10-1 Accounting for sales on account

10-2 Posting from a sales journal

10-4 Posting from a cash receipts journal

ACCOUNTS RECEIVABLE LEDGER

CUSTOMER _____   CUSTOMER NO. _____

DATE	ITEM	POST. REF.	DEBIT	CREDIT	DEBIT BALANCE

CUSTOMER FJT Plumbing   CUSTOMER NO. 120

DATE	ITEM	POST. REF.	DEBIT	CREDIT	DEBIT BALANCE
20-- June 1	Balance	✔			2 9 8 9 20

CUSTOMER Roberts College   CUSTOMER NO. 130

DATE	ITEM	POST. REF.	DEBIT	CREDIT	DEBIT BALANCE
20-- June 1	Balance	✔			3 8 1 60

SALES JOURNAL   PAGE ___

	DATE	ACCOUNT DEBITED	SALE. NO.	POST. REF.	ACCOUNTS RECEIVABLE DEBIT (1)	SALES CREDIT (2)	SALES TAX PAYABLE CREDIT (3)	
1								1
2								2
3								3
4								4
5								5
6								6

Column Title	Debit Totals	Credit Totals
Accounts Receivable Debit	_____	
Sales Credit		_____
Sales Tax Payable Credit		_____
Totals	══════	══════

ACCOUNT Cash   ACCOUNT NO. 1110

DATE		ITEM	POST. REF.	DEBIT	CREDIT	BALANCE DEBIT	BALANCE CREDIT
20-- June	1	Balance	✔			8 6 1 7 01	
	30		CP6		6 9 4 8 15	1 6 6 8 86	

ACCOUNT Accounts Receivable   ACCOUNT NO. 1130

DATE		ITEM	POST. REF.	DEBIT	CREDIT	BALANCE DEBIT	BALANCE CREDIT
20-- June	1	Balance	✔			3 5 5 5 80	

ACCOUNT Sales Tax Payable   ACCOUNT NO. 2120

DATE		ITEM	POST. REF.	DEBIT	CREDIT	BALANCE DEBIT	BALANCE CREDIT
20-- June	1	Balance	✔				6 4 8 18

ACCOUNT Sales   ACCOUNT NO. 4110

DATE		ITEM	POST. REF.	DEBIT	CREDIT	BALANCE DEBIT	BALANCE CREDIT
20-- June	1	Balance	✔				94 8 1 8 25

ACCOUNT Sales Discount   ACCOUNT NO. 4120

DATE		ITEM	POST. REF.	DEBIT	CREDIT	BALANCE DEBIT	BALANCE CREDIT
20-- June	1	Balance	✔			6 1 2 18	

10-3 and 10-4 ON YOUR OWN, p. 301, and 309

10-3 Accounting for cash and credit card sales

10-4 Posting from a cash receipts journal

CASH RECEIPTS JOURNAL

PAGE _____

				GENERAL		ACCOUNTS RECEIVABLE CREDIT	SALES CREDIT	SALES TAX PAYABLE CREDIT	SALES DISCOUNT DEBIT	CASH DEBIT	
DATE	ACCOUNT TITLE	DOC. NO.	POST. REF.	DEBIT	CREDIT						
											1
											2
											3
											4
											5
											6
											7
											8
											9

2.

Column Title	Debit Totals	Credit Totals
General Debit..............................	_____	
General Credit.............................		_____
Accounts Receivable Credit.....................		_____
Sales Credit...............................		_____
Sales Tax Payable Credit......................		_____
Sales Discount Debit.........................	_____	
Cash Debit................................	_____	
Totals	_____	_____

3.

Cash on hand at the beginning of the month
(June 1 balance of general ledger Cash account) ....

Plus total cash received during the month
(Cash Debit column total, cash receipts journal) .... _____

Equal total...................................

Less total cash paid during the month
(General ledger posting in Cash account) .... _____

Equals cash balance on hand at the end of the month............... _____

Checkbook balance on the next unused check stub................. _____

6.

10-1, 10-2, and 10-4 APPLICATION PROBLEMS (LO2, 3, 6, 7), pp. 313 and 314

10-1 Journalizing sales on account

10-2 Posting from a sales journal

10-4 Posting from a cash receipts journal

SALES JOURNAL   PAGE

	DATE	ACCOUNT DEBITED	SALE NO.	POST. REF.	ACCOUNTS RECEIVABLE DEBIT (2)	SALES CREDIT (3)	SALES TAX PAYABLE CREDIT (4)	
1								1
2								2
3								3
4								4
5								5
6								6
7								7
8								8
9								9

10-2 Posting from a sales journal

10-4 Posting from a cash receipts journal

ACCOUNTS RECEIVABLE LEDGER

CUSTOMER Central Medical Clinic   CUSTOMER NO. 110

DATE		ITEM	POST. REF.	DEBIT	CREDIT	DEBIT BALANCE
20-- Nov.	1	Balance	✔			1 6 4 8 96

CUSTOMER Fairview Hospital   CUSTOMER NO. 120

DATE		ITEM	POST. REF.	DEBIT	CREDIT	DEBIT BALANCE
20-- Nov.	1	Balance	✔			4 2 1 8 19

CUSTOMER Mason College   CUSTOMER NO. 130

DATE		ITEM	POST. REF.	DEBIT	CREDIT	DEBIT BALANCE
20-- Nov.	1	Balance	✔			6 7 9 19

CUSTOMER Paulson Medical Clinic   CUSTOMER NO. 140

DATE		ITEM	POST. REF.	DEBIT	CREDIT	DEBIT BALANCE
20-- Nov.	1	Balance	✔			1 5 4 7 15

CUSTOMER Trannon Emergency Center   CUSTOMER NO. 150

DATE		ITEM	POST. REF.	DEBIT	CREDIT	DEBIT BALANCE
20-- Nov.	1	Balance	✔			2 1 8 4 14

10-2 and 10-4 APPLICATION PROBLEMS

Column Title	Debit Totals	Credit Totals
Accounts Receivable Debit......................	_____	
Sales Credit..................................		_____
Sales Tax Payable Credit......................		_____
Totals	_____	_____

GENERAL LEDGER

ACCOUNT Cash   ACCOUNT NO. 1110

DATE		ITEM	POST. REF.	DEBIT	CREDIT	BALANCE DEBIT	BALANCE CREDIT
20-- Nov.	1	Balance	✔			16 4 8 9 36	
	30		CP11		14 4 7 4 63	2 0 1 4 73	

ACCOUNT Accounts Receivable   ACCOUNT NO. 1130

DATE		ITEM	POST. REF.	DEBIT	CREDIT	BALANCE DEBIT	BALANCE CREDIT
20-- Nov.	1	Balance	✔			10 2 7 7 63	

ACCOUNT Sales Tax Payable   ACCOUNT NO. 2120

DATE		ITEM	POST. REF.	DEBIT	CREDIT	BALANCE DEBIT	BALANCE CREDIT
20-- Nov.	1	Balance	✔				9 4 5 18

ACCOUNT Sales   ACCOUNT NO. 4110

DATE		ITEM	POST. REF.	DEBIT	CREDIT	BALANCE DEBIT
20-- Nov.	1	Balance	✔			194 7 3 5 26

ACCOUNT Sales Discount   ACCOUNT NO. 4120

DATE		ITEM	POST. REF.	DEBIT	CREDIT	BALANCE DEBIT	BALANCE CREDIT
20-- Nov.	1	Balance	✔			4 1 8 19	

10-3 Journalizing cash receipts
10-4 Posting from a cash receipts journal

CASH RECEIPTS JOURNAL

PAGE

	DATE	ACCOUNT TITLE	DOC. NO.	POST. REF.	GENERAL DEBIT	GENERAL CREDIT	ACCOUNTS RECEIVABLE CREDIT	SALES CREDIT	SALES TAX PAYABLE CREDIT	SALES DISCOUNT DEBIT	CASH DEBIT	
					1	2	3	4	5	6	7	
1												1
2												2
3												3
4												4
5												5
6												6
7												7
8												8
9												9
10												10
11												11

10-4 **APPLICATION PROBLEMS (concluded)**

2.

Column Title	Debit Totals	Credit Totals
General Debit................................	_____	
General Credit...............................		_____
Accounts Receivable Credit.....................		_____
Sales Credit.................................		_____
Sales Tax Payable Credit......................		_____
Sales Discount Debit..........................	_____	
Cash Debit..................................	_____	
Totals	_____	_____

3.

Cash on hand at the beginning of the month
(Nov. 1 balance of general ledger Cash account) ....
Plus total cash received during the month
(Cash Debit column total, cash receipts journal) .... _____
Equal total..
Less total cash paid during the month
(General ledger posting in Cash account) .... _____
Equals cash balance on hand at the end of the month................ _____
Checkbook balance on the next unused check stub................. _____

6.

Journalizing sales and cash receipts transactions

1., 2., 3.

SALES JOURNAL   PAGE

	DATE		ACCOUNT DEBITED	SALE. NO.	POST. REF.	ACCOUNTS RECEIVABLE DEBIT	SALES CREDIT	SALES TAX PAYABLE CREDIT	
						1	2	3	
1									1
2									2
3									3
4									4
5									5
6									6

2.

Column Title	Debit Totals	Credit Totals
Accounts Receivable Debit......................	_____	
Sales Credit....................................		_____
Sales Tax Payable Credit........................		_____
Totals	_____	_____

10-M MASTERY PROBLEM (continued)

1., 4., 6., 7.

CASH RECEIPTS JOURNAL

PAGE 7

DATE	ACCOUNT TITLE	DOC. NO.	POST. REF.	GENERAL DEBIT (1)	GENERAL CREDIT (2)	ACCOUNTS RECEIVABLE CREDIT (3)	SALES CREDIT (4)	SALES TAX PAYABLE CREDIT (5)	SALES DISCOUNT DEBIT (6)	CASH DEBIT (7)
1										
2										
3										
4										
5										
6										
7										
8										
9										
10										
11										

4.

Column Title	Debit Totals	Credit Totals
General Debit		
General Credit		
Accounts Receivable Credit		
Sales Credit		
Sales Tax Payable Credit		
Sales Discount Debit		
Cash Debit		
Totals		

1. ACCOUNTS RECEIVABLE LEDGER

CUSTOMER Daniel Smith Promotions   CUSTOMER NO. 110

DATE		ITEM	POST. REF.	DEBIT	CREDIT	DEBIT BALANCE
Mar.	1	Balance	✔			3 1 1 5 08

CUSTOMER Jenkins & Sanders LLP   CUSTOMER NO. 120

DATE		ITEM	POST. REF.	DEBIT	CREDIT	DEBIT BALANCE
Mar.	1	Balance	✔			1 8 4 9 00

CUSTOMER Luxury Suites   CUSTOMER NO. 130

DATE		ITEM	POST. REF.	DEBIT	CREDIT	DEBIT BALANCE
Mar.	1	Balance	✔			4 2 1 9 00

CUSTOMER Southwestern University   CUSTOMER NO. 140

DATE		ITEM	POST. REF.	DEBIT	CREDIT	DEBIT BALANCE
Mar.	1	Balance	✔			9 4 8 00

CUSTOMER Trailor Stores   CUSTOMER NO. 150

DATE		ITEM	POST. REF.	DEBIT	CREDIT	DEBIT BALANCE

5.

Cash on hand at the beginning of the month
(Mar. 1 balance of general ledger Cash account) . . . .
Plus total cash received during the month
(Cash Debit column total, cash receipts journal) . . . . _____
Equal total. . . . .
Less total cash paid during the month
(General ledger posting in Cash account) . . . . _____
Equals cash balance on hand at the end of the month. . . . . ========
Checkbook balance on the next unused check stub. . . . . ========

10-M MASTERY PROBLEM (continued)

3., 7.

ACCOUNT Cash   ACCOUNT NO. 1110

DATE		ITEM	POST. REF.	DEBIT	CREDIT	BALANCE DEBIT	BALANCE CREDIT
Mar.	1	Balance	✔			6 5 4 4 15	
	31		CP3		4 1 7 4 46	2 3 6 9 69	

ACCOUNT Accounts Receivable   ACCOUNT NO. 1130

DATE		ITEM	POST. REF.	DEBIT	CREDIT	BALANCE DEBIT	BALANCE CREDIT
Mar.	1	Balance	✔			10 1 3 1 08	

ACCOUNT Sales Tax Payable   ACCOUNT NO. 2120

DATE		ITEM	POST. REF.	DEBIT	CREDIT	BALANCE DEBIT	BALANCE CREDIT
Mar.	1	Balance	✔				4 8 9 18

ACCOUNT Sales   ACCOUNT NO. 4110

DATE		ITEM	POST. REF.	DEBIT	CREDIT	BALANCE DEBIT	BALANCE CREDIT
Mar.	1	Balance	✔				24 1 5 9 15

ACCOUNT Sales Discount   ACCOUNT NO. 4120

DATE		ITEM	POST. REF.	DEBIT	CREDIT	BALANCE DEBIT	BALANCE CREDIT
Mar.	1	Balance	✔			1 9 4 03	

8.

10-S SOURCE DOCUMENTS PROBLEM (LO2, 3, 4, 5, 6), p. 315

Journalizing sales and cash receipts transactions; proving and ruling journals

---

Golfer's Paradise
142 Glade Road
Crossville, TN 38555-8102

RECEIPT

FROM: _Mary Ann Ingram_

DATE: 11/13/--
RECEIPT NO.: 528

PAYMENT METHOD	CHECK NO.	CUSTOMER ACCT. NO.	RECEIVED BY
Check	5326	150	Tom Andrews

DESCRIPTION	INVOICE	GROSS AMOUNT	DISCOUNT	CASH RECEIVED
On account	428	$ 150.00	$ —	$ 150.00
		TOTAL DISCOUNT		
			TOTAL	$ 150.00

Golfer's Paradise
142 Glade Road
Crossville, TN 38555-8102

RECEIPT

FROM: _Adams Driving Range_

DATE: 11/24/--
RECEIPT NO.: 529

PAYMENT METHOD	CHECK NO.	CUSTOMER ACCT. NO.	RECEIVED BY
Check	481	110	Sally Richards

DESCRIPTION	INVOICE	GROSS AMOUNT	DISCOUNT	CASH RECEIVED
On account	444	$ 435.91	$ 8.72	$ 427.19
		TOTAL DISCOUNT	$ 8.72	
			TOTAL	$ 427.19

Golfer's Paradise
142 Glade Road
Crossville, TN 38555-8102

INVOICE

SOLD TO: Daniel Pearson
2345 Lakeview Drive
Crossville, TN 38555-5819

DATE: 11/5/--
INV. NO.: 443
TERMS: n/30
CUST. NO.: 260

QUANTITY	PART NO.	DESCRIPTION	UNIT PRICE	TOTAL
1	2432	9 degree titanium driver	$439.50	**$439.50**
5	745	Practice golf balls, dz.	10.00	50.00
		SUBTOTAL		**$489.50**
		TAX		36.71
		TOTAL		**$526.21**

Serving Crossville and Fairfield Glade with all your recreational equipment

Golfer's Paradise
142 Glade Road
Crossville, TN 38555-8102

INVOICE

SOLD TO: Adams Driving Range
594 Eagles Nest Road
Crossville, TN 38555-5819

DATE: 11/16/--
INV. NO.: 444
TERMS: 2/10, n/30
CUST. NO.: 110

QUANTITY	PART NO.	DESCRIPTION	UNIT PRICE	TOTAL
1	BG-34	Oversized irons, graphite shafts	$405.50	**$405.50**
		SUBTOTAL		**$405.50**
		TAX		30.41
		TOTAL		**$435.91**

Serving Crossville and Fairfield Glade with all your recreational equipment

10-S SOURCE DOCUMENTS PROBLEM (continued)

Golfer's Paradise 142 Glade Road Crossville, TN 38555-8102		INVOICE			
	SOLD TO:	Mountain View Golf 1001 Lakeview Drive Crossville, TN 38555-5819	DATE: INV. NO.: TERMS: CUST. NO.:	11/26/-- 445 2/10, n/30 490	
QUANTITY	PART NO.	DESCRIPTION	UNIT PRICE	TOTAL	
75	9448	X-out golf balls, dz.	$6.50	$487.50	
35	490	Gloves	5.50	192.50	
		SUBTOTAL		$680.00	
		TAX			
		TOTAL		$680.00	
Serving Crossville and Fairfield Glade with all your recreational equipment					

1., 2.

SALES JOURNAL

PAGE _____

	DATE	ACCOUNT DEBITED	SALE. NO.	POST. REF.	ACCOUNTS RECEIVABLE DEBIT 1	SALES CREDIT 2	SALES TAX PAYABLE CREDIT 3	
1								1
2								2
3								3
4								4
5								5
6								6
7								7
8								8

TERMINAL SUMMARY
Golfer's Paradise

CODE:		36
DATE:		11/4/--
TIME:		18:34

VISA	028	
Sales		1,548.95
Sales Tax		92.94
Total		1,641.89

MasterCard	031	
Sales		2,458.08
Sales Tax		147.48
Total		2,605.56

Debit Cards	048	
Sales		1,947.63
Sales Tax		116.86
Total		2,064.49

Cash	158	
Sales		3,154.14
Sales Tax		189.25
Total		3,343.39

Totals		
Sales		9,108.80
Sales Tax		546.53
Total		9,655.33

BATCH REPORT

MERCHANT:	498418 145
TERMINAL:	1548
DATE:	11/4/-- 18:34
BATCH:	36

VISA	
COUNT	028
SALES	1,704.04
RETURNS	62.15
NET	1,641.89

MASTERCARD	
COUNT	031
SALES	2,651.45
RETURNS	45.89
NET	2,605.56

DEBIT CARDS	
COUNT	048
SALES	2,222.64
RETURNS	158.15
NET	2,064.49

TOTALS	
COUNT	107
SALES	6,578.13
RETURNS	266.19
NET	6,311.94

CONTROL NUMBER: 001486486

10-S SOURCE DOCUMENTS PROBLEM (continued)

TERMINAL SUMMARY Golfer's Paradise	
CODE:	37
DATE:	11/23/--
TIME:	18:34
VISA	033
Sales	1,648.21
Sales Tax	98.89
Total	1,747.10
MasterCard	025
Sales	1,473.19
Sales Tax	88.39
Total	1,561.58
Debit Cards	044
Sales	1,497.21
Sales Tax	89.83
Total	1,587.04
Cash	173
Sales	2,849.16
Sales Tax	170.95
Total	3,020.11
Totals	
Sales	7,467.77
Sales Tax	448.06
Total	7,915.83

BATCH REPORT	
MERCHANT:	498418 145
TERMINAL:	1548
DATE:	11/23/-- 18:48
BATCH:	37
VISA	
COUNT	033
SALES	1,809.25
RETURNS	62.15
NET	1,747.10
MASTERCARD	
COUNT	025
SALES	1,607.47
RETURNS	45.89
NET	1,561.58
DEBIT CARDS	
COUNT	044
SALES	1,745.19
RETURNS	158.15
NET	1,587.04
TOTALS	
COUNT	102
SALES	5,161.91
RETURNS	266.19
NET	4,895.72
CONTROL NUMBER: 001489875	

1., 3.

CASH RECEIPTS JOURNAL

PAGE

				1	2		3	4	5	6	7
				GENERAL		ACCOUNTS RECEIVABLE CREDIT	SALES CREDIT	SALES TAX PAYABLE CREDIT	SALES DISCOUNT DEBIT	CASH DEBIT
DATE	ACCOUNT TITLE	DOC. NO.	POST. REF.	DEBIT	CREDIT						

10-C CHALLENGE PROBLEM (LO2, 3, 4, 5, 6), p. 316

Journalizing sales and cash receipts transactions

1., 2.

SALES JOURNAL   PAGE _____

	DATE	ACCOUNT DEBITED	SALE. NO.	POST. REF.	ACCOUNTS RECEIVABLE DEBIT 1	SALES CREDIT 2	SALES TAX PAYABLE CREDIT 3	
1								1
2								2
3								3
4								4
5								5
6								6
7								7
8								8
9								9

2.

Column Title	Debit Totals	Credit Totals
Accounts Receivable Debit	_____	
Sales Credit		_____
Sales Tax Payable Credit		_____
Totals	_____	_____

1., 2.

CASH RECEIPTS JOURNAL

PAGE 7

	DATE	ACCOUNT TITLE	DOC. NO.	POST. REF.	GENERAL DEBIT	GENERAL CREDIT	ACCOUNTS RECEIVABLE CREDIT	SALES CREDIT	SALES TAX PAYABLE DEBIT	SALES TAX PAYABLE CREDIT	SALES DISCOUNT DEBIT	CASH DEBIT	
					1	2	3	4	5	6	7		
1													1
2													2
3													3
4													4
5													5
6													6
7													7
8													8
9													9
10													10

2.

Column Title	Debit Totals	Credit Totals
General Debit		
General Credit		
Accounts Receivable Credit		
Sales Credit		
Sales Tax Payable Debit		
Sales Tax Payable Credit		
Sales Discount Debit		
Cash Debit		
Totals		

10-C CHALLENGE PROBLEM (continued)

1.   **ACCOUNTS RECEIVABLE LEDGER**

customer Andersen & Smith LLP   customer no. 110

DATE		ITEM	POST. REF.	DEBIT	CREDIT	DEBIT BALANCE
20-- Nov.	1	Balance	✔			4 2 0 9 40
	12		CR11		2 8 1 9 41	1 3 8 9 99
	20		CR11		1 3 8 9 99	——
	23	S893	S11	1 5 8 6 80		1 5 8 6 80

customer Jenson College   customer no. 120

DATE		ITEM	POST. REF.	DEBIT	CREDIT	DEBIT BALANCE
20-- Nov.	1	Balance	✔			6 2 4 7 25
	26	S894	S11	3 0 0 7 93		9 2 5 5 18
	28		CR11		6 2 4 7 25	3 0 0 7 93

customer Northern Regional Airlines   customer no. 130

DATE		ITEM	POST. REF.	DEBIT	CREDIT	DEBIT BALANCE
20-- Nov.	1	Balance	✔			3 4 8 1 47
	22	S896	S11	6 1 8 4 02		9 6 6 5 49
	30		CR11		3 4 8 1 47	6 1 8 4 02

CUSTOMER Olsen Manufacturing   CUSTOMER NO. 140

DATE		ITEM	POST. REF.	DEBIT	CREDIT	DEBIT BALANCE
Nov. 20--	1	Balance	✔			1 5 4 9 01
	14	S892	S11	6 4 8 08		2 1 9 7 09
	25		CR11		1 5 4 9 01	6 4 8 08
	29	S897	S11	1 3 2 9 99		1 9 7 8 07

CUSTOMER Randle Distribution Centers   CUSTOMER NO. 150

DATE		ITEM	POST. REF.	DEBIT	CREDIT	DEBIT BALANCE
Nov. 20--	1	Balance	✔			3 4 7 0 59
	4		CR11		3 4 7 0 59	—
	28	S895	S11	4 2 1 9 64		4 2 1 9 64

Name	Perfect Score	Your Score
Identifying Accounting Terms	11 Pts.	
Analyzing Accounting Concepts and Practices	20 Pts.	
Analyzing Transactions Recorded in Journals	15 Pts.	
Total	46 Pts.	

Study Guide 11

Part One—Identifying Accounting Terms

Directions: Select the one term in Column I that best fits each definition in Column II. Print the letter identifying your choice in the Answers column.

Column I	Column II	Answers
A. board of directors	1. A journal with two amount columns in which all kinds of entries can be recorded. (p. 320)	1. _____
B. credit memorandum	2. Credit allowed for the purchase price of returned merchandise, resulting in a decrease in the customer's account payable to the vendor. (p. 322)	2. _____
C. debit memorandum	3. Credit allowed for part of the purchase price of merchandise that is not returned, resulting in a decrease in the customer's account payable to the vendor. (p. 322)	3. _____
D. declaring a dividend	4. A form prepared by the customer showing the price deduction taken by the customer for a return or an allowance. (p. 322)	4. _____
E. dividends	5. Credit allowed to a customer for the sales price of returned merchandise, resulting in a decrease in the accounts receivable of the merchandising business. (p. 327)	5. _____
F. general journal	6. Credit allowed to a customer for part of the sales price of merchandise that is not returned, resulting in a decrease in the accounts receivable of the merchandising business. (p. 327)	6. _____
G. purchases allowance	7. A form prepared by the vendor showing the amount deducted for returns and allowances. (p. 327)	7. _____
H. purchases return	8. An amount earned by a corporation and not yet distributed to stockholders. (p. 332)	8. _____
I. retained earnings	9. Earnings distributed to stockholders. (p. 332)	9. _____
J. sales allowance	10. A group of persons elected by the stockholders to govern a corporation. (p. 333)	10. _____
K. sales return	11. Action by a board of directors to distribute corporate earnings to stockholders. (p. 333)	11. _____

Part Two—Analyzing Accounting Concepts and Practices

Directions: Place a *T* for True or an *F* for False in the Answers column to show whether each of the following statements is true or false.

		Answers
1.	Transactions that cannot be recorded in a special journal are recorded in a general journal. (p. 320)	1. _____
2.	A general journal entry posted to Accounts Payable will also be posted to a subsidiary ledger account. (p. 321)	2. _____
3.	Credit allowed for part of the purchase price of merchandise that is not returned results in an increase in the customer's account. (p. 322)	3. _____
4.	A debit memorandum prepared by a customer results in the customer recording a debit to the vendor account. (p. 322)	4. _____
5.	An entry recorded in a general journal will either increase all accounts or decrease all accounts affected by the entry. (p. 323)	5. _____
6.	The normal account balance of Purchases Returns and Allowances is a debit. (p. 323)	6. _____
7.	An entry in the general journal that affects Accounts Payable also affects a vendor's account in the accounts payable ledger. (p. 324)	7. _____
8.	In a computerized accounting system, transactions recorded in a general journal are posted immediately after they are entered. (p. 325)	8. _____
9.	A completed general journal page should always be reviewed to be sure that all postings have been made. (p. 325)	9. _____
10.	A credit memorandum issued by a vendor results in the vendor recording a debit to the customer's account. (p. 327)	10. _____
11.	The normal account balance of Sales Returns and Allowances is a debit. (p. 327)	11. _____
12.	A sales return that credits the customer's account is not recorded in a cash receipts journal because the transaction does not involve cash. (p. 328)	12. _____
13.	Entries in the general journal only affect account balances in general ledger accounts. (p. 329)	13. _____
14.	The correcting entry to correct a sale on account recorded to the wrong customer in the sales journal involves only subsidiary ledger accounts. (p. 330)	14. _____
15.	Net income increases a corporation's total stockholders' equity. (p. 332)	15. _____
16.	A corporation's Dividends account is a permanent account similar to a proprietorship's drawing account. (p. 332)	16. _____
17.	Dividends can be distributed to stockholders only by formal action of a corporation's chief financial officer. (p. 333)	17. _____
18.	All corporations are required to declare dividends. (p. 333)	18. _____
19.	The stockholders' equity account, Dividends, has a normal debit balance. (p. 333)	19. _____
20.	Most corporations pay a dividend by writing a single check to an agent, such as a bank, that distributes checks to individual stockholders. (p. 334)	20. _____

© 2019 Cengage®. May not be scanned, copied or duplicated, or posted to a publicly accessible website, in whole or in part.

Part Three—Analyzing Transactions Recorded in Journals

Directions: In Answers Column l, print the abbreviation for the journal in which each transaction is to be recorded. In Answers Columns 2 and 3, print the letters identifying the subsidiary and general ledger accounts to be debited and credited for each transaction.

GJ—General journal; **CPJ**—Cash payments journal

Account Titles	Transactions	Answers		
		1	**2**	**3**
		Journal	**Debit**	**Credit**
A. Accounts Payable	**1-2-3.** Bought office supplies on account from Walton Supply. (p. 321)	**1.** _____	**2.** _____	**3.** _____
B. Accounts Receivable				
C. Cash	**4-5-6.** Returned merchandise to Yeats Corporation. (p. 323)	**4.** _____	**5.** _____	**6.** _____
D. Dividends				
E. Dividends Payable	**7-8-9.** Granted credit to Tim Thorton for merchandise returned, plus sales tax. (p. 328)	**7.** _____	**8.** _____	**9.** _____
F. Purchases				
G. Purchases Returns and Allowances	**10-11-12.** The board of directors declared a quarterly dividend. (p. 333)	**10.** _____	**11.** _____	**12.** _____
H. Sales	**13-14-15.** Paid cash for quarterly dividend declared December 15. (p. 334)	**13.** _____	**14.** _____	**15.** _____
I. Sales Return and Allowances				
J. Sales Tax Payable				
K. Supplies—Office				
L. Tim Thorton				
M. Walton Supply				
N. Yeats Corporation				

Across

1. Credit allowed to a customer for part of the sales price of merchandise that is not returned, resulting in a decrease in the accounts receivable of the merchandising business.

4. Credit allowed for the purchase price of returned merchandise, resulting in a decrease in the customer's account.

7. A form prepared by the customer showing the price deduction taken by the customer for a return or an allowance.

8. A group of persons elected by the stockholders to govern a corporation.

9. Credit allowed for part of the purchase price of merchandise that is not returned, resulting in a decrease in the customer's account.

10. A journal with two amount columns in which all kinds of entries can be recorded.

11. Action by a board of directors to distribute corporate earnings to stockholders.

12. Earnings distributed to stockholders.

Down

2. Credit allowed to a customer for the sales price of returned merchandise, resulting in a decrease in the accounts receivable of the merchandising business.

3. Processes and procedures employed within a business to ensure that its operations are conducted ethically, accurately, and reliably.

5. An amount earned by a corporation and not yet distributed to stockholders.

6. A form prepared by the vendor showing the amount deducted for returns and allowances.

11-1 WORK TOGETHER, p. 326

Journalizing and posting transactions using a general journal

1., 2.

GENERAL JOURNAL   PAGE

	DATE		ACCOUNT TITLE	DOC. NO.	POST. REF.	DEBIT	CREDIT	
1								1
2								2
3								3
4								4
5								5

2.

VENDOR Griffin, Inc.   VENDOR NO. 220

	DATE		ITEM	POST. REF.	DEBIT	CREDIT	CREDIT BALANCE
	20-- Dec.	1	Balance	✔			9 5 8 00

VENDOR Milam Corp.   VENDOR NO. 250

	DATE		ITEM	POST. REF.	DEBIT	CREDIT	CREDIT BALANCE
	20-- Dec.	1	Balance	✔			1 4 4 3 00

2.

ACCOUNT Supplies—Office   ACCOUNT NO. 1145

DATE		ITEM	POST. REF.	DEBIT	CREDIT	BALANCE	
						DEBIT	CREDIT
20-- Dec.	1	Balance	✔			2 9 4 8 00	

ACCOUNT Accounts Payable   ACCOUNT NO. 2110

DATE		ITEM	POST. REF.	DEBIT	CREDIT	BALANCE	
						DEBIT	CREDIT
20-- Dec.	1	Balance	✔				8 4 9 3 50

ACCOUNT Purchases Returns and Allowances   ACCOUNT NO. 5130

DATE		ITEM	POST. REF.	DEBIT	CREDIT	BALANCE	
						DEBIT	CREDIT
20-- Dec.	1	Balance	✔				4 1 9 4 60

11-1 ON YOUR OWN, p. 326

Journalizing and posting transactions using a general journal

1., 2.

GENERAL JOURNAL   PAGE _____

	DATE	ACCOUNT TITLE	DOC. NO.	POST. REF.	DEBIT	CREDIT	
1							1
2							2
3							3
4							4
5							5
6							6
7							7
8							8
9							9

2.

VENDOR **Branker Supply**   VENDOR NO. 210

DATE		ITEM	POST. REF.	DEBIT	CREDIT	CREDIT BALANCE
20-- Dec.	1	Balance	✔			3 4 8 00

VENDOR **Gould Depot**   VENDOR NO. 220

DATE		ITEM	POST. REF.	DEBIT	CREDIT	CREDIT BALANCE
20-- Dec.	1	Balance	✔			6 9 4 00

VENDOR **Olen, Inc.**   VENDOR NO. 230

DATE		ITEM	POST. REF.	DEBIT	CREDIT	CREDIT BALANCE
20-- Dec.	1	Balance	✔			8 1 9 00

VENDOR **Plette Corp.**   VENDOR NO. 240

DATE		ITEM	POST. REF.	DEBIT	CREDIT	CREDIT BALANCE
20-- Dec.	1	Balance	✔			1 1 8 3 00

2.

ACCOUNT Supplies—Office   ACCOUNT NO. 1145

DATE	ITEM	POST. REF.	DEBIT	CREDIT	BALANCE DEBIT	BALANCE CREDIT
20-- Dec. 1	Balance	✔			3 0 4 9 60	

ACCOUNT Supplies—Store   ACCOUNT NO. 1150

DATE	ITEM	POST. REF.	DEBIT	CREDIT	BALANCE DEBIT	BALANCE CREDIT
20-- Dec. 1	Balance	✔			4 1 8 30	

ACCOUNT Accounts Payable   ACCOUNT NO. 2110

DATE	ITEM	POST. REF.	DEBIT	CREDIT	BALANCE DEBIT	BALANCE CREDIT
20-- Dec. 1	Balance	✔				3 0 4 4 00

ACCOUNT Purchases Returns and Allowances   ACCOUNT NO. 5130

DATE	ITEM	POST. REF.	DEBIT	CREDIT	BALANCE DEBIT	BALANCE CREDIT
20-- Dec. 1	Balance	✔				6 4 9 8 10

11-2 WORK TOGETHER, p. 331

Accounting for sales returns and allowances using a general journal

1., 2.

GENERAL JOURNAL

PAGE _____

	DATE	ACCOUNT TITLE	DOC. NO.	POST. REF.	DEBIT	CREDIT	
1							1
2							2
3							3
4							4
5							5
6							6
7							7
8							8
9							9
10							10
11							11

2.

CUSTOMER Abraham Corporation   CUSTOMER NO. 110

DATE		ITEM	POST. REF.	DEBIT	CREDIT	DEBIT BALANCE
20-- June	1	Balance	✔			1 6 4 9 50

CUSTOMER Ashston & Lindsay LLP   CUSTOMER NO. 120

DATE		ITEM	POST. REF.	DEBIT	CREDIT	DEBIT BALANCE
20-- June	1	Balance	✔			6 8 4 25

CUSTOMER Karson Properties   CUSTOMER NO. 130

DATE		ITEM	POST. REF.	DEBIT	CREDIT	DEBIT BALANCE
20-- June	1	Balance	✔			1 6 4 7 60

CUSTOMER Keller Associates   CUSTOMER NO. 140

DATE		ITEM	POST. REF.	DEBIT	CREDIT	DEBIT BALANCE
20-- June	1	Balance	✔			1 7 1 6 40

CUSTOMER Lambert Schools   CUSTOMER NO. 150

DATE		ITEM	POST. REF.	DEBIT	CREDIT	DEBIT BALANCE
20-- June	1	Balance	✔			3 4 9 0 00

11-2 **WORK TOGETHER (concluded)**

2.

ACCOUNT Accounts Receivable   ACCOUNT NO. 1130

DATE		ITEM	POST. REF.	DEBIT	CREDIT	BALANCE	
						DEBIT	CREDIT
20-- June	1	Balance	✔			9 1 8 7 75	

ACCOUNT Sales Tax Payable   ACCOUNT NO. 2120

DATE		ITEM	POST. REF.	DEBIT	CREDIT	BALANCE	
						DEBIT	CREDIT
20-- June	1	Balance	✔				6 4 8 10

ACCOUNT Sales Returns and Allowances   ACCOUNT NO. 4130

DATE		ITEM	POST. REF.	DEBIT	CREDIT	BALANCE	
						DEBIT	CREDIT
20-- June	1	Balance	✔			2 4 8 7 60	

Accounting for sales returns and allowances using a general journal

1., 2.

GENERAL JOURNAL

PAGE

	DATE		ACCOUNT TITLE	DOC. NO.	POST. REF.	DEBIT	CREDIT	
1								1
2								2
3								3
4								4
5								5
6								6
7								7
8								8
9								9
10								10
11								11

11-2 ON YOUR OWN (continued)

2.

CUSTOMER Bettsworth Hospital   CUSTOMER NO. 110

DATE		ITEM	POST. REF.	DEBIT	CREDIT	DEBIT BALANCE
20-- July	1	Balance	✔			1 6 4 9 50

CUSTOMER City Food Bank   CUSTOMER NO. 120

DATE		ITEM	POST. REF.	DEBIT	CREDIT	DEBIT BALANCE
20-- July	1	Balance	✔			6 8 4 25

CUSTOMER Learning Playhouse   CUSTOMER NO. 130

DATE		ITEM	POST. REF.	DEBIT	CREDIT	DEBIT BALANCE
20-- July	1	Balance	✔			1 6 4 7 60

CUSTOMER Paulson Café   CUSTOMER NO. 140

DATE		ITEM	POST. REF.	DEBIT	CREDIT	DEBIT BALANCE
20-- July	1	Balance	✔			1 7 1 6 40

CUSTOMER RPL Corporation   CUSTOMER NO. 150

DATE		ITEM	POST. REF.	DEBIT	CREDIT	DEBIT BALANCE
20-- July	1	Balance	✔			3 4 9 0 00

2.

ACCOUNT Accounts Receivable ACCOUNT NO. 1130

DATE		ITEM	POST. REF.	DEBIT	CREDIT	BALANCE	
						DEBIT	CREDIT
July	1	Balance	✔			9 1 8 7 75	

ACCOUNT Sales Tax Payable ACCOUNT NO. 2120

DATE		ITEM	POST. REF.	DEBIT	CREDIT	BALANCE	
						DEBIT	CREDIT
July	1	Balance	✔				6 4 8 10

ACCOUNT Sales Returns and Allowances ACCOUNT NO. 4130

DATE		ITEM	POST. REF.	DEBIT	CREDIT	BALANCE	
						DEBIT	CREDIT
July	1	Balance	✔			2 4 8 7 60	

11-3 WORK TOGETHER, p. 336

Journalizing the declaration and payment of dividends

GENERAL JOURNAL

PAGE _____

	DATE	ACCOUNT TITLE	DOC. NO.	POST. REF.	DEBIT	CREDIT	
13							13
14							14
15							15
16							16

CASH PAYMENTS JOURNAL

PAGE 5

	DATE	ACCOUNT TITLE	CK. NO.	POST. REF.	GENERAL DEBIT	GENERAL CREDIT	ACCOUNTS PAYABLE DEBIT	PURCHASES DISCOUNT CREDIT	CASH CREDIT	
					1	2	3	4	5	
16										16
17										17
18										18

Journalizing the declaration and payment of dividends

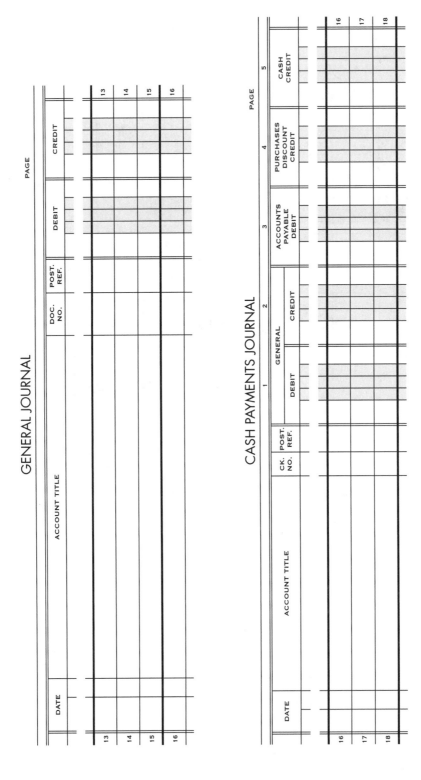

GENERAL JOURNAL

PAGE

DATE	ACCOUNT TITLE	DOC. NO.	POST. REF.	DEBIT	CREDIT	
						13
						14
						15
						16

CASH PAYMENTS JOURNAL

PAGE

				1	2	3	4	5	
DATE	ACCOUNT TITLE	CK. NO.	POST. REF.	GENERAL DEBIT	GENERAL CREDIT	ACCOUNTS PAYABLE DEBIT	PURCHASES DISCOUNT CREDIT	CASH CREDIT	
									16
									17
									18

11-1 **APPLICATION PROBLEM (LO2, 3), p. 339**

Journalizing and posting purchases transactions using a general journal

1., 2.

GENERAL JOURNAL   PAGE _____

	DATE	ACCOUNT TITLE	DOC. NO.	POST. REF.	DEBIT	CREDIT	
1							1
2							2
3							3
4							4
5							5
6							6
7							7
8							8
9							9

2.

VENDOR Daniels Supply   VENDOR NO. 210

DATE		ITEM	POST. REF.	DEBIT	CREDIT	CREDIT BALANCE
20-- Dec.	1	Balance	✔			1 1 2 3 00

VENDOR Harris Paints   VENDOR NO. 220

DATE		ITEM	POST. REF.	DEBIT	CREDIT	CREDIT BALANCE
20-- Dec.	1	Balance	✔			1 5 6 0 00

VENDOR Mason Molds   VENDOR NO. 230

DATE		ITEM	POST. REF.	DEBIT	CREDIT	CREDIT BALANCE
20-- Dec.	1	Balance	✔			6 4 0 00

VENDOR Office Zone   VENDOR NO. 240

DATE		ITEM	POST. REF.	DEBIT	CREDIT	CREDIT BALANCE
20-- Dec.	1	Balance	✔			7 9 5 00

11-1 APPLICATION PROBLEM (concluded)

2.

ACCOUNT Supplies—Office   ACCOUNT NO. 1145

DATE		ITEM	POST. REF.	DEBIT	CREDIT	BALANCE	
						DEBIT	CREDIT
20-- Dec.	1	Balance	✔			4 2 6 0 00	

ACCOUNT Supplies—Store   ACCOUNT NO. 1150

DATE		ITEM	POST. REF.	DEBIT	CREDIT	BALANCE	
						DEBIT	CREDIT
20-- Dec.	1	Balance	✔			1 5 7 0 00	

ACCOUNT Accounts Payable   ACCOUNT NO. 2110

DATE		ITEM	POST. REF.	DEBIT	CREDIT	BALANCE	
						DEBIT	CREDIT
20-- Dec.	1	Balance	✔				6 4 9 1 00

ACCOUNT Purchases Returns and Allowances   ACCOUNT NO. 5130

DATE		ITEM	POST. REF.	DEBIT	CREDIT	BALANCE	
						DEBIT	CREDIT
20-- Dec.	1	Balance	✔				3 0 4 7 25

Accounting for sales returns and allowances using a general journal

1., 2.

GENERAL JOURNAL

PAGE

	DATE	ACCOUNT TITLE	DOC. NO.	POST. REF.	DEBIT	CREDIT	
1							1
2							2
3							3
4							4
5							5
6							6
7							7
8							8
9							9
10							10
11							11

11-2 APPLICATION PROBLEM (continued)

2.

CUSTOMER John Auburn   CUSTOMER NO. 110

DATE	ITEM	POST. REF.	DEBIT	CREDIT	DEBIT BALANCE
Sept. 1	Balance	✔			5 8 9 15

CUSTOMER Mary Best   CUSTOMER NO. 120

DATE	ITEM	POST. REF.	DEBIT	CREDIT	DEBIT BALANCE
Sept. 1	Balance	✔			1 5 6 2 00

CUSTOMER Burns & Associates   CUSTOMER NO. 130

DATE	ITEM	POST. REF.	DEBIT	CREDIT	DEBIT BALANCE
Sept. 1	Balance	✔			4 8 9 58

CUSTOMER Cassidy Corporation   CUSTOMER NO. 140

DATE	ITEM	POST. REF.	DEBIT	CREDIT	DEBIT BALANCE
Sept. 1	Balance	✔			2 1 9 9 19

CUSTOMER Anna Jackson   CUSTOMER NO. 150

DATE	ITEM	POST. REF.	DEBIT	CREDIT	DEBIT BALANCE
Sept. 1	Balance	✔			1 9 4 8 25

CUSTOMER Metsville Schools   CUSTOMER NO. 160

DATE	ITEM	POST. REF.	DEBIT	CREDIT	DEBIT BALANCE
Sept. 1	Balance	✔			2 7 9 4 18

2.

ACCOUNT Accounts Receivable

ACCOUNT NO. 1130

DATE		ITEM	POST. REF.	DEBIT	CREDIT	BALANCE	
						DEBIT	CREDIT
Sept.	1	Balance	✔			9 5 8 2 35	

ACCOUNT Sales Tax Payable

ACCOUNT NO. 2120

DATE		ITEM	POST. REF.	DEBIT	CREDIT	BALANCE	
						DEBIT	CREDIT
Sept.	1	Balance	✔				6 4 8 10

ACCOUNT Sales Returns and Allowances

ACCOUNT NO. 4130

DATE		ITEM	POST. REF.	DEBIT	CREDIT	BALANCE	
						DEBIT	CREDIT
Sept.	1	Balance	✔			2 4 8 7 60	

11-3 **APPLICATION PROBLEM (LO8), p. 339**

Journalizing the declaration and payment of dividends

GENERAL JOURNAL

PAGE _____

DATE	ACCOUNT TITLE	DOC. NO.	POST. REF.	DEBIT	CREDIT	
						13
						14
						15
						16

CASH PAYMENTS JOURNAL

PAGE _____

DATE	ACCOUNT TITLE	CK. NO.	POST. REF.	GENERAL DEBIT	GENERAL CREDIT	ACCOUNTS PAYABLE DEBIT	PURCHASES DISCOUNT CREDIT	CASH CREDIT	
									16
									17
									18

Journalizing and posting transactions using a general journal and a cash payments journal

1., 2.

GENERAL JOURNAL

PAGE

	DATE		ACCOUNT TITLE	DOC. NO.	POST. REF.	DEBIT	CREDIT	
1								1
2								2
3								3
4								4
5								5
6								6
7								7
8								8
9								9
10								10
11								11
12								12
13								13
14								14
15								15
16								16

1., 3.

CASH PAYMENTS JOURNAL

PAGE

						1	2	3	4	5		
	DATE	ACCOUNT TITLE	CK. NO.	POST. REF.		GENERAL		ACCOUNTS PAYABLE DEBIT	PURCHASES DISCOUNT CREDIT	CASH CREDIT		
						DEBIT	CREDIT					
16												16
17												17
18												18

11-M.1 MASTERY PROBLEM (continued)

2. ACCOUNTS PAYABLE LEDGER

VENDOR Century Foods   VENDOR NO. 220

DATE		ITEM	POST. REF.	DEBIT	CREDIT	CREDIT BALANCE
Dec.	1	Balance	✔			1 9 4 8 25

VENDOR Great Lakes Produce   VENDOR NO. 260

DATE		ITEM	POST. REF.	DEBIT	CREDIT	CREDIT BALANCE
Dec.	1	Balance	✔			3 1 8 4 26

VENDOR Kelsar Supply   VENDOR NO. 280

DATE		ITEM	POST. REF.	DEBIT	CREDIT	CREDIT BALANCE
Dec.	1	Balance	✔			9 6 8 28

2. **ACCOUNTS RECEIVABLE LEDGER**

CUSTOMER Connie's Bakery   CUSTOMER NO. 120

DATE		ITEM	POST. REF.	DEBIT	CREDIT	DEBIT BALANCE
20-- Dec.	1	Balance	✔			5 8 9 15

CUSTOMER JD's Café   CUSTOMER NO. 160

DATE		ITEM	POST. REF.	DEBIT	CREDIT	DEBIT BALANCE
20-- Dec.	1	Balance	✔			1 5 6 2 00

CUSTOMER Restaurant Deville   CUSTOMER NO. 180

DATE		ITEM	POST. REF.	DEBIT	CREDIT	DEBIT BALANCE
20-- Dec.	1	Balance	✔			9 7 0 36

CUSTOMER Rib Shack   CUSTOMER NO. 190

DATE		ITEM	POST. REF.	DEBIT	CREDIT	DEBIT BALANCE
20-- Dec.	1	Balance	✔			5 7 4 05

11-M.1 MASTERY PROBLEM (continued)

2., 3.   **GENERAL LEDGER**

ACCOUNT Accounts Receivable   ACCOUNT NO. 1130

DATE		ITEM	POST. REF.	DEBIT	CREDIT	BALANCE DEBIT	BALANCE CREDIT
20-- Dec.	1	Balance	✔			16 4 8 2 15	

ACCOUNT Supplies—Store   ACCOUNT NO. 1150

DATE		ITEM	POST. REF.	DEBIT	CREDIT	BALANCE DEBIT	BALANCE CREDIT
20-- Dec.	1	Balance	✔			3 0 4 9 24	

ACCOUNT Accounts Payable   ACCOUNT NO. 2110

DATE		ITEM	POST. REF.	DEBIT	CREDIT	BALANCE DEBIT	BALANCE CREDIT
20-- Dec.	1	Balance	✔				18 4 3 1 18

ACCOUNT Sales Tax Payable   ACCOUNT NO. 2120

DATE		ITEM	POST. REF.	DEBIT	CREDIT	BALANCE DEBIT	BALANCE CREDIT
20-- Dec.	1	Balance	✔				8 9 4 17

2., 3.

ACCOUNT Dividends Payable   ACCOUNT NO. 2180

DATE	ITEM	POST. REF.	DEBIT	CREDIT	BALANCE DEBIT	BALANCE CREDIT

ACCOUNT Dividends   ACCOUNT NO. 3130

DATE	ITEM	POST. REF.	DEBIT	CREDIT	BALANCE DEBIT	BALANCE CREDIT
20-- Dec. 1	Balance	✔			8 7 7 2 00	

ACCOUNT Sales Returns and Allowances   ACCOUNT NO. 4130

DATE	ITEM	POST. REF.	DEBIT	CREDIT	BALANCE DEBIT	BALANCE CREDIT
20-- Dec. 1	Balance	✔			8 4 1 7 10	

ACCOUNT Purchases Returns and Allowances   ACCOUNT NO. 5130

DATE	ITEM	POST. REF.	DEBIT	CREDIT	BALANCE DEBIT	BALANCE CREDIT
20-- Dec. 1	Balance	✔				4 1 8 9 94

11-M.2 MASTERY PROBLEM (Review of Chapters 9, 10, and 11), p. 340

Journalizing and posting transactions

1.

GENERAL JOURNAL   PAGE

	DATE		ACCOUNT TITLE	DOC. NO.	POST. REF.	DEBIT	CREDIT	
1								1
2								2
3								3
4								4
5								5
6								6
7								7
8								8
9								9
10								10
11								11
12								12
13								13
14								14

1., 2.

SALES JOURNAL

PAGE

	DATE	ACCOUNT DEBITED	SALE NO.	POST. REF.	ACCOUNTS RECEIVABLE DEBIT 1	SALES CREDIT 2	SALES TAX PAYABLE CREDIT 3	
1								1
2								2
3								3
4								4
5								5
6								6
7								7

2. Sales Journal Proof

Column Title	Debit Totals	Credit Totals
Accounts Receivable Debit		
Sales Credit		
Sales Tax Payable Credit		
Totals		

1., 3.

PURCHASES JOURNAL

PAGE

	DATE	ACCOUNT CREDITED	PURCH. NO.	POST. REF.	PURCHASES DR. ACCTS. PAY. CR.	
1						1
2						2
3						3
4						4
5						5
6						6
7						7
8						8
9						9

11-M.2 MASTERY PROBLEM (continued)

1., 4.

CASH RECEIPTS JOURNAL

PAGE 7

DATE	ACCOUNT TITLE	DOC. NO.	POST. REF.	GENERAL DEBIT (1)	GENERAL CREDIT (2)	ACCOUNTS RECEIVABLE CREDIT (3)	SALES CREDIT (4)	SALES TAX PAYABLE CREDIT (5)	SALES DISCOUNT DEBIT (6)	CASH DEBIT (7)

4. Cash Receipts Journal Proof

Column Title	Debit Totals	Credit Totals
General Debit		
General Credit		
Accounts Receivable Credit		
Sales Credit		
Sales Tax Payable Credit		
Sales Discount Debit		
Cash Debit		
Totals		

1., 5.

CASH PAYMENTS JOURNAL

PAGE 5

					1	2	3	4	5
DATE	ACCOUNT TITLE	CK. NO.	POST. REF.	GENERAL DEBIT	GENERAL CREDIT	ACCOUNTS PAYABLE DEBIT	PURCHASES DISCOUNT CREDIT	CASH CREDIT	
									1
									2
									3
									4
									5
									6
									7
									8
									9
									10
									11
									12
									13
									14
									15

5. Cash Payments Journal Proof

Column Title	Debit Totals	Credit Totals
General Debit		
General Credit		
Accounts Payable Debit		
Purchases Discount Credit		
Cash Debit		
Totals		

11-M.2 MASTERY PROBLEM (continued)

1.   ACCOUNTS RECEIVABLE LEDGER

CUSTOMER LaDonna Atkins   CUSTOMER NO. 110

DATE		ITEM	POST. REF.	DEBIT	CREDIT	DEBIT BALANCE
20-- Dec.	1	Balance	✔			2 2 1 1 98

CUSTOMER Coastal County Schools   CUSTOMER NO. 120

DATE		ITEM	POST. REF.	DEBIT	CREDIT	DEBIT BALANCE
20-- Dec.	1	Balance	✔			1 6 4 7 50

CUSTOMER Joseph Greggs   CUSTOMER NO. 130

DATE		ITEM	POST. REF.	DEBIT	CREDIT	DEBIT BALANCE
20-- Dec.	1	Balance	✔			3 4 9 4 50

CUSTOMER Kelsey Pittman   CUSTOMER NO. 140

DATE		ITEM	POST. REF.	DEBIT	CREDIT	DEBIT BALANCE
20-- Dec.	1	Balance	✔			2 4 1 7 50

CUSTOMER Larry Simpson   CUSTOMER NO. 150

DATE		ITEM	POST. REF.	DEBIT	CREDIT	DEBIT BALANCE

7.

1.

ACCOUNTS PAYABLE LEDGER

VENDOR Barger Office Supply   VENDOR NO. 210

DATE		ITEM	POST. REF.	DEBIT	CREDIT	CREDIT BALANCE
20-- Dec.	1	Balance	✔			2 2 8 4 00

VENDOR Francis Industries   VENDOR NO. 220

DATE		ITEM	POST. REF.	DEBIT	CREDIT	CREDIT BALANCE
20-- Dec.	1	Balance	✔			1 5 9 5 00

VENDOR Jing Corporation   VENDOR NO. 230

DATE		ITEM	POST. REF.	DEBIT	CREDIT	CREDIT BALANCE
20-- Dec.	1	Balance	✔			3 2 9 0 00

VENDOR Quitman Manufacturing   VENDOR NO. 240

DATE		ITEM	POST. REF.	DEBIT	CREDIT	CREDIT BALANCE
20-- Dec.	1	Balance	✔			1 5 8 9 00

VENDOR Wilson Metals   VENDOR NO. 250

DATE		ITEM	POST. REF.	DEBIT	CREDIT	CREDIT BALANCE

7.

_____

11-M.2 MASTERY PROBLEM (continued)

1., 2., 3., 4., 5.

GENERAL LEDGER

ACCOUNT Cash   ACCOUNT NO. 1110

DATE		ITEM	POST. REF.	DEBIT	CREDIT	BALANCE DEBIT	BALANCE CREDIT
20-- Dec.	1	Balance	✔			21 3 5 9 50	

ACCOUNT Petty Cash   ACCOUNT NO. 1120

DATE		ITEM	POST. REF.	DEBIT	CREDIT	BALANCE DEBIT	BALANCE CREDIT
20-- Dec.	1	Balance	✔			1 5 0 00	

ACCOUNT Accounts Receivable   ACCOUNT NO. 1130

DATE		ITEM	POST. REF.	DEBIT	CREDIT	BALANCE DEBIT	BALANCE CREDIT
20-- Dec.	1	Balance	✔			9 7 7 1 48	

ACCOUNT Supplies—Office   ACCOUNT NO. 1145

DATE		ITEM	POST. REF.	DEBIT	CREDIT	BALANCE DEBIT	BALANCE CREDIT
20-- Dec.	1	Balance	✔			1 6 4 8 66	

ACCOUNT Accounts Payable   ACCOUNT NO. 2110

DATE		ITEM	POST. REF.	DEBIT	CREDIT	BALANCE DEBIT	BALANCE CREDIT
20-- Dec.	1	Balance	✔				8 7 5 8 00

ACCOUNT Sales Tax Payable   ACCOUNT NO. 2120

DATE	ITEM	POST. REF.	DEBIT	CREDIT	BALANCE DEBIT	BALANCE CREDIT
20-- Dec. 1	Balance	✔				4 1 8 05

ACCOUNT Dividends Payable   ACCOUNT NO. 2180

DATE	ITEM	POST. REF.	DEBIT	CREDIT	BALANCE DEBIT	BALANCE CREDIT

ACCOUNT Dividends   ACCOUNT NO. 3130

DATE	ITEM	POST. REF.	DEBIT	CREDIT	BALANCE DEBIT	BALANCE CREDIT

ACCOUNT Sales   ACCOUNT NO. 4110

DATE	ITEM	POST. REF.	DEBIT	CREDIT	BALANCE DEBIT	BALANCE CREDIT
20-- Dec. 1	Balance	✔				162 7 8 9 11

ACCOUNT Sales Discount   ACCOUNT NO. 4120

DATE	ITEM	POST. REF.	DEBIT	CREDIT	BALANCE DEBIT	BALANCE CREDIT
20-- Dec. 1	Balance	✔			6 1 8 90	

11-M.2 MASTERY PROBLEM (continued)

ACCOUNT Sales Returns and Allowances   ACCOUNT NO. 4130

DATE		ITEM	POST. REF.	DEBIT	CREDIT	BALANCE DEBIT	BALANCE CREDIT
20-- Dec.	1	Balance	✔			3 4 9 1 10	

ACCOUNT Purchases   ACCOUNT NO. 5110

DATE		ITEM	POST. REF.	DEBIT	CREDIT	BALANCE DEBIT	BALANCE CREDIT
20-- Dec.	1	Balance	✔			114 9 1 0 84	

ACCOUNT Purchases Discount   ACCOUNT NO. 5120

DATE		ITEM	POST. REF.	DEBIT	CREDIT	BALANCE DEBIT	BALANCE CREDIT
20-- Dec.	1	Balance	✔				3 4 7 1 80

ACCOUNT Purchases Returns and Allowances   ACCOUNT NO. 5130

DATE		ITEM	POST. REF.	DEBIT	CREDIT	BALANCE DEBIT	BALANCE CREDIT
20-- Dec.	1	Balance	✔				2 4 7 1 62

ACCOUNT Advertising Expense   ACCOUNT NO. 6105

DATE		ITEM	POST. REF.	DEBIT	CREDIT	BALANCE DEBIT	BALANCE CREDIT
20-- Dec.	1	Balance	✔			8 4 9 7 20	

ACCOUNT Cash Short and Over   ACCOUNT NO. 6110

DATE		ITEM	POST. REF.	DEBIT	CREDIT	BALANCE DEBIT	BALANCE CREDIT
20-- Dec.	1	Balance	✔			6 15	

ACCOUNT Miscellaneous Expense   ACCOUNT NO. 6135

DATE		ITEM	POST. REF.	DEBIT	CREDIT	BALANCE DEBIT	BALANCE CREDIT
20-- Dec.	1	Balance	✔			4 1 7 3 56	

ACCOUNT Rent Expense   ACCOUNT NO. 6145

DATE		ITEM	POST. REF.	DEBIT	CREDIT	BALANCE DEBIT	BALANCE CREDIT
20-- Dec.	1	Balance	✔			8 8 0 0 00	

ACCOUNT Utilities Expense   ACCOUNT NO. 6170

DATE		ITEM	POST. REF.	DEBIT	CREDIT	BALANCE DEBIT	BALANCE CREDIT
20-- Dec.	1	Balance	✔			4 4 8 1 19	

6. Cash Proof

Cash on hand at the beginning of the month . . . .

Plus total cash received during the month . . . . _____

Equals total. . . . .

Less total cash paid during the month. . . . . _____

Equals cash balance on hand at the end of the month . . . . =========

Checkbook balance on the next unused check stub. . . . . =========

11-C CHALLENGE PROBLEM (LO2, 6), p. 341

Journalizing business transactions

GENERAL JOURNAL

PAGE _____

	DATE	ACCOUNT TITLE	DOC. NO.	POST. REF.	DEBIT	CREDIT	
1							1
2							2
3							3
4							4
5							5
6							6
7							7
8							8
9							9
10							10
11							11
12							12
13							13

Study Guide 12

Name	Perfect Score	Your Score
Identifying Accounting Terms	24 Pts.	
Analyzing Payroll Procedures	5 Pts.	
Identifying Accounting Practices	25 Pts.	
Total	54 Pts.	

Part One—Identifying Accounting Terms

Directions: Select the one term in Column I that best fits each definition in Column II. Print the letter identifying your choice in the Answers column.

Contains accounting terms for Lessons 12-1 and 12-2.

Column I	Column II	Answers
A. 401(k)	1. The amount paid to an employee for every hour worked. (p. 346)	1. _____
B. accumulated earnings	2. A fixed annual sum of money divided among equal pay periods. (p. 346)	2. _____
C. commission	3. A method of paying an employee based on the amount of sales the employee generates. (p. 346)	3. _____
D. individual retirement account	4. The total amount paid by a business for an employee's work, earned by a wage, salary, or commission. (p. 346)	4. _____
E. Medicare tax	5. The number of days or weeks of work covered by an employee's paycheck. (p. 346)	5. _____
F. pay period	6. The total amount earned by all employees for a pay period. (p. 346)	6. _____
G. payroll	7. The accounting staff position that compiles and computes payroll data, then prepares, journalizes, and posts payroll transactions. (p. 346)	7. _____
H. payroll clerk	8. A device used to record the dates and times of every employee's arrivals and departures. (p. 347)	8. _____
I. payroll deduction	9. Taxes based on the payroll of a business. (p. 351)	9. _____
J. payroll taxes	10. A deduction from total earnings for each person legally supported by a taxpayer, including the employee. (p. 352)	10. _____
K. qualified retirement plan	11. Any amount withheld from an employee's gross earnings. (p. 352)	11. _____
L. Roth individual retirement account	12. A federal tax paid for old-age, survivors, and disability insurance. (p. 355)	12. _____
M. salary	13. A federal tax paid for hospital insurance. (p. 355)	13. _____
N. social security tax	14. The total gross earnings year to date for an employee. (p. 355)	14. _____
O. tax base	15. The maximum amount of gross earnings on which a tax is calculated. (p. 355)	15. _____
P. time clock	16. A retirement savings plan approved by the Internal Revenue Service that provides individuals with a tax benefit. (p. 356)	16. _____
Q. total earnings	17. A qualified retirement plan sponsored by an employer. (p. 356)	17. _____
R. wage	18. A qualified retirement plan that provides most individuals with a deferred federal income tax benefit. (p. 356)	18. _____
S. withholding allowance	19. A qualified retirement plan that allows tax-free withdrawals from the account. (p. 356)	19. _____

Chapter 12 Preparing Payroll Records • **311**

Directions: Select the one term in Column I that best fits each definition in Column II. Print the letter identifying your choice in the Answers column.

Contains accounting terms for Lessons 12-3 and 12-4.

Column I	Column II	Answers
A. direct deposit	**20.** An accounting form that summarizes the earnings, deductions, and net pay of all employees for one pay period. (p. 358)	**20.**_____
B. employee earnings record	**21.** The total earnings paid to an employee after payroll taxes and other deductions. (p. 359)	**21.**_____
C. net pay	**22.** A business form used to record details of an employee's earnings and deductions. (p. 360)	**22.**_____
D. payroll register	**23.** A check with a detachable check stub that contains detailed information about the cash payment. (p. 364)	**23.**_____
E. voucher check	**24.** The payment of an employee's net pay using electronic funds transfer. (p. 366)	**24.**_____

Part Two—Analyzing Payroll Procedures

Directions: For each of the following items, select the choice that best completes the statement. Print the letter of your choice in the Answers column.

Answers

1. How many hours were worked by an employee who arrived at 8:10 A.M. and departed at 12:10 P.M.? (A) 4 hours (B) 5 hours (C) 4 hours and 10 minutes (D) none of these. (p. 347)   **1.**_____

2. How many hours were worked by an employee who arrived at 7:05 A.M. and departed at 6:05 P.M. with one hour off for lunch? (A) 11 hours (B) 10 hours (C) 12 hours (D) none of these. (p. 347)   **2.**_____

3. Employee regular earnings are calculated as (A) regular hours times regular rate (B) total hours divided by regular rate (C) total hours plus overtime rate (D) overtime hours minus overtime rate. (p. 349)   **3.**_____

4. Social security tax is calculated on (A) total earnings and marital status (B) number of withholding allowances (C) total earnings and number of withholding allowances (D) employee earnings up to a maximum paid in a calendar year. (p. 355)   **4.**_____

5. A separate payroll checking account is used primarily to (A) simplify the payroll accounting system (B) help reduce the cost of preparing a payroll (C) provide additional protection and control payroll payments (D) eliminate employer earnings records. (p. 364)   **5.**_____

Part Three—Identifying Accounting Practices

Directions: Place a *T* for True or an *F* for False in the Answers column to show whether each of the following statements is true or false.

Answers

1. A business may decide to pay employee salaries every week, every two weeks, twice a month, or once a month. (p. 346)

1. _____

3. Total earnings are sometimes referred to as net pay or net earnings. (p. 346)

2. _____

2. Today's time clocks can feed data directly into a company's computer system. (p. 348)

3. _____

4. An hourly employee's total earnings are calculated as regular hours × regular rate, plus overtime hours × overtime rate. (p. 349)

4. _____

5. Payroll taxes withheld represent a liability for an employer until payment is made to the government. (p. 351)

5. _____

6. Employers are required to have a current Form W-4, Employee's Withholding Allowance Certificate, for all employees. (p. 352)

6. _____

7. Federal income tax is one example of a payroll deduction. (p. 352)

7. _____

8. The amount of income tax withheld from each employee's total earnings is determined from the number of withholding allowances and by the employee's marital status. (p. 352)

8. _____

9. A single person will have less income tax withheld than a married employee earning the same amount. (p. 352)

9. _____

10. The larger the number of withholding allowances claimed, the larger the amount of income tax withheld. (p. 352)

10. _____

11. An employee can be exempt from having federal income tax withheld under certain conditions. (p. 352)

11. _____

12. Social security tax is only paid by the employer. (p. 355)

12. _____

13. An act of Congress can change the social security tax base and tax rate at any time. (p. 355)

13. _____

14. When an employee's accumulated earnings exceed the tax base, no more social security tax is deducted. (p. 355)

14. _____

15. Qualified retirement plans are approved by the Internal Revenue Service (p. 356)

15. _____

16. Employee contributions to a 401(k) reduce the amount of earnings subject to payroll taxes. (p. 356)

16. _____

17. The investment income of a 401(k) account is taxable to the employee in the year earned. (p. 356)

17. _____

18. Taxes on the contributions and investment income of an IRA are deferred until the funds are withdrawn. (p. 356)

18. _____

19. Contributions to a Roth IRA do not provide a current tax benefit. (p. 356)

19. _____

20. The investment income in a Roth IRA is subject to federal income taxes when withdrawn. (p. 356)

20. _____

21. The columns of the employee earnings record consist of the amount columns in a payroll register and an Accumulated Earnings column. (p. 360)

21. _____

22. A check for each employee's total net pay is written on the general checking account of the business. (p. 364)

22. _____

23. The original voucher check, with the voucher attached, is mailed to the vendor. (p. 365)

23. _____

24. The voucher of a payroll check contains current pay period and year-to-date earnings and deduction information. (p. 365)

24. _____

25. When EFT is used, the employee does not receive an individual check. (p. 366)

25. _____

12-1 WORK TOGETHER, p. 350

Calculating hourly employee total earnings

1.

	MORNING		AFTERNOON		EVENING		HOURS	
Day	IN	OUT	IN	OUT	IN	OUT	REG	OT
Mon 01	7^{54}	11^{57}	12^{56}	5^{02}				
Tue 02	8^{00}	11^{52}	1^{06}	5^{02}				
Wed 03	7^{56}	12^{01}	1^{04}	5^{01}				
Thu 04	7^{59}	11^{57}	12^{59}	4^{59}	6^{01}	9^{33}		
Fri 05			12^{58}	4^{56}	6^{01}	10^{10}		
Mon 08	8^{01}	11^{57}	1^{00}	4^{53}				
Tue 09	8^{01}	12^{03}	12^{57}	6^{06}				
Wed 10	7^{54}	11^{52}	1^{02}	5^{03}				
Thu 11	7^{58}	12^{01}	12^{58}	5^{00}				
Fri 12	8^{01}	1^{04}	2^{02}	5^{05}				
Sat 13	10^{05}	1^{05}						
Mon 15	7^{52}	12^{00}	12^{59}	4^{53}				
					PERIOD TOTALS			

EMPLOYEE NO. 4

NAME Alice R. Webster

PAY PERIOD ENDED October 15, 20--

APPROVED BY _____

2.

Employee Number	Hours Worked		Regular Rate	Earnings		Total Earnings
	Regular	Overtime		Regular	Overtime	
1	80	5	$ 9.00	_____	_____	_____
2	80	3	12.50	_____	_____	_____
3	70	0	9.75	_____	_____	_____
4			11.00	_____	_____	_____

Calculating hourly employee total earnings

1.

EMPLOYEE NO. 34

NAME Mary Carol Prestwood

PAY PERIOD ENDED June 30, 20--

Day	MORNING IN	MORNING OUT	AFTERNOON IN	AFTERNOON OUT	EVENING IN	EVENING OUT	HOURS REG	HOURS OT
Mon 16	8^{55}	11^{53}	12^{52}	6^{05}				
Tue 17	9^{06}	11^{58}	1^{00}	6^{02}				
Thu 19	8^{57}	12^{00}	1^{00}	6^{03}				
Fri 20	8^{55}	11^{57}	12^{59}	5^{52}	6^{01}	9^{10}		
Sat 21	8^{56}	12^{01}	12^{52}	5^{53}				
Mon 23	9^{04}	11^{55}	1^{01}	5^{53}				
Tue 24	9^{05}	12^{02}	12^{59}	5^{54}				
Thu 26			1^{05}	6^{04}				
Fri 27	8^{58}	12^{00}	12^{55}	6^{00}	7^{05}	9^{05}		
Sat 28	9^{03}	11^{56}	12^{56}	5^{52}				
Mon 30	8^{52}	11^{57}	12^{57}	5^{56}				
			PERIOD TOTALS					

APPROVED BY _____

2.

Employee Number	Hours Worked Regular	Hours Worked Overtime	Regular Rate	Earnings Regular	Earnings Overtime	Total Earnings
25	88	5	$10.00	_____	_____	_____
28	72	3	14.50	_____	_____	_____
32	88	4	13.75	_____	_____	_____
34			12.50	_____	_____	_____

Name _____ Date _____ Class _____

Determining payroll tax withholding

1., 2.

No.	Employee Name	Marital Status	Number of Withholding Allowances	Total Earnings	Federal Income Tax Withholding	Social Security Tax Withholding	Medicare Withholding
1	Clauson, John P.	M	2	$1,360.00			
9	Edison, Janice A.	S	1	980.00			
5	Lambert, Terri C.	M	3	1,510.00			
2	Simpson, Anthony W.	S	2	1,125.00			

Determining payroll tax withholding

1., 2.

No.	Employee Name	Marital Status	Number of Withholding Allowances	Total Earnings	Federal Income Tax Withholding	Social Security Tax Withholding	Medicare Withholding
3	Gilmore, Harris J.	S	2	$1,020.00			
8	Keller, Francis P.	M	3	1,810.00			
4	Millhouse, Gary R.	S	1	1,205.00			
1	Williamson, Mary A.	M	1	1,405.00			

Preparing payroll records

(Note: The payroll register and employee earnings record used in this problem are also used in Work Together 12-4.)

1., 2.

PAYROLL REGISTER

SEMIMONTHLY PERIOD ENDED _____

DATE OF PAYMENT _____

				1	2	3	4	5	6	7	8	9	10	
				EARNINGS			DEDUCTIONS							
EMPL. NO.	EMPLOYEE'S NAME	MARI-TAL STATUS	NO. OF ALLOW-ANCES	REGULAR	OVERTIME	TOTAL	FEDERAL INCOME TAX	SOCIAL SECURITY TAX	MEDICARE TAX	HEALTH INSURANCE	RETIREMENT PLAN	TOTAL	NET PAY	CHECK NO.
2	Johnson, Edward P.	M	2	1 3 2 0 00	1 1 2 50	1 4 3 2 50								1
4	Nelson, Janice E.	S	1	9 2 0 00	5 1 75	9 7 1 75								2
														3
														4
														5

3.

EARNINGS RECORD FOR QUARTER ENDED _____

EMPLOYEE NO. _____   LAST NAME _____   FIRST _____   MIDDLE INITIAL _____   MARITAL STATUS _____   WITHHOLDING ALLOWANCES _____

RATE OF PAY _____   PER HOUR _____   SOCIAL SECURITY NO. _____   POSITION _____

	1	2	3	4	5	6	7	8	9	10	11
PAY PERIOD	EARNINGS			DEDUCTIONS							
NO.	ENDED	REGULAR	OVERTIME	TOTAL	FEDERAL INCOME TAX	SOCIAL SECURITY TAX	MEDICARE TAX	HEALTH INSURANCE	RETIREMENT PLAN	TOTAL	NET PAY	ACCUMULATED EARNINGS
1												
7	TOTALS											

12-3 | **ON YOUR OWN, p. 363**

Preparing payroll records

(*Note: The payroll register used in this problem is also used in On Your Own 12-4.*)

1., 2.

PAYROLL REGISTER

SEMIMONTHLY PERIOD ENDED _____ DATE OF PAYMENT _____

EMPL. NO.	EMPLOYEE'S NAME	MARI-TAL STATUS	NO. OF ALLOW-ANCES	EARNINGS			DEDUCTIONS						NET PAY	CHECK NO.
				REGULAR	OVERTIME	TOTAL	FEDERAL INCOME TAX	SOCIAL SECURITY TAX	MEDICARE TAX	HEALTH INSURANCE	RETIREMENT PLAN	TOTAL		
				1	2	3	4	5	6	7	8	9	10	
1	3	Patterson, James T.	S	2	1 6 0 1 60	5 4 60	1 6 5 6 20								1
2	6	Reeves, Glenda R.	M	3	1 5 8 4 00	9 4 50	1 6 7 8 50								2
3															3
4															4
5															5

3.

EARNINGS RECORD FOR QUARTER ENDED _____

EMPLOYEE NO. _____ LAST NAME _____ FIRST _____ MIDDLE INITIAL _____ MARITAL STATUS _____ WITHHOLDING ALLOWANCES _____

SOCIAL SECURITY NO. _____ POSITION _____

RATE OF PAY _____ PER HOUR _____

PAY PERIOD		EARNINGS			DEDUCTIONS					NET PAY	ACCUMULATED EARNINGS
NO.	ENDED	REGULAR	OVERTIME	TOTAL	FEDERAL INCOME TAX	SOCIAL SECURITY TAX	MEDICARE TAX	HEALTH INSURANCE	RETIREMENT PLAN	TOTAL	
		1	2	3	4	5	6	7	8	9	10	11
1												
7	TOTALS											

Preparing payroll checks

(Note: The payroll register used in this problem was also used in Work Together 12-3.)

1.

JUDY'S FASHIONS		DATE	No. **895**
PAYEE			

ACCOUNT	TITLE	DESCRIPTION	AMOUNT

JUDY'S FASHIONS
1534 South College Street
Auburn, AL 36830

FIRST COMMUNITY BANK
320 N. Dean Road
Auburn, AL 36830

No. **895**

GENERAL ACCOUNT

DATE   AMOUNT

$ _____

_____ Dollars

FOR CLASSROOM USE ONLY

PAY TO THE
ORDER OF

⑈:9⊦894861⑊: 5⊦848⊦⊦58⑊⊦ 0895

12-4 WORK TOGETHER (continued)

2.

EMPLOYEE	Edward P. Johnson					DATE	June 30, 20--	
TYPE	**HOURS**	**RATE**	**GROSS PAY**		**DEDUCTIONS**		**CURRENT**	**YTD**
					Federal Income Tax		43.00	522.00
Regular	84.00	15.00	1,260.00		Social Security Tax		80.91	1,067.52
Overtime	2.00	22.50	45.00		Medicare Tax		18.92	249.66
					Health Insurance		60.00	720.00
					Retirement		15.00	180.00
Current Total Earnings			1,305.00		Totals		217.83	2,739.18
YTD Total Earnings			17,218.00		Net Pay		1,087.17	14,478.82

EMPLOYEE						DATE		
TYPE	**HOURS**	**RATE**	**GROSS PAY**		**DEDUCTIONS**		**CURRENT**	**YTD**
					Federal Income Tax		_____	_____
Regular	88.00	15.00	_____		Social Security Tax		_____	_____
Overtime	5.00	22.50	_____		Medicare Tax		_____	_____
					Health Insurance		_____	_____
					Retirement		_____	_____
Current Total Earnings			_____		Totals		_____	_____
YTD Total Earnings			_____		Net Pay		_____	_____

PAYROLL ACCOUNT   _____   66-311 / 513

JUDY'S FASHIONS   **No. 261**

PAY TO THE
ORDER OF _____ $ _____

_____ Dollars

FOR CLASSROOM USE ONLY

FIRST COMMUNITY BANK
AUBURN, AL 36830   _____

⑈918948611⑈ 148164118⑈ 261

EMPLOYEE	Janice E. Nelson					DATE	June 30, 20--
TYPE	HOURS	RATE	GROSS PAY	DEDUCTIONS		CURRENT	YTD
				Federal Income Tax		79.00	892.00
Regular	82.00	11.50	943.00	Social Security Tax		61.67	736.10
Overtime	3.00	17.25	51.75	Medicare Tax		14.42	172.15
				Health Insurance		60.00	720.00
				Retirement		15.00	180.00
Current Total Earnings			994.75	Totals		230.09	2,700.25
YTD Total Earnings			11,872.50	Net Pay		764.66	9,172.25

EMPLOYEE						DATE	
TYPE	HOURS	RATE	GROSS PAY	DEDUCTIONS		CURRENT	YTD
				Federal Income Tax		_____	_____
Regular	80.00	11.50	_____	Social Security Tax		_____	_____
Overtime	3.00	17.25	_____	Medicare Tax		_____	_____
				Health Insurance		_____	_____
				Retirement		_____	_____
Current Total Earnings			_____	Totals		_____	_____
YTD Total Earnings			_____	Net Pay		_____	_____

PAYROLL ACCOUNT

$\dfrac{66\text{-}311}{513}$

JUDY'S FASHIONS **No. 262**

PAY TO THE
ORDER OF _____ $ _____

_____ Dollars

FOR CLASSROOM USE ONLY

FIRST COMMUNITY BANK
AUBURN, AL 36830

⑆91894861⑆ 148164118⑈ 262

12-4 ON YOUR OWN, p. 368

Preparing payroll checks
(Note: The payroll register used in this problem was also used in On Your Own 12-3.)

1.

RUSSELL COMPANY		DATE		No. **921**
PAYEE				
ACCOUNT	**TITLE**	**DESCRIPTION**		**AMOUNT**

- -

RUSSELL COMPANY
1534 Military Road
Columbus, MS 39701

FIRST AMERICAN BANK
656 S. 7th Street
Columbus, MS 39701

No. **921**

GENERAL ACCOUNT

DATE _____

AMOUNT

$ _____

_____ Dollars
FOR CLASSROOM USE ONLY

**PAY TO THE
ORDER OF**

_____

⑆648188841⑆ 7184848⑈ 0921

2.

EMPLOYEE	James T. Patterson				DATE	June 30, 20--
TYPE	**HOURS**	**RATE**	**GROSS PAY**	**DEDUCTIONS**	**CURRENT**	**YTD**
				Federal Income Tax	137.00	1,583.00
Regular	80.00	18.20	1,456.00	Social Security Tax	95.35	1,187.30
Overtime	3.00	27.30	81.90	Medicare Tax	22.30	277.68
				Health Insurance	75.00	900.00
				Retirement	30.00	360.00
Current Total Earnings			1,537.90	Totals	359.65	4,307.98
YTD Total Earnings			19,150.00	Net Pay	1,178.25	14,842.02

EMPLOYEE					DATE	
TYPE	**HOURS**	**RATE**	**GROSS PAY**	**DEDUCTIONS**	**CURRENT**	**YTD**
				Federal Income Tax	_____	_____
Regular	88.00	18.20	_____	Social Security Tax	_____	_____
Overtime	2.00	27.30	_____	Medicare Tax	_____	_____
				Health Insurance	_____	_____
				Retirement	_____	_____
Current Total Earnings			_____	Totals	_____	_____
YTD Total Earnings			_____	Net Pay	_____	_____

PAYROLL ACCOUNT   _____   66-311 / 513

RUSSELL COMPANY   **No. 148**

PAY TO THE
ORDER OF _____ $ _____

_____ Dollars
FOR CLASSROOM USE ONLY

FIRST AMERICAN BANK
    Columbus, MS 39701   _____

⑆648188841⑆ 7484767⑈ 148

12-4 ON YOUR OWN (concluded)

EMPLOYEE Glenda R. Reeves					DATE June 30, 20--	
TYPE	HOURS	RATE	GROSS PAY	DEDUCTIONS	CURRENT	YTD
				Federal Income Tax	44.00	408.00
Regular	80.00	18.00	1,440.00	Social Security Tax	90.95	836.32
Overtime	1.00	27.00	27.00	Medicare Tax	21.27	195.59
				Health Insurance	75.00	675.00
				Retirement	30.00	270.00
Current Total Earnings			1,467.00	Totals	261.22	2,384.91
YTD Total Earnings			13,489.00	Net Pay	1,205.78	11,104.09

EMPLOYEE					DATE	
TYPE	HOURS	RATE	GROSS PAY	DEDUCTIONS	CURRENT	YTD
				Federal Income Tax	_____	_____
Regular	88.00	18.00	_____	Social Security Tax	_____	_____
Overtime	3.50	27.00	_____	Medicare Tax	_____	_____
				Health Insurance	_____	_____
				Retirement	_____	_____
Current Total Earnings			_____	Totals	_____	_____
YTD Total Earnings			_____	Net Pay	_____	_____

PAYROLL ACCOUNT   _____   66-311 / 513

RUSSELL COMPANY   **No. 149**

PAY TO THE
ORDER OF _____ $ _____

_____ Dollars
FOR CLASSROOM USE ONLY

FIRST AMERICAN BANK
Columbus, MS 39701   _____

⑈648188846⑈ 748476 7⑈ 149

Calculating total earnings

1.

EMPLOYEE NO. 7

NAME Marcus T. Groves

PAY PERIOD ENDED   December 15, 20--

Day	MORNING IN	MORNING OUT	AFTERNOON IN	AFTERNOON OUT	EVENING IN	EVENING OUT	HOURS REG	HOURS OT
Mon 01	5^{58}	11^{53}	12^{59}	3^{54}				
Tue 02	8^{56}	12^{01}	12^{53}	5^{56}	6^{53}	9^{53}		
Wed 03			1^{00}	6^{02}	7^{55}	9^{55}		
Thu 04			12^{54}	5^{56}	6^{53}	10^{06}		
Fri 05			12^{54}	5^{58}				
Sat 06	9^{04}	11^{56}	12^{56}	5^{56}	6^{28}	9^{26}		
Mon 08	6^{04}	12^{02}	12^{59}	3^{54}				
Tue 09	9^{02}	11^{55}	1^{56}	6^{03}				
Wed 10			12^{58}	6^{59}	7^{57}	9^{57}		
Thu 11			12^{57}	5^{56}	6^{54}	10^{04}		
Fri 12			12^{54}	5^{55}				
Sat 13			12^{59}	5^{59}	6^{34}	9^{56}		
Mon 15	9^{01}	11^{55}	1^{03}	6^{00}				
					PERIOD TOTALS		

APPROVED BY _____

2.

Employee Number	Hours Worked Regular	Hours Worked Overtime	Regular Rate	Earnings Regular	Earnings Overtime	Total Earnings
2	80	12	$15.00	_____	_____	_____
4	80	2	16.50	_____	_____	_____
6	60	2.5	18.00	_____	_____	_____
7			14.50	_____	_____	_____

12-2 APPLICATION PROBLEM (LO3, 4), p. 371

Determining payroll tax withholding

1., 2.

No.	Employee Name	Marital Status	Number of Withholding Allowances	Total Earnings	Federal Income Tax Withholding	Social Security Tax Withholding	Medicare Withholding
1	Kelly, Sandra P.	S	3	$1,485.00			
9	Miller, Kelly T.	M	2	1,621.00			
5	Cleveland, Patti A.	S	1	1,595.00			
2	Maxwell, Jon T.	M	4	1,348.00			
3	King, David R.	M	2	1,492.00			
8	Greene, Mary S.	S	0	215.00			
4	Hazelwood, Ellie J.	S	1	1,642.00			
7	Sharpe, Molli E.	M	3	1,489.00			

Preparing payroll records

1.

PAYROLL REGISTER

SEMIMONTHLY PERIOD ENDED _____ DATE OF PAYMENT _____

EMPL. NO.	EMPLOYEE'S NAME	MARITAL STATUS	NO. OF ALLOWANCES	EARNINGS			DEDUCTIONS						NET PAY	CHECK NO.
				REGULAR	OVERTIME	TOTAL	FEDERAL INCOME TAX	SOCIAL SECURITY TAX	MEDICARE TAX	HEALTH INSURANCE	RETIREMENT PLAN	TOTAL		
9	Gamble, Ed P.	S	1	1 3 4 2 00		1 3 4 2 00				4 5 00	1 0 00			395
7	Holtz, Thomas E.	M	2	1 0 5 8 00	4 8 50	1 1 0 6 50				6 0 00	2 5 00			396
6	Jones, Virginia W.	S	4	1 0 7 4 00	8 4 00	1 1 5 8 00				9 0 00	2 0 00			397
8	Lowe, Mary C.	M	2	1 4 8 6 00	1 0 8 00	1 5 9 4 00				6 0 00	5 0 00			398
1	Muldoon, Janice T.	M	2	1 6 4 8 00	5 5 50	1 7 0 3 50				6 0 00	5 0 00			399
11	Myers, Samuel L.	S	0	2 3 5 00		2 3 5 00				4 5 00	6 0 00			400
12	Spiller, Nathan R.	S	3	1 6 2 8 00		1 6 2 8 00				7 5 00	4 0 00			401
2	Terrell, Mary A.	M	2	1 6 0 0 00	3 0 00	1 6 3 0 00				6 0 00	3 0 00			402

12-3 APPLICATION PROBLEM (concluded)

2., 3.

EARNINGS RECORD FOR QUARTER ENDED — September 30, 20--

EMPLOYEE NO.	2
LAST NAME	Terrell
FIRST	Mary
MIDDLE INITIAL	A.
SOCIAL SECURITY NO.	947-15-4487
RATE OF PAY	$20.00 PER HOUR
MARITAL STATUS	M
WITHHOLDING ALLOWANCES	2
POSITION	Purchasing Manager

NO.	PAY PERIOD ENDED	EARNINGS REGULAR	EARNINGS OVERTIME	TOTAL	DEDUCTIONS FEDERAL INCOME TAX	SOCIAL SECURITY TAX	MEDICARE TAX	HEALTH INSURANCE	RETIREMENT PLAN	TOTAL	NET PAY	ACCUMULATED EARNINGS
												20640.00
1	7/15	1760.00	60.00	1820.00	121.00	112.84	26.39	60.00	30.00	350.23	1469.77	22460.00
2	7/31	1600.00	90.00	1690.00	100.00	104.78	24.51	60.00	30.00	319.29	1370.71	24150.00
3	8/15	1540.00	75.00	1615.00	88.00	100.13	23.42	60.00	30.00	301.55	1313.45	25765.00
4	8/31	1760.00	108.00	1868.00	127.00	115.82	27.09	60.00	30.00	359.91	1508.09	27633.00
5	9/15	1600.00	55.50	1655.50	94.00	102.64	24.00	60.00	30.00	310.64	1344.86	29288.50
6												
7												
TOTALS												

Preparing payroll checks

1.

CASTLE ELECTRONICS		DATE		No. 1056
PAYEE				
ACCOUNT	TITLE	DESCRIPTION		AMOUNT

- -

CASTLE ELECTRONICS
940 Dean Street
St. Charles, Illinois 60174

THE PEOPLES BANK
180 N. Jefferson Street
Batavia, Illinois 60510

No. 1056

GENERAL ACCOUNT

DATE _____

AMOUNT

$ _____

_____ Dollars

FOR CLASSROOM USE ONLY

PAY TO THE
ORDER OF

_____

⑆154861⑆ 5186644⑆ 1056

12-4 APPLICATION PROBLEM (continued)

2.

TYPE	HOURS	RATE	GROSS PAY	DEDUCTIONS	CURRENT	YTD
EMPLOYEE Mitchell R. Haynes					**DATE** April 30, 20--	
				Federal Income Tax	56.00	409.00
Regular	72.00	16.00	1,152.00	Social Security Tax	77.38	610.20
Overtime	4.00	24.00	96.00	Medicare Tax	18.10	142.71
				Health Insurance	50.00	400.00
				Retirement	25.00	200.00
Current Total Earnings			1,248.00	Totals	226.48	1,761.91
YTD Total Earnings			9,842.00	Net Pay	1,021.52	8,080.09

TYPE	HOURS	RATE	GROSS PAY	DEDUCTIONS	CURRENT	YTD
EMPLOYEE					**DATE**	
				Federal Income Tax	_____	_____
Regular	80.00	16.00	_____	Social Security Tax	_____	_____
Overtime	2.50	24.00	_____	Medicare Tax	_____	_____
				Health Insurance	_____	_____
				Retirement	_____	_____
Current Total Earnings			_____	Totals	_____	_____
YTD Total Earnings			_____	Net Pay	_____	_____

PAYROLL ACCOUNT _____ 77-126 / 169

CASTLE ELECTRONICS **No. 658**

PAY TO THE
ORDER OF _____ $ _____

_____ Dollars
FOR CLASSROOM USE ONLY

THE PEOPLES BANK
Batavia, Illinois 60510

⑆015486⑆2⑆ 5⑆848⑆⑆48⑈ 658   _____

EMPLOYEE	Sharon V. Bricken					DATE	April 30, 20--
TYPE	HOURS	RATE	GROSS PAY	DEDUCTIONS		CURRENT	YTD
				Federal Income Tax		101.00	792.00
Regular	80.00	14.50	1,160.00	Social Security Tax		80.01	629.80
Overtime	6.00	21.75	130.50	Medicare Tax		18.71	147.29
				Health Insurance		65.00	520.00
				Retirement		40.00	320.00
Current Total Earnings			1,290.50	Totals		304.72	2,409.09
YTD Total Earnings			10,158.00	Net Pay		985.78	7,748.91

EMPLOYEE						DATE	
TYPE	HOURS	RATE	GROSS PAY	DEDUCTIONS		CURRENT	YTD
				Federal Income Tax		_____	_____
Regular	80.00	14.50	_____	Social Security Tax		_____	_____
Overtime	1.70	21.75	_____	Medicare Tax		_____	_____
				Health Insurance		_____	_____
				Retirement		_____	_____
Current Total Earnings			_____	Totals		_____	_____
YTD Total Earnings			_____	Net Pay		_____	_____

PAYROLL ACCOUNT
77-126
169

CASTLE ELECTRONICS

No. 659

PAY TO THE
ORDER OF _____ $ _____

_____ Dollars
FOR CLASSROOM USE ONLY

THE PEOPLES BANK
Batavia, Illinois 60510

⑆0154861 2⑈ 518481148⑈ 659

Preparing a semimonthly payroll

1., 3.

PAYROLL REGISTER

SEMIMONTHLY PERIOD ENDED August 15, 20--   DATE OF PAYMENT August 15, 20--

	EMPL. NO.	EMPLOYEE'S NAME	MARITAL STATUS	NO. OF ALLOW-ANCES	EARNINGS			DEDUCTIONS						NET PAY	CHECK NO.	
					REGULAR	OVERTIME	TOTAL	FEDERAL INCOME TAX	SOCIAL SECURITY TAX	MEDICARE TAX	HEALTH INSURANCE	RETIREMENT PLAN	TOTAL			
					1	2	3	4	5	6	7	8	9	10		
1	2	Davis, Henry W.	M	2	1188 00	131 63	1319 63				50 00	20 00				1
2	11	Garcia, Juan S.	M	1	1276 00	97 88	1373 88				20 00	25 00				2
3	7	Lewis, Jack P.	S	3	940 00	105 75	1045 75				80 00	20 00				3
4	9	Lopez, Gloria P.	S	2	1460 00	—	1460 00				50 00	20 00				4
5	3	Nelson, Evelyn Y.	M	4	1188 00	178 20	1366 20				100 00	25 00				5
6	4	Robinson, Joshua T.	S	2	1500 00	105 00	1605 00				50 00	60 00				6
7	13	Rodriguez, Jean A.	M	3	1240 00	171 00	1411 00				80 00	20 00				7
8	6	Walker, Mildred M.	S	1	1104 00	—	1104 00				20 00	35 00				8
9																9
10																10
11																11
12																12
13																13
14																14
15																15
16																16
17																17
18																18
19																19
20																20
21																21

2.

MALONE COMPANY		DATE		NO. 1895
PAYEE				
ACCOUNT	**TITLE**	**DESCRIPTION**		**AMOUNT**

MALONE COMPANY
1290 N. Fry Road
Katy, Texas 77450

FIRST AMERICAN BANK
2680 S. Mason Road
Katy, Texas 77450

No. 1895

GENERAL ACCOUNT

DATE

AMOUNT

$

_____ Dollars

FOR CLASSROOM USE ONLY

**PAY TO THE
ORDER OF**

⑈318489⑈: 6510554881⑈ 1895

12-M   MASTERY PROBLEM (continued)

3.

EMPLOYEE Henry W. Davis				DEDUCTIONS	DATE July 31, 20--	
TYPE	**HOURS**	**RATE**	**GROSS PAY**	**DEDUCTIONS**	**CURRENT**	**YTD**
				Federal Income Tax	35.00	525.00
Regular	88.00	13.50	1,188.00	Social Security Tax	76.17	1,130.91
Overtime	2.00	20.25	40.50	Medicare Tax	17.81	264.49
				Health Insurance	50.00	700.00
				Retirement	20.00	280.00
Current Total Earnings			1,228.50	Totals	198.98	2,900.40
YTD Total Earnings			18,240.48	Net Pay	1,029.52	15,340.08

EMPLOYEE				DEDUCTIONS	DATE	
TYPE	**HOURS**	**RATE**	**GROSS PAY**	**DEDUCTIONS**	**CURRENT**	**YTD**
				Federal Income Tax	____	____
Regular	88.00	13.50	____	Social Security Tax	____	____
Overtime	6.50	20.25	____	Medicare Tax	____	____
				Health Insurance	____	____
				Retirement	____	____
Current Total Earnings			____	Totals	____	____
YTD Total Earnings			____	Net Pay	____	____

**PAYROLL
ACCOUNT**   _____   66-311
                                                                        513

MALONE COMPANY   **No. 452**

PAY TO THE
ORDER OF _____ $ _____

_____ Dollars
                    FOR CLASSROOM USE ONLY

FIRST AMERICAN BANK
      Katy, Texas 77450   _____

⑆318⑈4899⑆: 3455972⑈ 452

EMPLOYEE	Juan S. Garcia					DATE	July 31, 20--
TYPE	**HOURS**	**RATE**	**GROSS PAY**	**DEDUCTIONS**	**CURRENT**	**YTD**
				Federal Income Tax	80.00	1,085.00
Regular	88.00	14.50	1,276.00	Social Security Tax	87.88	1,150.25
Overtime	6.50	21.75	141.38	Medicare Tax	20.55	269.01
				Health Insurance	20.00	280.00
				Retirement	25.00	350.00
Current Total Earnings			1,417.38	Totals	233.43	3,134.26
YTD Total Earnings			18,552.40	Net Pay	1,183.95	15,418.14

EMPLOYEE						DATE	
TYPE	**HOURS**	**RATE**	**GROSS PAY**	**DEDUCTIONS**	**CURRENT**	**YTD**
				Federal Income Tax	_____	_____
Regular	88.00	14.50	_____	Social Security Tax	_____	_____
Overtime	4.50	21.75	_____	Medicare Tax	_____	_____
				Health Insurance	_____	_____
				Retirement	_____	_____
Current Total Earnings			_____	Totals	_____	_____
YTD Total Earnings			_____	Net Pay	_____	_____

PAYROLL ACCOUNT _____ 66-311 / 513

MALONE COMPANY   **No. 453**

PAY TO THE
ORDER OF _____ $ _____

_____ Dollars

FOR CLASSROOM USE ONLY

FIRST AMERICAN BANK
Katy, Texas 77450   _____

⑈:31848991⑈: 34559721⑈ 453

Name _____ Date _____ Class _____

Preparing a semimonthly payroll

Hour Summary				
Payroll Period: 12/1/20-- to 12/15/20--				
Employee No.: 3			Hourly Rate:	$15.50
Employee Name: Michael P. Hogan				
Date	**Day**	**Regular**	**Overtime**	**Total**
12/1/20--	Mon	8.0		8.0
12/2/20--	Tue	8.0	1.0	9.0
12/3/20--	Wed	8.0	1.0	9.0
12/4/20--	Thu	8.0		8.0
12/5/20--	Fri	8.0		8.0
12/8/20--	Mon	8.0		8.0
12/9/20--	Tue	8.0		8.0
12/10/20--	Wed	8.0		8.0
12/11/20--	Thu	8.0		8.0
12/12/20--	Fri	8.0		8.0
12/13/20--	Sat		4.0	4.0
12/15/20--	Mon	8.0		8.0
Totals		88.0	6.0	94.0
Employee No.: 4			Hourly Rate:	$14.00
Employee Name: Rickey J. McGuire				
Date	**Day**	**Regular**	**Overtime**	**Total**
12/2/20--	Tue	8.0		8.0
12/3/20--	Wed	8.0		8.0
12/4/20--	Thu	8.0	3.0	11.0
12/5/20--	Fri	8.0		8.0
12/8/20--	Mon	8.0		8.0
12/9/20--	Tue	8.0		8.0
12/10/20--	Wed	8.0		8.0
12/11/20--	Thu	8.0		8.0
12/12/20--	Fri	8.0		8.0
12/15/20--	Mon	8.0		8.0
Totals		80.0	3.0	83.0

Employee No.: 5			Hourly Rate:	$15.00
Employee Name: Candace M. Powers				

Date	Day	Regular	Overtime	Total
12/2/20--	Tue	4.0		4.0
12/3/20--	Wed	8.0		8.0
12/4/20--	Thu	8.0		8.0
12/5/20--	Fri	4.0		4.0
12/8/20--	Mon	8.0		8.0
12/9/20--	Tue	8.0		8.0
12/10/20--	Wed	8.0		8.0
12/11/20--	Thu	8.0		8.0
12/12/20--	Fri	8.0		8.0
12/13/20--	Sat		6.0	6.0
12/15/20--	Mon	8.0		8.0
Totals		72.0	6.0	78.0

Employee No.: 7			Hourly Rate:	$17.20
Employee Name: Damon B. Whorton				

Date	Day	Regular	Overtime	Total
12/2/20--	Tue	4.0		4.0
12/3/20--	Wed	8.0	3.0	11.0
12/4/20--	Thu	8.0	4.0	12.0
12/8/20--	Mon	8.0		8.0
12/9/20--	Tue	8.0		8.0
12/10/20--	Wed	8.0		8.0
12/11/20--	Thu	8.0		8.0
12/12/20--	Fri	8.0		8.0
12/15/20--	Mon	8.0		8.0
Totals		68.0	7.0	75.0

Preparing a semimonthly payroll

1.

PAYROLL REGISTER

SEMIMONTHLY PERIOD ENDED December 15, 20--   DATE OF PAYMENT December 15, 20--

EMPL. NO.	EMPLOYEE'S NAME	MARI-TAL STATUS	NO. OF ALLOW-ANCES	EARNINGS REGULAR (1)	OVERTIME (2)	TOTAL (3)	FEDERAL INCOME TAX (4)	DEDUCTIONS SOCIAL SECURITY TAX (5)	MEDICARE TAX (6)	HEALTH INSURANCE (7)	RETIREMENT PLAN (8)	TOTAL (9)	NET PAY (10)	CHECK NO.
3	Hogan, Michael P.	S	2							40 00	30 00			1
4	McGuire, Rickey J.	M	1							30 00	15 00			2
5	Powers, Candace M.	M	3							60 00	40 00			3
7	Whorton, Damon B.	M	2							40 00	30 00			4
	Totals													5
														6

2.

EARNINGS RECORD FOR QUARTER ENDED December 31, 20--

EMPLOYEE NO. 3   LAST NAME Hogan   FIRST Michael   MIDDLE INITIAL P.

SOCIAL SECURITY NO. 904-51-4891   MARITAL STATUS S   WITHHOLDING ALLOWANCES 2

RATE OF PAY $15.50   PER HOUR   POSITION Manager

PAY PERIOD NO.	ENDED	EARNINGS REGULAR (1)	OVERTIME (2)	TOTAL (3)	FEDERAL INCOME TAX (4)	DEDUCTIONS SOCIAL SECURITY TAX (5)	MEDICARE TAX (6)	HEALTH INSURANCE (7)	RETIREMENT PLAN (8)	TOTAL (9)	NET PAY (10)	ACCUMULATED EARNINGS (11)
1	10/15	1 3 0 2 00	1 3 9 50	1 4 4 1 50	1 2 5 00	8 9 37	2 0 90	4 0 00	3 0 00	3 0 5 27	1 1 3 6 23	24 5 0 5 50
2	10/31	1 3 6 4 00		1 3 6 4 00	1 1 3 00	8 4 57	1 9 78	4 0 00	3 0 00	2 8 7 35	1 0 7 6 65	25 9 4 7 00
3	11/15	1 1 1 6 00	9 3 00	1 2 0 9 00	8 9 00	7 4 96	1 7 53	4 0 00	3 0 00	2 5 1 49	9 5 7 51	27 3 1 1 00
4	11/30	1 1 1 6 00	1 8 6 00	1 3 0 2 00	1 0 4 00	8 0 72	1 8 88	4 0 00	3 0 00	2 7 3 60	1 0 2 8 40	28 5 2 0 00
5												29 8 2 0 00
6	TOTALS											

Earnings Record — Employee No. 4

EARNINGS RECORD FOR QUARTER ENDED December 31, 20--

LAST NAME: McGuire FIRST: Rickey MIDDLE INITIAL: J.
RATE OF PAY: $14.00 PER HOUR SOCIAL SECURITY NO. 987-15-0058
MARITAL STATUS: M POSITION: Carpenter WITHHOLDING ALLOWANCES: 1

	PAY PERIOD	EARNINGS			DEDUCTIONS						NET PAY	ACCUMULATED EARNINGS
NO.	ENDED	REGULAR (1)	OVERTIME (2)	TOTAL (3)	FEDERAL INCOME TAX (4)	SOCIAL SECURITY TAX (5)	MEDICARE TAX (6)	HEALTH INSURANCE (7)	RETIREMENT PLAN (8)	TOTAL (9)	(10)	(11)
1	10/15	1 1 7 6 00	1 2 6 00	1 3 0 2 00	6 5 00	8 0 72	1 8 88	3 0 00	1 5 00	2 0 9 60	1 0 9 2 40	1 9 5 3 0 00
2	10/31	1 2 3 2 00	4 2 00	1 2 7 4 00	5 9 00	7 8 99	1 8 47	3 0 00	1 5 00	2 0 1 46	1 0 7 2 54	2 0 8 3 2 00
3	11/15	1 0 9 2 00		1 0 9 2 00	3 7 00	6 7 70	1 5 83	3 0 00	1 5 00	1 6 5 53	9 2 6 47	2 2 1 0 6 00
4	11/30	1 0 0 8 00	1 0 5 00	1 1 1 3 00	3 9 00	6 9 01	1 6 14	3 0 00	1 5 00	1 6 9 15	9 4 3 85	2 3 1 9 8 00
5												2 4 3 1 1 00
6												
	TOTALS											

Earnings Record — Employee No. 5

EARNINGS RECORD FOR QUARTER ENDED December 31, 20--

LAST NAME: Powers FIRST: Candace MIDDLE INITIAL: M.
RATE OF PAY: $15.00 PER HOUR SOCIAL SECURITY NO. 905-15-1849
MARITAL STATUS: M POSITION: Office Manager WITHHOLDING ALLOWANCES: 3

	PAY PERIOD	EARNINGS			DEDUCTIONS						NET PAY	ACCUMULATED EARNINGS
NO.	ENDED	REGULAR (1)	OVERTIME (2)	TOTAL (3)	FEDERAL INCOME TAX (4)	SOCIAL SECURITY TAX (5)	MEDICARE TAX (6)	HEALTH INSURANCE (7)	RETIREMENT PLAN (8)	TOTAL (9)	(10)	(11)
1	10/15	1 2 6 0 00		1 2 6 0 00	2 4 00	7 8 12	1 8 27	6 0 00	4 0 00	2 2 0 39	1 0 3 9 61	2 0 1 6 0 00
2	10/31	1 3 2 0 00		1 3 2 0 00	3 0 00	8 1 84	1 9 14	6 0 00	4 0 00	2 3 0 98	1 0 8 9 02	2 1 4 2 0 00
3	11/15	1 0 8 0 00	1 3 5 00	1 2 1 5 00	1 8 00	7 5 33	1 7 62	6 0 00	4 0 00	2 1 0 95	1 0 0 4 05	2 2 7 4 0 00
4	11/30	1 0 8 0 00	1 8 0 00	1 2 6 0 00	2 4 00	7 8 12	1 8 27	6 0 00	4 0 00	2 2 0 39	1 0 3 9 61	2 3 9 5 5 00
5												2 5 2 1 5 00
6												
	TOTALS											

EARNINGS RECORD FOR QUARTER ENDED _____ December 31, 20--

EMPLOYEE NO. 7			
LAST NAME Whorton	FIRST Damon	MIDDLE INITIAL B.	MARITAL STATUS M WITHHOLDING ALLOWANCES 2
RATE OF PAY $17.20	PER HOUR	SOCIAL SECURITY NO. 945-06-8473	POSITION Carpenter

NO.	PAY PERIOD ENDED	EARNINGS REGULAR	OVERTIME	TOTAL	DEDUCTIONS FEDERAL INCOME TAX	SOCIAL SECURITY TAX	MEDICARE TAX	HEALTH INSURANCE	RETIREMENT PLAN	TOTAL	NET PAY	ACCUMULATED EARNINGS
		1	2	3	4	5	6	7	8	9	10	11
1	10/15	1444 80	77 40	1522 20	76 00	94 38	22 07	40 00	30 00	262 45	1259 75	2435520
2	10/31	1513 60	103 20	1616 80	88 00	100 24	23 44	40 00	30 00	281 68	1335 12	2587740
3	11/15	1238 40	51 60	1290 00	41 00	79 98	18 71	40 00	30 00	209 69	1080 31	2749420
4	11/30	1238 40	154 80	1393 20	55 00	86 38	20 20	40 00	30 00	231 58	1116 62	2878420
5												3017740
6												
7												
	TOTALS											

3.

JENKINS CABINETS	DATE		No. **689**

PAYEE			
ACCOUNT	**TITLE**	**DESCRIPTION**	**AMOUNT**

JENKINS CABINETS
6001 Atlantic Avenue
Florence, CA 90201

First National Savings Bank
890 W. Manchester Blvd.
Inglewood, CA 90045

No. **689**

GENERAL ACCOUNT

DATE   AMOUNT

$ _____

_____ Dollars

FOR CLASSROOM USE ONLY

PAY TO THE
ORDER OF

⑆848919841⑆ 848480058⑈ 0689

4.

EMPLOYEE Michael P. Hogan					DATE December 1, 20--		
TYPE	**HOURS**	**RATE**	**GROSS PAY**	**DEDUCTIONS**	**CURRENT**	**YTD**
				Federal Income Tax	104.00	2,984.00
Regular	72.00	15.50	1,116.00	Social Security Tax	80.72	1,848.96
Overtime	8.00	23.25	186.00	Medicare Tax	18.88	432.42
				Health Insurance	40.00	880.00
				Retirement	30.00	660.00
Current Total Earnings			1,302.00	Totals	273.60	6,805.38
YTD Total Earnings			29,822.00	Net Pay	1,028.40	23,016.62

EMPLOYEE					DATE		
TYPE	**HOURS**	**RATE**	**GROSS PAY**	**DEDUCTIONS**	**CURRENT**	**YTD**
				Federal Income Tax	_____	_____
Regular	88.00	15.50	_____	Social Security Tax	_____	_____
Overtime	6.00	23.25	_____	Medicare Tax	_____	_____
				Health Insurance	_____	_____
				Retirement	_____	_____
Current Total Earnings		_____		Totals	_____	_____
YTD Total Earnings		_____		Net Pay	_____	_____

PAYROLL ACCOUNT _____ 66-311 / 513

JENKINS CABINETS   **No. 234**

PAY TO THE
ORDER OF _____ $ _____

_____ Dollars
FOR CLASSROOM USE ONLY

First National Savings Bank
Inglewood, CA 90045   _____

⑆848919841⑆ 4811544881⑈ 234

EMPLOYEE	Rickey J. McGuire				DATE	December 1, 20--	
TYPE	**HOURS**	**RATE**	**GROSS PAY**	**DEDUCTIONS**	**CURRENT**	**YTD**	
				Federal Income Tax	39.00	1,018.00	
Regular	72.00	14.00	1,008.00	Social Security Tax	69.01	1,507.28	
Overtime	5.00	21.00	105.00	Medicare Tax	16.14	352.51	
				Health Insurance	30.00	660.00	
				Retirement	15.00	330.00	
Current Total Earnings			1,113.00	Totals	169.15	3,867.79	
YTD Total Earnings			24,311.00	Net Pay	943.85	20,443.21	

EMPLOYEE					DATE		
TYPE	**HOURS**	**RATE**	**GROSS PAY**	**DEDUCTIONS**	**CURRENT**	**YTD**	
				Federal Income Tax	_____	_____	
Regular	80.00	14.00	_____	Social Security Tax	_____	_____	
Overtime	3.00	21.00	_____	Medicare Tax	_____	_____	
				Health Insurance	_____	_____	
				Retirement	_____	_____	
Current Total Earnings			_____	Totals	_____	_____	
YTD Total Earnings			_____	Net Pay	_____	_____	

PAYROLL ACCOUNT

66-311
513

JENKINS CABINETS **No. 235**

_____

PAY TO THE
ORDER OF _____ $ _____

_____ Dollars

FOR CLASSROOM USE ONLY

First National Savings Bank
Inglewood, CA 90045

⑆648 18884⑆ 48 11544 88⑈ 235

_____

12-S   SOURCE DOCUMENTS PROBLEM (continued)

EMPLOYEE Candace M. Powers				DATE December 1, 20--		
TYPE	**HOURS**	**RATE**	**GROSS PAY**	**DEDUCTIONS**	**CURRENT**	**YTD**
				Federal Income Tax	24.00	365.00
Regular	72.00	15.00	1,080.00	Social Security Tax	78.12	1,563.33
Overtime	8.00	22.50	180.00	Medicare Tax	18.27	365.62
				Health Insurance	60.00	1,200.00
				Retirement	40.00	800.00
Current Total Earnings			1,260.00	Totals	220.39	4,293.95
YTD Total Earnings			25,215.00	Net Pay	1,039.61	20,921.05

EMPLOYEE				DATE		
TYPE	**HOURS**	**RATE**	**GROSS PAY**	**DEDUCTIONS**	**CURRENT**	**YTD**
				Federal Income Tax	_____	_____
Regular	72.00	15.00	_____	Social Security Tax	_____	_____
Overtime	6.00	22.50	_____	Medicare Tax	_____	_____
				Health Insurance	_____	_____
				Retirement	_____	_____
Current Total Earnings			_____	Totals	_____	_____
YTD Total Earnings			_____	Net Pay	_____	_____

PAYROLL ACCOUNT _____   66-311 / 513

JENKINS CABINETS   **No. 236**

PAY TO THE
ORDER OF _____ $ _____

_____ Dollars
FOR CLASSROOM USE ONLY

First National Savings Bank
Inglewood, CA 90045   _____

⑆648188841⑆ 481154488⑈ 236

EMPLOYEE Damon B. Whorton					DATE December 1, 20--	
TYPE	HOURS	RATE	GROSS PAY	DEDUCTIONS	CURRENT	YTD
				Federal Income Tax	55.00	1,402.00
Regular	72.00	17.20	1,238.40	Social Security Tax	86.38	1,870.97
Overtime	6.00	25.80	154.80	Medicare Tax	20.20	437.57
				Health Insurance	40.00	800.00
				Retirement	30.00	600.00
Current Total Earnings			1,393.20	Totals	231.58	5,110.54
YTD Total Earnings			30,177.00	Net Pay	1,161.62	25,066.46

EMPLOYEE					DATE	
TYPE	HOURS	RATE	GROSS PAY	DEDUCTIONS	CURRENT	YTD
				Federal Income Tax	_____	_____
Regular	68.00	17.20	_____	Social Security Tax	_____	_____
Overtime	7.00	25.80	_____	Medicare Tax	_____	_____
				Health Insurance	_____	_____
				Retirement	_____	_____
Current Total Earnings			_____	Totals	_____	_____
YTD Total Earnings			_____	Net Pay	_____	_____

PAYROLL ACCOUNT   66-311 / 513

JENKINS CABINETS   **No. 237**

PAY TO THE
ORDER OF _____ $ _____

_____ Dollars

FOR CLASSROOM USE ONLY

First National Savings Bank
Inglewood, CA 90045   _____

⑈648188841⑈ 481154488⑈ 237

CHALLENGE PROBLEM (LO3, 4, 6), p. 374

Preparing a semimonthly payroll with pretax medical and retirement plans

1.

PAYROLL REGISTER

SEMIMONTHLY PERIOD ENDED August 15, 20-- DATE OF PAYMENT August 15, 20--

EMPL. NO.	EMPLOYEE'S NAME	MARITAL STATUS	NO. OF ALLOWANCES	EARNINGS REGULAR	EARNINGS OVERTIME	EARNINGS TOTAL	FEDERAL INCOME TAX	SOCIAL SECURITY TAX	MEDICARE TAX	HEALTH INSURANCE	RETIREMENT PLAN	TOTAL	NET PAY	CHECK NO.
2	Davis, Henry W.	M	2	1 1 8 8 00	1 3 1 63	1 3 1 9 63				5 0 00	2 0 00			
11	Garcia, Juan S.	M	1	1 2 7 6 00	9 7 88	1 3 7 3 88				2 0 00	2 5 00			
7	Lewis, Jack P.	S	3	9 4 0 00	1 0 5 75	1 0 4 5 75				8 0 00	2 0 00			
9	Lopez, Gloria P.	S	2	1 4 6 0 00	—	1 4 6 0 00				5 0 00	2 0 00			
3	Nelson, Evelyn Y.	M	4	1 1 8 8 00	1 7 8 20	1 3 6 6 20				1 0 0 00	2 5 00			
4	Robinson, Joshua T.	S	2	1 5 0 0 00	1 0 5 00	1 6 0 5 00				5 0 00	6 0 00			
13	Rodriguez, Jean A.	M	3	1 2 4 0 00	1 7 1 00	1 4 1 1 00				8 0 00	2 0 00			
6	Walker, Mildred M.	S	1	1 1 0 4 00	—	1 1 0 4 00				2 0 00	3 5 00			

2.

Net Pay with Voluntary Deductions			
Employee	**Taxable**	**Nontaxable**	**Difference**
Davis, Henry W.			
Garcia, Juan S.			
Lewis, Jack P.			
Lopez, Gloria P.			
Nelson, Evelyn Y.			
Robinson, Joshua T.			
Rodriguez, Jean A.			
Walker, Mildred M.			

Chapter 12 Preparing Payroll Records • **347**

Name	Perfect Score	Your Score
Analyzing Payroll Records	15 Pts.	
Analyzing Transactions Affecting Payroll	5 Pts.	
Analyzing Form W-2	10 Pts.	
Total	30 Pts.	

Part One—Analyzing Payroll Records

Directions: For each of the following items, select the choice that best completes the statement. Print the letter identifying your choice in the Answers column.

Answers

1. All the payroll information needed to prepare payroll and tax reports is found on (A) Form W-4 and the employee earnings record (B) Form W-4 and the payroll register (C) the payroll register and the employee earnings record (D) Form W-4. (p. 378)

   1. _____

2. The payroll journal entry is based on the totals of the payroll register (A) Total Earnings column, each deduction column, and the Net Pay column (B) Total Earnings, Earnings Regular, Earnings Overtime, and Deductions Total columns (C) Earnings Regular, Earnings Overtime, and Deductions Total columns (D) Total Earnings, Earnings Regular, and Earnings Overtime Total columns. (p. 379)

   2. _____

3. The Total Earnings column total of a payroll register is journalized as a debit to (A) Cash (B) Salary Expense (C) Employee Income Tax Payable (D) Social Security Tax Payable. (p. 379)

   3. _____

4. The total of the Federal Income Tax column of a payroll register is credited to (A) a revenue account (B) an expense account (C) a liability account (D) an asset account. (p. 379)

   4. _____

5. The total of the Net Pay column of the payroll register is credited to (A) a revenue account (B) an expense account (C) an asset account (D) a liability account. (p. 379)

   5. _____

6. When a semimonthly payroll is paid, the credit to Cash is equal to the (A) total earnings of all employees (B) total deductions for income tax and social security tax (C) total deductions (D) net pay of all employees. (p. 380)

   6. _____

7. Employer payroll taxes are (A) assets (B) expenses (C) revenues (D) none of these. (p. 382)

   7. _____

8. Payroll taxes that are paid by both the employer and the employee are (A) federal unemployment tax and social security tax (B) federal unemployment tax and Medicare tax (C) social security tax and Medicare tax (D) federal income tax, social security tax, and Medicare tax. (p. 382)

   8. _____

9. A tax paid to administer the unemployment program is the (A) social security tax (B) Medicare tax (C) federal unemployment tax (D) state unemployment tax. (p. 382)

   9. _____

10. A state tax used to pay benefits to unemployed workers is the (A) social security tax (B) Medicare tax (C) federal unemployment tax (D) state unemployment tax. (p. 382)

    10. _____

11. An employee's earnings subject to unemployment taxes are referred to as (A) gross earnings (B) net earnings (C) FUTA earnings (D) accumulated earnings. (p. 383)

    11. _____

12. Each employer who withholds income tax, social security tax, and Medicare tax from employee earnings must furnish each employee an (A) IRS Form W-4 (B) IRS Form W-2 (C) IRS Form W-3 (D) IRS Form 941. (p. 387)

    12. _____

13. Each employer is required by law to report payroll taxes on an (A) IRS Form W-4 (B) IRS Form 941 (C) IRS Form W-2 (D) IRS Form W-3. (p. 389)

    13. _____

14. The form used to report annual earnings and payroll taxes for all employees to the Social Security Administration is the (A) W-2 (B) Form 941 (C) W-3 (D) W-4. (p. 390)

    14. _____

15. To record the payment of federal unemployment tax, the account debited is (A) a revenue account (B) an expense account (C) a liability account (D) an asset account. (p. 396)

    15. _____

Part Two—Analyzing Transactions Affecting Payroll

Directions: Analyze each of the following transactions into debit and credit parts. Print the letters identifying your choices in the proper Answers column.

Account Titles	Transactions	Answers Debit	Credit
A. Cash	**1.** Paid cash for semimonthly payroll. (p. 380)	_____	_____
B. Employee Income Tax Payable	**2.** Recorded employer payroll taxes expense. (p. 384)	_____	_____
C. Health Insurance Premiums Payable	**3.** Paid cash for liability for employee income tax, social security tax, and Medicare tax. (p. 394)	_____	_____
D. Medicare Tax Payable	**4.** Paid cash for federal unemployment tax liability. (p. 396)	_____	_____
E. Payroll Taxes Expense	**5.** Paid cash for state unemployment tax liability. (p. 396)	_____	_____
F. Retirement Benefits Payable			
G. Salary Expense			
H. Social Security Tax Payable			
I. Unemployment Tax Payable—Federal			
J. Unemployment Tax Payable—State			

Part Three—Analyzing Form W-2

Directions: Analyze the following statements about a Form W-2, Wage and Tax Statement. Use the Form W-2 below to answer the specific questions about John Butler. Place a T for True or an F for False in the Answers column to show whether each of the following statements is true or false. (p. 387)

22222	a Employee's social security number 194-81-5823	OMB No. 1545-0008		
b Employer identification number (EIN) 31-0429632			1 Wages, tips, other compensation 30,273.75	2 Federal income tax withheld 620.00
c Employer's name, address, and ZIP code ThreeGreen Products, Inc. 1501 Commerce Street Carlisle, PA 17013			3 Social security wages 30,273.75	4 Social security tax withheld 1,876.97
			5 Medicare wages and tips 30,273.75	6 Medicare tax withheld 438.97
			7 Social security tips	8 Allocated tips
d Control number			9	10 Dependent care benefits
e Employee's first name and initial Last name John P. Butler Suff.			11 Nonqualified plans	12a
			13 Statutory employee Retirement plan Third-party sick pay	12b
1014 Bosler Ave. Carlisle, PA 17013			14 Other	12c
				12d
f Employee's address and ZIP code				
15 State Employer's state ID number	16 State wages, tips, etc.	17 State income tax	18 Local wages, tips, etc.	19 Local income tax 20 Locality name

Form **W-2** Wage and Tax Statement **20--**
Copy 1—For State, City, or Local Tax Department
Department of the Treasury—Internal Revenue Service

Answers

1. John Butler's total salary is more than his total social security salary. — 1. _____

2. This Form W-2 shows John Butler's net pay for the entire year. — 2. _____

3. The amount withheld for Mr. Butler's social security tax was more than the amount withheld for his federal income tax. — 3. _____

4. State income tax was withheld from Mr. Butler's salary. — 4. _____

5. All deductions from Mr. Butler's salary for taxes and retirement plan contributions are shown on his Form W-2. — 5. _____

6. This Form W-2 would indicate whether Mr. Butler had more than one employer during the year. — 6. _____

7. If an employee works for several employers during the year, that employee must receive a Form W-2 from each employer. — 7. _____

8. An employer is required to provide employees with a Form W-2 no later than January 31 of the year following the one for which the report has been completed. — 8. _____

9. When John Butler files his federal income tax return, he must attach Copy A of Form W-2 to his return. — 9. _____

10. Businesses in states with state income tax must prepare additional copies of Form W-2. — 10. _____

Across

5. The total of gross earnings for all employees earning hourly wages, salaries, and commissions.

6. The 12-month period that ends on June 30th of the prior year that is used to determine how frequently a business must deposit payroll taxes.

Down

1. A state tax paid by employers that is used to pay benefits to unemployed workers.

2. The payment of payroll taxes to the government.

3. The chief accountant in an organization, having responsibility for both financial and managerial accounting activities. Sometimes called comptroller.

4. A process that requires an employer to withhold a portion of an employee's paycheck to pay a court-ordered debt settlement.

13-1 WORK TOGETHER, p. 381

Recording a payroll

1.

Salary Expense

Employee Income Tax Payable

Social Security Tax Payable

Medicare Tax Payable

Cash

2.

CASH PAYMENTS JOURNAL

PAGE _____

| | | | | GENERAL | | ACCOUNTS PAYABLE DEBIT | PURCHASES DISCOUNT CREDIT | CASH CREDIT |
DATE	ACCOUNT TITLE	CK. NO.	POST. REF.	DEBIT	CREDIT			
				1	2	3	4	5

Recording a payroll

1.

Salary Expense

Employee Income Tax Payable

Social Security Tax Payable

Medicare Tax Payable

Cash

2.

CASH PAYMENTS JOURNAL

PAGE

			GENERAL		ACCOUNTS PAYABLE DEBIT	PURCHASES DISCOUNT CREDIT	CASH CREDIT	
DATE	ACCOUNT TITLE	CK. NO.	POST. REF.	DEBIT	CREDIT			
				1	2	3	4	5
1								
2								
3								
4								
5								
6								

Name _____ Date _____ Class _____

13-2 WORK TOGETHER, p. 386

Recording employer payroll taxes

1., 2.

1	2	3	4	5
Employee Name	**Prior Accumulated Earnings**	**Earnings to Equal FUTA Tax Base**	**Earnings for Current Pay Period**	**FUTA Earnings**
Ellis, Nick C.	$6,100.00	$ 900.00	$ 762.50	_____
Jennings, Evan P.	7,980.00	0.00	1,040.00	_____
Powers, Virginia A.	4,380.00	2,620.00	527.00	_____
Wolfe, Kerry T.	6,850.00	150.00	849.50	_____
	Totals		_____	_____

Social Security Tax Payable, 6.2% _____

Medicare Tax Payable, 1.45% _____

Unemployment Tax Payable—Federal, 0.8% _____

Unemployment Tax Payable—State, 5.4% _____

   Total Payroll Taxes _____

3.

GENERAL JOURNAL

PAGE _____

	DATE	ACCOUNT TITLE	DOC. NO.	POST. REF.	DEBIT	CREDIT	
7							7
8							8
9							9
10							10
11							11
12							12
13							13
14							14
15							15
16							16
17							17
18							18
19							19
20							20

Chapter 13 Accounting for Payroll and Payroll Taxes • **355**

© 2019 Cengage®. May not be scanned, copied or duplicated, or posted to a publicly accessible website, in whole or in part.

Recording employer payroll taxes

1., 2.

1	2	3	4	5
Employee Name	**Prior Accumulated Earnings**	**Earnings to Equal FUTA Tax Base**	**Earnings for Current Pay Period**	**FUTA Earnings**
Holt, Stephanie L.	$6,380.00	$ 620.00	$ 653.00	_____
Klein, Jacob S.	3,840.00	3,160.00	521.00	_____
Singh, Irene M.	7,290.00	0.00	736.50	_____
Tate, Joyce B.	6,270.00	730.00	614.00	_____
	Totals		═══════	═══════

Social Security Tax Payable, 6.2%	_____
Medicare Tax Payable, 1.45%	_____
Unemployment Tax Payable—Federal, 0.8%	_____
Unemployment Tax Payable—State, 5.4%	_____
Total Payroll Taxes	═══════

3.

GENERAL JOURNAL   PAGE

	DATE	ACCOUNT TITLE	DOC. NO.	POST. REF.	DEBIT	CREDIT	
7							7
8							8
9							9
10							10
11							11
12							12
13							13
14							14
15							15
16							16
17							17
18							18
19							19
20							20

13-3 WORK TOGETHER, p. 391

Reporting withholding and payroll taxes

1.

Form **941 for 20--:** **Employer's QUARTERLY Federal Tax Return**   951110
(Rev. October 20--)   Department of the Treasury — Internal Revenue Service   OMB No. 1545-0029

(EIN)
Employer identification number ☐☐ – ☐☐☐☐☐☐☐

Name (not your trade name) _____

Trade name (if any) _____

Address _____
    Number   Street   Suite or room number
    _____
    City   State   ZIP code

Report for this Quarter of 20--
(Check one.)

☐ **1:** January, February, March
☐ **2:** April, May, June
☐ **3:** July, August, September
☐ **4:** October, November, December

Read the separate instructions before you complete Form 941. Type or print within the boxes.

Part 1: Answer these questions for this quarter.

1	Number of employees who received wages, tips, or other compensation for the pay period including: *Mar. 12* (Quarter 1), *June 12* (Quarter 2), *Sept. 12* (Quarter 3), or *Dec. 12* (Quarter 4)	1 ___
2	Wages, tips, and other compensation	2 ___
3	Income tax withheld from wages, tips, and other compensation	3 ___
4	If no wages, tips, and other compensation are subject to social security or Medicare tax	☐ Check and go to line 6e.

Report wages/tips for this quarter, including those paid to qualified new employees, on lines 5a–5c. The social security tax exemption on wages/tips will be figured on lines 6c and 6d and will reduce the tax on line 6e.

		Column 1		Column 2
5a	Taxable social security wages* .	___	× .124 =	___
5b	Taxable social security tips* . .	___	× .124 =	___
5c	Taxable Medicare wages & tips*	___	× .029 =	___
5d	Add *Column 2* line 5a, *Column 2* line 5b, and *Column 2* line 5c		5d ___

See instructions for definitions of qualified employee and exempt wages/tips.

6a	Number of qualified employees *first* paid exempt wages/tips this quarter	___	
6b	Number of qualified employees paid exempt wages/tips this quarter	___	
6c	Exempt wages/tips paid to qualified employees this quarter	___ × .062 =	6d ___
6e	Total taxes before adjustments (line 3 + line 5d – line 6d = line 6e)		6e ___
7a	Current quarter's adjustment for fractions of cents		7a ___
7b	Current quarter's adjustment for sick pay		7b ___
7c	Current quarter's adjustments for tips and group-term life insurance		7c ___
8	Total taxes after adjustments. Combine lines 6e through 7c		8 ___
9	Advance earned income credit (EIC) payments made to employees		9 ___
10	Total taxes after adjustment for advance EIC (line 8 – line 9 = line 10)		10 ___
11	Total deposits, including prior quarter overpayments		11 ___
12a	COBRA premium assistance payments (see instructions)		12a ___
12b	Number of individuals provided COBRA premium assistance . .	___	
12c	Number of qualified employees paid exempt wages/tips March 19–31	___	
12d	Exempt wages/tips paid to qualified employees March 19–31	___ × .062 =	12e ___
13	Add lines 11, 12a, and 12e		13 ___
14	Balance due. If line 10 is more than line 13, enter the difference and see instructions . . .		14 ___
15	Overpayment. If line 13 is more than line 10, enter the difference ___		Check one: ☐ Apply to next return. ☐ Send a refund.

Complete lines 12c, 12d, and 12e only for the 2nd quarter of 20--.

▶ **You MUST complete both pages of Form 941 and SIGN it.**   Next ▶

For Privacy Act and Paperwork Reduction Act Notice, see the back of the Payment Voucher.   Cat. No. 17001Z   Form **941** (Rev. 10-20--)

950210

Name *(not your trade name)*	Employer identification number (EIN)

Part 2: Tell us about your deposit schedule and tax liability for this quarter.

If you are unsure about whether you are a monthly schedule depositor or a semiweekly schedule depositor, see *Pub. 15 (Circular E)*, section 11.

16 ☐☐ Write the state abbreviation for the state where you made your deposits OR write "MU" if you made your deposits in *multiple* states.

17 Check one: ☐ Line 10 on this return is less than $2,500 or line 10 on the return for the preceding quarter was less than $2,500, and you did not incur a $100,000 next-day deposit obligation during the current quarter. Go to Part 3.

☐ **You were a monthly schedule depositor for the entire quarter.** Enter your tax liability for each month and total liability for the quarter.

Tax liability:	Month 1	▪
	Month 2	▪
	Month 3	▪
Total liability for quarter		▪	**Total must equal line 10.**

☐ **You were a semiweekly schedule depositor for any part of this quarter.** Complete *Schedule B (Form 941): Report of Tax Liability for Semiweekly Schedule Depositors,* and attach it to Form 941.

13-3 **ON YOUR OWN, p. 391**

Reporting withholding and payroll taxes

1.

Form **941 for 20--:** Employer's QUARTERLY Federal Tax Return			951110
(Rev. October 20--) Department of the Treasury — Internal Revenue Service			OMB No. 1545-0029

(EIN)
Employer identification number ☐☐ – ☐☐☐☐☐☐☐

Name (not your trade name)

Trade name (if any)

Address
Number Street Suite or room number

City State ZIP code

Report for this Quarter of 20--
(Check one.)

☐ 1: January, February, March
☐ 2: April, May, June
☐ 3: July, August, September
☐ 4: October, November, December

Read the separate instructions before you complete Form 941. Type or print within the boxes.

Part 1: Answer these questions for this quarter.

1	Number of employees who received wages, tips, or other compensation for the pay period including: *Mar. 12* (Quarter 1), *June 12* (Quarter 2), *Sept. 12* (Quarter 3), or *Dec. 12* (Quarter 4)	1	
2	Wages, tips, and other compensation	2	.
3	Income tax withheld from wages, tips, and other compensation	3	.

4 If no wages, tips, and other compensation are subject to social security or Medicare tax ☐ **Check and go to line 6e.**

Report wages/tips for this quarter, including those paid to qualified new employees, on lines 5a–5c. The social security tax exemption on wages/tips will be figured on lines 6c and 6d and will reduce the tax on line 6e.

		Column 1		Column 2
5a	Taxable social security wages* .	.	× .124 =	.
5b	Taxable social security tips* . .	.	× .124 =	.
5c	Taxable Medicare wages & tips*	.	× .029 =	.

5d	Add *Column 2* line 5a, *Column 2* line 5b, and *Column 2* line 5c	5d	.
6a	Number of qualified employees *first* paid exempt wages/tips this quarter		

See instructions for definitions of qualified employee and exempt wages/tips.

6b	Number of qualified employees paid exempt wages/tips this quarter		
6c	Exempt wages/tips paid to qualified employees this quarter	. × .062 =	6d	.
6e	Total taxes before adjustments (line 3 + line 5d – line 6d = line 6e)	6e	.
7a	Current quarter's adjustment for fractions of cents	7a	.
7b	Current quarter's adjustment for sick pay	7b	.
7c	Current quarter's adjustments for tips and group-term life insurance	7c	.
8	Total taxes after adjustments. Combine lines 6e through 7c	8	.
9	Advance earned income credit (EIC) payments made to employees	9	.
10	Total taxes after adjustment for advance EIC (line 8 – line 9 = line 10)	10	.
11	Total deposits, including prior quarter overpayments	11	.
12a	COBRA premium assistance payments (see instructions)	12a	.
12b	Number of individuals provided COBRA premium assistance . .		

Complete lines 12c, 12d, and 12e only for the 2nd quarter of 20--.

12c	Number of qualified employees paid exempt wages/tips March 19–31		
12d	Exempt wages/tips paid to qualified employees March 19–31	. × .062 =	12e	.
13	Add lines 11, 12a, and 12e	13	.
14	Balance due. If line 10 is more than line 13, enter the difference and see instructions . . .	14	.
15	Overpayment. If line 13 is more than line 10, enter the difference	.	Check one: ☐ Apply to next return. ☐ Send a refund.

▶ **You MUST complete both pages of Form 941 and SIGN it.** Next ▶

For Privacy Act and Paperwork Reduction Act Notice, see the back of the Payment Voucher. Cat. No. 17001Z Form **941** (Rev. 10-20--)

950210

Name *(not your trade name)*	**Employer identification number (EIN)**

Part 2: Tell us about your deposit schedule and tax liability for this quarter.

If you are unsure about whether you are a monthly schedule depositor or a semiweekly schedule depositor, see *Pub. 15 (Circular E),* section 11.

16 [ ] [ ]   Write the state abbreviation for the state where you made your deposits OR write "MU" if you made your deposits in *multiple* states.

17   Check one: [ ]   Line 10 on this return is less than $2,500 or line 10 on the return for the preceding quarter was less than $2,500, and you did not incur a $100,000 next-day deposit obligation during the current quarter. Go to Part 3.

[ ]   **You were a monthly schedule depositor for the entire quarter.** Enter your tax liability for each month and total liability for the quarter.

Tax liability: Month 1   [.]

Month 2   [.]

Month 3   [.]

Total liability for quarter   [.]   **Total must equal line 10.**

[ ]   **You were a semiweekly schedule depositor for any part of this quarter.** Complete *Schedule B (Form 941): Report of Tax Liability for Semiweekly Schedule Depositors,* and attach it to Form 941.

13-4 WORK TOGETHER, p. 397

Paying withholding and payroll taxes

1., 2.

CASH PAYMENTS JOURNAL

PAGE

DATE	ACCOUNT TITLE	CK. NO.	POST. REF.	GENERAL DEBIT	GENERAL CREDIT	ACCOUNTS PAYABLE DEBIT	PURCHASES DISCOUNT CREDIT	CASH CREDIT

Paying withholding and payroll taxes
1., 2.

CASH PAYMENTS JOURNAL

PAGE

DATE	ACCOUNT TITLE	CK. NO.	POST. REF.	GENERAL DEBIT	GENERAL CREDIT	ACCOUNTS PAYABLE DEBIT	PURCHASES DISCOUNT CREDIT	CASH CREDIT	
				1	2	3	4	5	1
									2
									3
									4
									5
									6
									7
									8
									9
									10
									11
									12
									13
									14
									15
									16
									17
									18
									19
									20
									21
									22
									23
									24
									25

13-1 APPLICATION PROBLEM (LO2), p. 401

Recording a payroll

CASH PAYMENTS JOURNAL

						GENERAL		ACCOUNTS PAYABLE DEBIT	PURCHASES DISCOUNT CREDIT	CASH CREDIT
DATE	ACCOUNT TITLE	CK. NO.	POST. REF.	DEBIT		CREDIT				

Recording employer payroll taxes

1., 2., 4.

1	2	3	4	5	6	7	8	9
Employee Name	Prior Accumulated Earnings	Earnings to Equal FUTA Tax Base	Earnings for Current Pay Period	FUTA Earnings	Prior Accumulated Earnings	Earnings to Equal FUTA Tax Base	Earnings for Current Pay Period	FUTA Earnings
Campos, Regina P.	$4,980.00		$ 830.00				$ 850.00	
Duran, Erica A.	5,490.00		915.00				895.00	
Glover, Brandon T.	7,080.00		1,180.00				1,180.00	
Norton, Authur S.	5,340.00		890.00				795.00	
Rivas, Pearl S.	6,900.00		1,150.00				1,060.00	
Totals					Totals			

Social Security Tax Payable, 6.2%

Medicare Tax Payable, 1.45%

Unemployment Tax Payable—Federal, 0.8%

Unemployment Tax Payable—State, 5.4%

Total Payroll Taxes

3., 5.

GENERAL JOURNAL

PAGE

DATE	ACCOUNT TITLE	DOC. NO.	POST. REF.	DEBIT	CREDIT	
						1
						2
						3
						4
						5
						6
						7
						8
						9
						10

13-3 APPLICATION PROBLEM (LO4), p. 402

Reporting withholding and payroll taxes

1.

Form **941 for 20--:** Employer's QUARTERLY Federal Tax Return
(Rev. October 20--)
Department of the Treasury — Internal Revenue Service

951110

OMB No. 1545-0029

(EIN)
Employer identification number [ ][ ] – [ ][ ][ ][ ][ ][ ]

Name *(not your trade name)*

Trade name *(if any)*

Address
Number   Street   Suite or room number
City   State   ZIP code

Report for this Quarter of 20--
(Check one.)

☐ **1:** January, February, March

☐ **2:** April, May, June

☐ **3:** July, August, September

☐ **4:** October, November, December

Read the separate instructions before you complete Form 941. Type or print within the boxes.

Part 1: Answer these questions for this quarter.

1	Number of employees who received wages, tips, or other compensation for the pay period including: *Mar. 12* (Quarter 1), *June 12* (Quarter 2), *Sept. 12* (Quarter 3), or *Dec. 12* (Quarter 4)	1
2	Wages, tips, and other compensation	2
3	Income tax withheld from wages, tips, and other compensation	3
4	If no wages, tips, and other compensation are subject to social security or Medicare tax	☐ Check and go to line 6e.

Report wages/tips for this quarter, including those paid to qualified new employees, on lines 5a–5c. The social security tax exemption on wages/tips will be figured on lines 6c and 6d and will reduce the tax on line 6e.

		Column 1		Column 2
5a	Taxable social security wages* .		× .124 =	
5b	Taxable social security tips* . .		× .124 =	
5c	Taxable Medicare wages & tips*		× .029 =	
5d	Add *Column 2* line 5a, *Column 2* line 5b, and *Column 2* line 5c	5d	

See instructions for definitions of qualified employee and exempt wages/tips.

6a	Number of qualified employees *first* paid exempt wages/tips this quarter	
6b	Number of qualified employees paid exempt wages/tips this quarter	
6c	Exempt wages/tips paid to qualified employees this quarter	× .062 =	6d
6e	Total taxes before adjustments (line 3 + line 5d – line 6d = line 6e)	6e
7a	Current quarter's adjustment for fractions of cents	7a
7b	Current quarter's adjustment for sick pay	7b
7c	Current quarter's adjustments for tips and group-term life insurance	7c
8	Total taxes after adjustments. Combine lines 6e through 7c	8
9	Advance earned income credit (EIC) payments made to employees	9
10	Total taxes after adjustment for advance EIC (line 8 – line 9 = line 10)	10
11	Total deposits, including prior quarter overpayments	11
12a	COBRA premium assistance payments (see instructions)	12a
12b	Number of individuals provided COBRA premium assistance . .	
12c	Number of qualified employees paid exempt wages/tips March 19–31	
12d	Exempt wages/tips paid to qualified employees March 19–31	× .062 =	12e
13	Add lines 11, 12a, and 12e	13
14	Balance due. If line 10 is more than line 13, enter the difference and see instructions . . .	14
15	Overpayment. If line 13 is more than line 10, enter the difference	Check one: ☐ Apply to next return. ☐ Send a refund.

Complete lines 12c, 12d, and 12e only for the 2nd quarter of 20--.

▶ You MUST complete both pages of Form 941 and SIGN it.   Next ▶

For Privacy Act and Paperwork Reduction Act Notice, see the back of the Payment Voucher.   Cat. No. 17001Z   Form **941** (Rev. 10-20--)

950210

Name *(not your trade name)*	Employer identification number (EIN)

Part 2: Tell us about your deposit schedule and tax liability for this quarter.

If you are unsure about whether you are a monthly schedule depositor or a semiweekly schedule depositor, see *Pub. 15 (Circular E)*, section 11.

16 ☐ ☐ Write the state abbreviation for the state where you made your deposits OR write "MU" if you made your deposits in *multiple* states.

17 **Check one:** ☐ Line 10 on this return is less than $2,500 or line 10 on the return for the preceding quarter was less than $2,500, and you did not incur a $100,000 next-day deposit obligation during the current quarter. Go to Part 3.

☐ **You were a monthly schedule depositor for the entire quarter.** Enter your tax liability for each month and total liability for the quarter.

Tax liability: Month 1 ☐ .

Month 2 ☐ .

Month 3 ☐ .

Total liability for quarter ☐ . **Total must equal line 10.**

☐ **You were a semiweekly schedule depositor for any part of this quarter.** Complete *Schedule B (Form 941): Report of Tax Liability for Semiweekly Schedule Depositors,* and attach it to Form 941.

13-4 APPLICATION PROBLEM (LO5), p. 402

Paying withholding and payroll taxes

1., 2., 3.

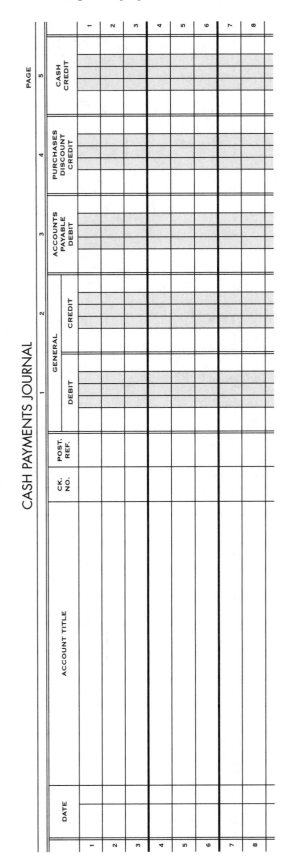

CASH PAYMENTS JOURNAL

Journalizing payroll transactions

CASH PAYMENTS JOURNAL

1., 2.

13-M MASTERY PROBLEM (concluded)

1.

GENERAL JOURNAL

PAGE _____

	DATE	ACCOUNT TITLE	DOC. NO.	POST. REF.	DEBIT	CREDIT	
1							1
2							2
3							3
4							4
5							5
6							6
7							7
8							8
9							9
10							10
11							11
12							12
13							13
14							14
15							15
16							16
17							17
18							18
19							19
20							20
21							21
22							22
23							23
24							24
25							25

Projecting employee expense

1.

Salary
Insurance

Tax	Taxable Amount	Tax Rate

Total expense for employee _____

2.

Salary
Insurance

Tax	Taxable Amount	Tax Rate

Total expense for employee _____

3.

REINFORCEMENT ACTIVITY 2, Part A, p. 406

An Accounting Cycle for a Corporation: Journalizing and Posting Transactions

1.

GENERAL JOURNAL

PAGE 12

	DATE		ACCOUNT TITLE	DOC. NO.	POST. REF.	DEBIT	CREDIT	
1								1
2								2
3								3
4								4
5								5
6								6
7								7
8								8
9								9
10								10
11								11
12								12
13								13
14								14
15								15
16								16
17								17
18								18
19								19
20								20
21								21
22								22
23								23

REINFORCEMENT ACTIVITY 2, Part A (continued)

1., 5.

PURCHASES JOURNAL PAGE 12

	DATE		ACCOUNT CREDITED	PURCH. NO.	POST. REF.	PURCHASES DR. ACCTS. PAY. CR.		
1								1
2								2
3								3
4								4
5								5
6								6
7								7
8								8
9								9
10								10
11								11
12								12
13								13
14								14
15								15
16								16
17								17
18								18
19								19
20								20
21								21
22								22
23								23
24								24
25								25

REINFORCEMENT ACTIVITY 2, Part A (continued)

1., 2., 7., 9.

CASH PAYMENTS JOURNAL

PAGE 23

DATE	ACCOUNT TITLE	CK. NO.	POST. REF.	GENERAL DEBIT (1)	GENERAL CREDIT (2)	ACCOUNTS PAYABLE DEBIT (3)	PURCHASES DISCOUNT CREDIT (4)	CASH CREDIT (5)	
									1
									2
									3
									4
									5
									6
									7
									8
									9
									10
									11
									12
									13
									14
									15
									16
									17
									18
									19
									20
									21
									22
									23
									24
									25

REINFORCEMENT ACTIVITY 2, Part A (continued)

1., 3., 6., 7., 9.

CASH PAYMENTS JOURNAL

PAGE 24

DATE	ACCOUNT TITLE	CK. NO.	POST. REF.	GENERAL DEBIT	GENERAL CREDIT	ACCOUNTS PAYABLE DEBIT	PURCHASES DISCOUNT CREDIT	CASH CREDIT
1								
2								
3								
4								
5								
6								
7								
8								
9								
10								
11								
12								
13								
14								
15								

Column Title	Debit Column Totals	Credit Column Totals
General Debit		
General Credit		
Accounts Payable Debit		
Purchases Discount Credit		
Cash Credit		
Totals		

REINFORCEMENT ACTIVITY 2, Part A (continued)

1., 4.

SALES JOURNAL   PAGE 12

	DATE	ACCOUNT DEBITED	SALE NO.	POST. REF.	ACCOUNTS RECEIVABLE DEBIT 1	SALES CREDIT 2	SALES TAX PAYABLE CREDIT 3	
1								1
2								2
3								3
4								4
5								5
6								6
7								7
8								8
9								9
10								10
11								11
12								12
13								13
14								14
15								15
16								16
17								17
18								18
19								19
20								20
21								21
22								22
23								23
24								24
25								25

1., 3., 6., 7., 8.

CASH RECEIPTS JOURNAL

PAGE 12

DATE	ACCOUNT TITLE	DOC. NO.	POST. REF.	GENERAL DEBIT	GENERAL CREDIT	ACCOUNTS RECEIVABLE CREDIT	SALES CREDIT	SALES TAX PAYABLE CREDIT	SALES DISCOUNT DEBIT	CASH DEBIT	
											1
											2
											3
											4
											5
											6
											7
											8
											9
											10
											11
											12
											13
											14
											15
											16

Column Title	Debit Totals	Credit Totals
General Debit		
General Credit		
Accounts Receivable Credit		
Sales Credit		
Sales Tax Payable Credit		
Sales Discount Debit		
Cash Debit		
Totals		

Cash on hand at the beginning of the month
(Dec. 1 balance of general ledger Cash account) . . . .
Plus total cash received during the month
(Cash Debit column total, cash receipts journal) . . . .
Equal total. . . . .
Less total cash paid during the month
(General ledger postings in Cash account) . . . .
Equals cash balance on hand at the end of the month . . . .
Checkbook balance on the next unused check stub . . . .

REINFORCEMENT ACTIVITY 2, Part A (continued)

1., 3., 10.

ACCOUNTS RECEIVABLE LEDGER

CUSTOMER Batesville Manufacturing   CUSTOMER NO. 110

DATE		ITEM	POST. REF.	DEBIT	CREDIT	DEBIT BALANCE
20-- Dec.	1	Balance	✔			5 8 1 9 35

CUSTOMER Chandler City Schools   CUSTOMER NO. 120

DATE		ITEM	POST. REF.	DEBIT	CREDIT	DEBIT BALANCE
20-- Dec.	1	Balance	✔			8 1 4 80

CUSTOMER Hubbard Medical Clinic   CUSTOMER NO. 130

DATE		ITEM	POST. REF.	DEBIT	CREDIT	DEBIT BALANCE
20-- Dec.	1	Balance	✔			4 6 4 9 80

CUSTOMER Musheer Orthopedics   CUSTOMER NO. 140

DATE		ITEM	POST. REF.	DEBIT	CREDIT	DEBIT BALANCE
20-- Dec.	1	Balance	✔			1 6 4 3 00

CUSTOMER Pacific Stores   CUSTOMER NO. 150

DATE	ITEM	POST. REF.	DEBIT	CREDIT	DEBIT BALANCE

CUSTOMER Western Theaters   CUSTOMER NO. 160

DATE		ITEM	POST. REF.	DEBIT	CREDIT	DEBIT BALANCE
20-- Dec.	1	Balance	✔			1 6 9 4 34

REINFORCEMENT ACTIVITY 2, Part A (continued)

1., 3., 10.

ACCOUNTS PAYABLE LEDGER

VENDOR Alpha Supply   VENDOR NO. 210

DATE		ITEM	POST. REF.	DEBIT	CREDIT	CREDIT BALANCE
20-- Dec.	1	Balance	✔			2 2 8 4 00

VENDOR Distinctive Garments   VENDOR NO. 220

DATE		ITEM	POST. REF.	DEBIT	CREDIT	CREDIT BALANCE
20-- Dec.	1	Balance	✔			1 5 9 5 00

VENDOR Klein Industries   VENDOR NO. 230

DATE		ITEM	POST. REF.	DEBIT	CREDIT	CREDIT BALANCE
20-- Dec.	1	Balance	✔			3 2 9 0 00

VENDOR Medical Clothiers   VENDOR NO. 240

DATE		ITEM	POST. REF.	DEBIT	CREDIT	CREDIT BALANCE
20-- Dec.	1	Balance	✔			5 4 8 00

VENDOR Singh Imports   VENDOR NO. 250

DATE		ITEM	POST. REF.	DEBIT	CREDIT	CREDIT BALANCE
Dec. 20--	1	Balance	✔			1 5 8 9 00

VENDOR Trevino Company   VENDOR NO. 260

DATE		ITEM	POST. REF.	DEBIT	CREDIT	CREDIT BALANCE

REINFORCEMENT ACTIVITY 2, Part A (continued)

1., 2., 3., 4., 5., 8., 9. **GENERAL LEDGER**

ACCOUNT Cash   ACCOUNT NO. 1110

DATE		ITEM	POST. REF.	DEBIT	CREDIT	BALANCE	
						DEBIT	CREDIT
20-- Dec.	1	Balance	✔			31 4 8 5 25	

ACCOUNT Petty Cash   ACCOUNT NO. 1120

DATE		ITEM	POST. REF.	DEBIT	CREDIT	BALANCE	
						DEBIT	CREDIT
20-- Dec.	1	Balance	✔			2 5 0 00	

ACCOUNT Accounts Receivable   ACCOUNT NO. 1130

DATE		ITEM	POST. REF.	DEBIT	CREDIT	BALANCE	
						DEBIT	CREDIT
20-- Dec.	1	Balance	✔			14 6 2 1 29	

ACCOUNT Allowance for Uncollectible Accounts   ACCOUNT NO. 1135

DATE		ITEM	POST. REF.	DEBIT	CREDIT	BALANCE	
						DEBIT	CREDIT
20-- Dec.	1	Balance	✔				2 1 6 9 25

ACCOUNT Merchandise Inventory   ACCOUNT NO. 1140

DATE		ITEM	POST. REF.	DEBIT	CREDIT	BALANCE	
						DEBIT	CREDIT
20-- Dec.	1	Balance	✔			49 1 5 4 84	

ACCOUNT Supplies—Office   ACCOUNT NO. 1145

DATE		ITEM	POST. REF.	DEBIT	CREDIT	BALANCE DEBIT	BALANCE CREDIT
Dec.	1	Balance	✔			2 5 9 8 48	

ACCOUNT Supplies—Store   ACCOUNT NO. 1150

DATE		ITEM	POST. REF.	DEBIT	CREDIT	BALANCE DEBIT	BALANCE CREDIT
Dec.	1	Balance	✔			3 4 8 1 20	

ACCOUNT Prepaid Insurance   ACCOUNT NO. 1160

DATE		ITEM	POST. REF.	DEBIT	CREDIT	BALANCE DEBIT	BALANCE CREDIT
Dec.	1	Balance	✔			14 4 0 0 00	

ACCOUNT Notes Receivable   ACCOUNT NO. 1170

DATE		ITEM	POST. REF.	DEBIT	CREDIT	BALANCE DEBIT	BALANCE CREDIT
Dec.	1	Balance	✔			4 0 0 0 00	

REINFORCEMENT ACTIVITY 2, Part A (continued)

ACCOUNT Interest Receivable   ACCOUNT NO. 1175

DATE	ITEM	POST. REF.	DEBIT	CREDIT	BALANCE DEBIT	BALANCE CREDIT

ACCOUNT Office Equipment   ACCOUNT NO. 1205

DATE	ITEM	POST. REF.	DEBIT	CREDIT	BALANCE DEBIT	BALANCE CREDIT
20-- Dec. 1	Balance	✔			23 2 4 5 97	

ACCOUNT Accumulated Depreciation—Office Equipment   ACCOUNT NO. 1210

DATE	ITEM	POST. REF.	DEBIT	CREDIT	BALANCE DEBIT	BALANCE CREDIT
20-- Dec. 1	Balance	✔				3 2 1 0 00

ACCOUNT Store Equipment   ACCOUNT NO. 1215

DATE	ITEM	POST. REF.	DEBIT	CREDIT	BALANCE DEBIT	BALANCE CREDIT
20-- Dec. 1	Balance	✔			36 4 8 9 20	

ACCOUNT Accumulated Depreciation—Store Equipment   ACCOUNT NO. 1220

DATE	ITEM	POST. REF.	DEBIT	CREDIT	BALANCE DEBIT	BALANCE CREDIT
20-- Dec. 1	Balance	✔				6 1 8 2 00

ACCOUNT Accounts Payable   ACCOUNT NO. 2110

DATE	ITEM	POST. REF.	DEBIT	CREDIT	BALANCE DEBIT	BALANCE CREDIT
20-- Dec. 1	Balance	✔				9 3 0 6 00

REINFORCEMENT ACTIVITY 2, Part A (continued)

ACCOUNT Sales Tax Payable   ACCOUNT NO. 2120

DATE		ITEM	POST. REF.	DEBIT	CREDIT	BALANCE DEBIT	BALANCE CREDIT
20-- Dec.	1	Balance	✔				3 2 4 00

ACCOUNT Employee Income Tax Payable   ACCOUNT NO. 2130

DATE		ITEM	POST. REF.	DEBIT	CREDIT	BALANCE DEBIT	BALANCE CREDIT
20-- Dec.	1	Balance	✔				4 7 1 00

ACCOUNT Social Security Tax Payable   ACCOUNT NO. 2135

DATE		ITEM	POST. REF.	DEBIT	CREDIT	BALANCE DEBIT	BALANCE CREDIT
20-- Dec.	1	Balance	✔				8 9 9 00

REINFORCEMENT ACTIVITY 2, Part A (continued)

ACCOUNT Medicare Tax Payable　　　　　　　ACCOUNT NO. 2140

DATE	ITEM	POST. REF.	DEBIT	CREDIT	BALANCE DEBIT	BALANCE CREDIT
20-- Dec. 1	Balance	✔				2 1 0 25

ACCOUNT Health Insurance Premiums Payable　　　　　　　ACCOUNT NO. 2145

DATE	ITEM	POST. REF.	DEBIT	CREDIT	BALANCE DEBIT	BALANCE CREDIT
20-- Dec. 1	Balance	✔				4 8 0 00

ACCOUNT Retirement Benefits Payable　　　　　　　ACCOUNT NO. 2150

DATE	ITEM	POST. REF.	DEBIT	CREDIT	BALANCE DEBIT	BALANCE CREDIT
20-- Dec. 1	Balance	✔				1 2 0 00

ACCOUNT Unemployment Tax Payable—Federal　　　　　　　ACCOUNT NO. 2160

DATE	ITEM	POST. REF.	DEBIT	CREDIT	BALANCE DEBIT	BALANCE CREDIT
20-- Dec. 1	Balance					1 0 76

ACCOUNT Unemployment Tax Payable—State   ACCOUNT NO. 2165

DATE		ITEM	POST. REF.	DEBIT	CREDIT	BALANCE DEBIT	BALANCE CREDIT
20-- Dec.	1	Balance	✔				7 2 63

ACCOUNT Federal Income Tax Payable   ACCOUNT NO. 2170

DATE		ITEM	POST. REF.	DEBIT	CREDIT	BALANCE DEBIT	BALANCE CREDIT

ACCOUNT Dividends Payable   ACCOUNT NO. 2180

DATE		ITEM	POST. REF.	DEBIT	CREDIT	BALANCE DEBIT	BALANCE CREDIT

ACCOUNT Capital Stock   ACCOUNT NO. 3110

DATE		ITEM	POST. REF.	DEBIT	CREDIT	BALANCE DEBIT	BALANCE CREDIT
20-- Dec.	1	Balance	✔				60 0 0 0 00

ACCOUNT Retained Earnings   ACCOUNT NO. 3120

DATE		ITEM	POST. REF.	DEBIT	CREDIT	BALANCE DEBIT	BALANCE CREDIT
20-- Dec.	1	Balance	✔				23 3 5 2 50

REINFORCEMENT ACTIVITY 2, Part A (continued)

ACCOUNT Dividends   ACCOUNT NO. 3130

DATE	ITEM	POST. REF.	DEBIT	CREDIT	BALANCE DEBIT	BALANCE CREDIT

ACCOUNT Income Summary   ACCOUNT NO. 3140

DATE	ITEM	POST. REF.	DEBIT	CREDIT	BALANCE DEBIT	BALANCE CREDIT

ACCOUNT Sales   ACCOUNT NO. 4110

DATE	ITEM	POST. REF.	DEBIT	CREDIT	BALANCE DEBIT	BALANCE CREDIT
20-- Dec. 1	Balance	✔				381 5 8 5 60

ACCOUNT Sales Discount   ACCOUNT NO. 4120

DATE	ITEM	POST. REF.	DEBIT	CREDIT	BALANCE DEBIT	BALANCE CREDIT
20-- Dec. 1	Balance	✔			3 1 5 00	

ACCOUNT Sales Returns and Allowances   ACCOUNT NO. 4130

DATE	ITEM	POST. REF.	DEBIT	CREDIT	BALANCE DEBIT	BALANCE CREDIT
20-- Dec. 1	Balance	✔			2 1 6 4 80	

ACCOUNT Purchases   ACCOUNT NO. 5110

DATE		ITEM	POST. REF.	DEBIT	CREDIT	BALANCE DEBIT	BALANCE CREDIT
20-- Dec.	1	Balance	✔			168 411 89	

ACCOUNT Purchases Discount   ACCOUNT NO. 5120

DATE		ITEM	POST. REF.	DEBIT	CREDIT	BALANCE DEBIT	BALANCE CREDIT
20-- Dec.	1	Balance	✔				2 194 89

ACCOUNT Purchases Returns and Allowances   ACCOUNT NO. 5130

DATE		ITEM	POST. REF.	DEBIT	CREDIT	BALANCE DEBIT	BALANCE CREDIT
20-- Dec.	1	Balance	✔				3 184 49

ACCOUNT Advertising Expense   ACCOUNT NO. 6105

DATE		ITEM	POST. REF.	DEBIT	CREDIT	BALANCE DEBIT	BALANCE CREDIT
20-- Dec.	1	Balance	✔			14 915 90	

ACCOUNT Cash Short and Over   ACCOUNT NO. 6110

DATE		ITEM	POST. REF.	DEBIT	CREDIT	BALANCE DEBIT	BALANCE CREDIT
20-- Dec.	1	Balance	✔			6 15	

REINFORCEMENT ACTIVITY 2, Part A (continued)

ACCOUNT Credit Card Fee Expense   ACCOUNT NO. 6115

DATE		ITEM	POST. REF.	DEBIT	CREDIT	BALANCE DEBIT	BALANCE CREDIT
Dec. 20--	1	Balance	✔			4 5 1 8 10	

ACCOUNT Depreciation Expense—Office Equipment   ACCOUNT NO. 6120

DATE	ITEM	POST. REF.	DEBIT	CREDIT	BALANCE DEBIT	BALANCE CREDIT

ACCOUNT Depreciation Expense—Store Equipment   ACCOUNT NO. 6125

DATE	ITEM	POST. REF.	DEBIT	CREDIT	BALANCE DEBIT	BALANCE CREDIT

ACCOUNT Insurance Expense   ACCOUNT NO. 6130

DATE	ITEM	POST. REF.	DEBIT	CREDIT	BALANCE DEBIT	BALANCE CREDIT

ACCOUNT Miscellaneous Expense   ACCOUNT NO. 6135

DATE		ITEM	POST. REF.	DEBIT	CREDIT	BALANCE DEBIT	BALANCE CREDIT
Dec. 20--	1	Balance	✔			5 1 6 8 90	

ACCOUNT Payroll Taxes Expense   ACCOUNT NO. 6140

DATE		ITEM	POST. REF.	DEBIT	CREDIT	BALANCE DEBIT	BALANCE CREDIT
Dec.	1	Balance	✔			6 3 8 1 20	

ACCOUNT Rent Expense   ACCOUNT NO. 6145

DATE		ITEM	POST. REF.	DEBIT	CREDIT	BALANCE DEBIT	BALANCE CREDIT
Dec.	1	Balance	✔			17 6 0 0 00	

ACCOUNT Salary Expense   ACCOUNT NO. 6150

DATE		ITEM	POST. REF.	DEBIT	CREDIT	BALANCE DEBIT	BALANCE CREDIT
Dec.	1	Balance	✔			77 6 1 6 00	

ACCOUNT Supplies Expense—Office   ACCOUNT NO. 6155

DATE		ITEM	POST. REF.	DEBIT	CREDIT	BALANCE DEBIT	BALANCE CREDIT

ACCOUNT Supplies Expense—Store   ACCOUNT NO. 6160

DATE		ITEM	POST. REF.	DEBIT	CREDIT	BALANCE DEBIT	BALANCE CREDIT

REINFORCEMENT ACTIVITY 2, Part A (concluded)

ACCOUNT Uncollectible Accounts Expense   ACCOUNT NO. 6165

DATE	ITEM	POST. REF.	DEBIT	CREDIT	BALANCE DEBIT	BALANCE CREDIT

ACCOUNT Utilities Expense   ACCOUNT NO. 6170

DATE	ITEM	POST. REF.	DEBIT	CREDIT	BALANCE DEBIT	BALANCE CREDIT
20-- Dec. 1	Balance	✔			6 9 4 8 20	

ACCOUNT Federal Income Tax Expense   ACCOUNT NO. 6205

DATE	ITEM	POST. REF.	DEBIT	CREDIT	BALANCE DEBIT	BALANCE CREDIT
20-- Dec. 1	Balance	✔			10 0 0 0 00	

ACCOUNT Interest Income   ACCOUNT NO. 7110

DATE	ITEM	POST. REF.	DEBIT	CREDIT	BALANCE DEBIT	BALANCE CREDIT

Name		Perfect Score	Your Score
	Identifying Accounting Terms	22 Pts.	
	Analyzing Accounts Receivable and Notes Receivable	20 Pts.	
	Journalizing Accounts Receivable and Notes Receivable Transactions	21 Pts.	
	Total	63 Pts.	

Part One—Identifying Accounting Terms

Directions: Select the one term in Column I that best fits each definition in Column II. Print the letter identifying your choice in the Answers column.

Column I	Column II	Answers
A. aging of accounts receivable	**1.** Accounts receivable that cannot be collected. (p. 412)	1. _____
B. allowance method	**2.** Crediting the estimated value of uncollectible accounts to a contra account. (p. 412)	2. _____
C. book value	**3.** The difference between an asset's account balance and its related contra account balance. (p. 412)	3. _____
D. book value of accounts receivable	**4.** The difference between the balance of Accounts Receivable and its contra account, Allowance for Uncollectible Accounts. (p. 412)	4. _____
E. direct write-off method	**5.** The amount of accounts receivable a business expects to collect. (p. 412)	5. _____
F. dishonored note	**6.** A method used to estimate uncollectible accounts receivable that assumes a percent of credit sales will become uncollectible. (p. 413)	6. _____
G. interest income	**7.** A method used to estimate uncollectible accounts receivable that uses an analysis of accounts receivable to estimate the amount that will be uncollectible. (p. 413)	7. _____
H. interest rate	**8.** Analyzing accounts receivable according to when they are due. (p. 414)	8. _____
I. maker of a note	**9.** Canceling the balance of a customer account because the customer does not pay. (p. 418)	9. _____
J. maturity date	**10.** Recording uncollectible accounts expense only when an amount is actually known to be uncollectible. (p. 419)	10. _____
K. maturity value	**11.** A written and signed promise to pay a sum of money at a specified time. (p. 425)	11. _____
L. net realizable value	**12.** A promissory note signed by a business and given to a creditor. (p. 425)	12. _____
M. note payable	**13.** A promissory note that a business accepts from a person or business. (p. 425)	13. _____
N. note receivable	**14.** The person or business that signs a note, and thus promises to make payment. (p. 425)	14. _____
O. payee	**15.** The person or business to whom the amount of a note is payable. (p. 425)	15. _____

Column I	Column II	Answers
P. percent of accounts receivable method	**16.** The original amount of a note, sometimes referred to as the face amount. (p. 425)	**16.**_____
Q. percent of sales method	**17.** The percentage of the principal that is due for the use of the funds secured by a note. (p. 425)	**17.**_____
R. principal	**18.** The date on which the principal of a note is due to be repaid. (p. 425)	**18.**_____
S. promissory note	**19.** The length of time from the signing date of a note to the maturity date. (p. 425)	**19.**_____
T. time of a note	**20.** The amount that is due on the maturity date of a note. (p. 427)	**20.**_____
U. uncollectible accounts	**21.** The interest earned on money loaned. (p. 428)	**21.**_____
V. writing off an account	**22.** A note that is not paid when due. (p. 429)	**22.**_____

Part Two—Analyzing Accounts Receivable and Notes Receivable

Directions: Place a *T* for True or an *F* for False in the Answers column to show whether each of the following statements is true or false.

1. The expense of an uncollectible account should be recorded in the accounting period that the account becomes uncollectible. (p. 412)   1. _____

2. The account, Allowance for Uncollectible Accounts, has a normal credit balance. (p. 412)   2. _____

3. A business usually knows at the end of the fiscal year which customer accounts will become uncollectible. (p. 412)   3. _____

4. The account, Allowance for Uncollectible Accounts, is reported on the income statement. (p. 412)   4. _____

5. The book value of accounts receivable must be a reasonable and unbiased estimate of the money the business expects to collect in the future. (p. 413)   5. _____

6. The percent of sales method of estimating uncollectible accounts expense assumes that a portion of every dollar of sales on account will become uncollectible. (p. 413)   6. _____

7. The accounting concept, Conservatism, is applied when the process of making accounting estimates is free from bias. (p. 413)   7. _____

8. The percent of each age group of an accounts receivable aging that is expected to become uncollectible is determined by the Securities and Exchange Commission. (p. 414)   8. _____

9. The adjusting entry for uncollectible accounts does not affect the balance of the Accounts Receivable account. (p. 415)   9. _____

10. A business having a $300.00 credit balance in Allowance for Uncollectible Accounts and estimating its uncollectible accounts to be $4,000.00 would record a $4,300.00 credit to Allowance for Uncollectible Accounts. (p. 415)   10. _____

11. When an account is written off as uncollectible, the business sends the customer a credit memo. (p. 418)   11. _____

12. When a customer account is written off under the allowance method, book value of accounts receivable decreases. (p. 418)   12. _____

13. The direct write-off method of accounting for uncollectible accounts does not comply with GAAP. (p. 419)   13. _____

14. When a previously written-off account is collected, Accounts Receivable is both debited and credited for the amount collected. (pp. 421–422)   14. _____

15. A note provides the business with legal evidence of the debt should it be necessary to go to court to collect. (p. 426)   15. _____

16. Total assets are reduced when a business accepts a note receivable from a customer needing an extension of time to pay an account receivable. (p. 426)   16. _____

17. Interest rates are stated as a percentage of the principal. (p. 427)   17. _____

18. Interest income is classified as an Other Revenue account. (p. 428)   18. _____

19. The method for calculating interest is the same for notes payable and notes receivable. (p. 428)   19. _____

20. Interest income should not be recorded on a dishonored note receivable. (p. 429)   20. _____

Part Three—Journalizing Accounts Receivable and Notes Receivable Transactions

Directions: In Answers Column l, print the abbreviation for the journal in which each transaction is to be recorded. In Answers Columns 2 and 3, print the letters identifying the accounts to be debited and credited for each transaction.

G—General journal **CR**—Cash receipts journal

Account Titles	Transactions	Answers 1 Journal	Answers 2 Debit	Answers 3 Credit
A. Accounts Receivable	**1-2-3.** Recorded adjusting entry for uncollectible accounts expense. (p. 415)	1. _____	2. _____	3. _____
B. Allowance for Uncollectible Accounts	**4-5-6.** Wrote off Sanderson Company's past-due account as uncollectible. (p. 418)	4. _____	5. _____	6. _____
C. Cash	Received cash in full payment of Sanderson Company's account, previously written off as uncollectible. *(Record two entries, 7-8-9 and 10-11-12, below.)*			
D. Interest Income	**7-8-9.** First entry. (p. 421)	7. _____	8. _____	9. _____
E. Notes Receivable	**10-11-12.** Second entry. (p. 422)	10. _____	11. _____	12. _____
F. Sanderson Company	**13-14-15.** Accepted a note from Sanderson Company for an extension of time on its account. (p. 426)	13. _____	14. _____	15. _____
G. Uncollectible Accounts Expense	**16-17-18.** Collected a note receivable from Sanderson Company. (p. 428)	16. _____	17. _____	18. _____
H. Williams Supply	**19-20-21.** Williams Supply dishonored a note receivable. (p. 429)	19. _____	20. _____	21. _____

14-1 WORK TOGETHER, p. 417

Journalizing the adjusting entry for Allowance for Uncollectible Accounts

1.

Age Group	Amount	Percent	Uncollectible
Current	$16,485.18	2.0%	
1–30	12,489.05	4.0%	
31–60	6,958.18	8.0%	
61–90	4,218.21	20.0%	
Over 90	3,157.10	70.0%	
	$43,307.72		
Current Balance of Allowance for Uncollectible Accounts			
Estimated Addition to Allowance for Uncollectible Accounts			

2.

GENERAL JOURNAL

PAGE 13

	DATE		ACCOUNT TITLE	DOC. NO.	POST. REF.	DEBIT	CREDIT	
1								1
2								2
3								3
4								4

14-1 ON YOUR OWN, p. 417

Journalizing the adjusting entry for Allowance for Uncollectible Accounts

1.

Age Group	Amount	Percent	Uncollectible
Current	$25,114.16	1.0%	
1–30	32,458.15	2.5%	
31–60	12,489.58	7.5%	
61–90	6,154.25	30.0%	
Over 90	7,189.28	80.0%	
	$83,405.42		
Current Balance of Allowance for Uncollectible Accounts			
Estimated Addition to Allowance for Uncollectible Accounts			

2.

GENERAL JOURNAL PAGE 13

	DATE		ACCOUNT TITLE	DOC. NO.	POST. REF.	DEBIT	CREDIT	
1								1
2								2
3								3
4								4

14-2 WORK TOGETHER, p. 424

Recording entries related to uncollectible accounts receivable

1., 2.

GENERAL JOURNAL   PAGE 15

	DATE	ACCOUNT TITLE	DOC. NO.	POST. REF.	DEBIT	CREDIT	
1							1
2							2
3							3
4							4
5							5
6							6
7							7
8							8
9							9
10							10
11							11
12							12

1.   **ACCOUNTS RECEIVABLE LEDGER**

ACCOUNT Fischer Industries   CUSTOMER NO. 110

DATE	ITEM	POST. REF.	DEBIT	CREDIT	DEBIT BALANCE
20-- Nov. 1	Balance	✔			1 3 6 0 00

ACCOUNT Horne Co.　　　　　　　　　　　　　　　CUSTOMER NO. 120

DATE		ITEM	POST. REF.	DEBIT	CREDIT	DEBIT BALANCE
20-- Nov.	1	Balance	✔			1 5 4 8 00

ACCOUNT Mellon Corp.　　　　　　　　　　　　　　CUSTOMER NO. 130

DATE		ITEM	POST. REF.	DEBIT	CREDIT	DEBIT BALANCE
20-- Nov.	1	Balance	✔			4 9 4 00

2.　　　　　　　　　　　　　**GENERAL LEDGER**

ACCOUNT Accounts Receivable　　　　　　　　　　ACCOUNT NO. 1130

DATE		ITEM	POST. REF.	DEBIT	CREDIT	BALANCE DEBIT	BALANCE CREDIT
20-- Nov.	1	Balance	✔			35 1 4 8 85	

ACCOUNT Allowance for Uncollectible Accounts　　ACCOUNT NO. 1135

DATE		ITEM	POST. REF.	DEBIT	CREDIT	BALANCE DEBIT	BALANCE CREDIT
20-- Nov.	1	Balance	✔				3 1 5 8 47

14-2 **WORK TOGETHER (concluded)**

1., 2.

CASH RECEIPTS JOURNAL

PAGE 24

DATE	ACCOUNT TITLE	DOC. NO.	POST. REF.	GENERAL DEBIT	GENERAL CREDIT	ACCOUNTS RECEIVABLE CREDIT	SALES CREDIT	SALES TAX PAYABLE CREDIT	SALES DISCOUNT DEBIT	CASH DEBIT
				1	2	3	4	5	6	7
1										
2										
3										

Recording entries related to uncollectible accounts receivable

1., 2.

GENERAL JOURNAL   PAGE 10

	DATE		ACCOUNT TITLE	DOC. NO.	POST. REF.	DEBIT	CREDIT	
1								1
2								2
3								3
4								4
5								5
6								6
7								7
8								8
9								9
10								10
11								11
12								12

1.   **ACCOUNTS RECEIVABLE LEDGER**

ACCOUNT Nancy Brown   CUSTOMER NO. 110

DATE		ITEM	POST. REF.	DEBIT	CREDIT	DEBIT BALANCE
20-- Oct.	1	Balance	✔			4 2 8 00

ACCOUNT Janice Harrell   CUSTOMER NO. 120

DATE		ITEM	POST. REF.	DEBIT	CREDIT	DEBIT BALANCE
20-- Oct.	1	Balance	✔			5 2 7 00

14-2 **ON YOUR OWN (continued)**

ACCOUNT Daniel Pruitt   CUSTOMER NO. 130

DATE	ITEM	POST. REF.	DEBIT	CREDIT	DEBIT BALANCE
20-- Oct. 1	Balance	✔			2 4 9 00

ACCOUNT Tom Sloan   CUSTOMER NO. 140

DATE	ITEM	POST. REF.	DEBIT	CREDIT	DEBIT BALANCE

2.   **GENERAL LEDGER**

ACCOUNT Accounts Receivable   ACCOUNT NO. 1130

DATE	ITEM	POST. REF.	DEBIT	CREDIT	BALANCE DEBIT	BALANCE CREDIT
20-- Oct. 1	Balance	✔			19 4 8 2 58	

ACCOUNT Allowance for Uncollectible Accounts   ACCOUNT NO. 1135

DATE	ITEM	POST. REF.	DEBIT	CREDIT	BALANCE DEBIT	BALANCE CREDIT
20-- Oct. 1	Balance	✔				3 6 5 8 97

1., 2.

CASH RECEIPTS JOURNAL

PAGE 22

				1 GENERAL	2	3 ACCOUNTS RECEIVABLE CREDIT	4 SALES CREDIT	5 SALES TAX PAYABLE CREDIT	6 SALES DISCOUNT DEBIT	7 CASH DEBIT
DATE	ACCOUNT TITLE	DOC. NO.	POST. REF.	DEBIT	CREDIT					
1										
2										
3										

14-3 WORK TOGETHER, p. 430

Recording notes receivable

1.

Note	Date	Principal	Interest Rate	Time in Days	Interest	Maturity Date	Maturity Value
NR3	June 5	$20,000.00	8%	90			
NR4	June 12	$10,000.00	6%	120			

Calculations:

Note	Maturity Date			Interest	Maturity Value
		Days from the Month	Days Remaining		
NR3	Term of the Note		90		
NR4	Term of the Note	Days from the Month	Days Remaining		
			120		

2., 3.

GENERAL JOURNAL

PAGE 7

DATE	ACCOUNT TITLE	DOC. NO.	POST. REF.	DEBIT	CREDIT	
						4
						5
						6
						7
						8
						9

2., 3.

CASH RECEIPTS JOURNAL

PAGE 8

				1	2	3	4	5	6	7	
DATE	ACCOUNT TITLE	DOC. NO.	POST. REF.	GENERAL DEBIT	GENERAL CREDIT	ACCOUNTS RECEIVABLE CREDIT	SALES CREDIT	SALES TAX PAYABLE CREDIT	SALES DISCOUNT DEBIT	CASH DEBIT	
											13
											14
											15

14-3 WORK TOGETHER (concluded)

2., 3.   **ACCOUNTS RECEIVABLE LEDGER**

ACCOUNT Dennis Craft   CUSTOMER NO. 110

DATE	ITEM	POST. REF.	DEBIT	CREDIT	DEBIT BALANCE

ACCOUNT Gary Kinney   CUSTOMER NO. 120

DATE	ITEM	POST. REF.	DEBIT	CREDIT	DEBIT BALANCE
July 1	Balance	✔			1 8 0 0 00

3.   **GENERAL LEDGER**

ACCOUNT Accounts Receivable   ACCOUNT NO. 1130

DATE	ITEM	POST. REF.	DEBIT	CREDIT	BALANCE DEBIT	BALANCE CREDIT
July 1	Balance	✔			42 1 8 1 97	

ACCOUNT Notes Receivable   ACCOUNT NO. 1170

DATE	ITEM	POST. REF.	DEBIT	CREDIT	BALANCE DEBIT	BALANCE CREDIT
July 1	Balance	✔			16 2 0 0 00	

ACCOUNT Interest Income   ACCOUNT NO. 7110

DATE	ITEM	POST. REF.	DEBIT	CREDIT	BALANCE DEBIT	BALANCE CREDIT
July 1	Balance	✔				4 5 8 00

Recording notes receivable

1.

Note	Date	Principal	Interest Rate	Time in Days	Interest	Maturity Date	Maturity Value
NR12	March 22	$8,000.00	6%	120			
NR13	April 7	$6,000.00	7%	90			

Calculations:

Note	Maturity Date			Interest	Maturity Value
		Days from the Month	Days Remaining		
NR12	Term of the Note		120		
		Days from the Month	Days Remaining		
NR13	Term of the Note		90		

2., 3.

GENERAL JOURNAL

PAGE 15

DATE	ACCOUNT TITLE	DOC. NO.	POST. REF.	DEBIT	CREDIT	
						7
						8
						9
						10
						11
						12

2., 3.

CASH RECEIPTS JOURNAL

PAGE 20

DATE	ACCOUNT TITLE	DOC. NO.	POST. REF.	GENERAL DEBIT	GENERAL CREDIT	ACCOUNTS RECEIVABLE CREDIT	SALES CREDIT	SALES TAX PAYABLE CREDIT	SALES DISCOUNT DEBIT	CASH DEBIT	
											19
											20
											21

2., 3. **ACCOUNTS RECEIVABLE LEDGER**

ACCOUNT Roger Hamm   CUSTOMER NO. 110

DATE	ITEM	POST. REF.	DEBIT	CREDIT	DEBIT BALANCE

ACCOUNT Marshall Sykes   CUSTOMER NO. 120

DATE	ITEM	POST. REF.	DEBIT	CREDIT	DEBIT BALANCE
20-- May 1	Balance	✔			3 2 0 0 00

3. **GENERAL LEDGER**

ACCOUNT Accounts Receivable   ACCOUNT NO. 1130

DATE	ITEM	POST. REF.	DEBIT	CREDIT	BALANCE DEBIT	BALANCE CREDIT
20-- May 1	Balance	✔			56 1 8 4 50	

ACCOUNT Notes Receivable   ACCOUNT NO. 1170

DATE	ITEM	POST. REF.	DEBIT	CREDIT	BALANCE DEBIT	BALANCE CREDIT
20-- May 1	Balance	✔			14 3 0 0 00	

ACCOUNT Interest Income   ACCOUNT NO. 7110

DATE	ITEM	POST. REF.	DEBIT	CREDIT	BALANCE DEBIT	BALANCE CREDIT
20-- May 1	Balance	✔				6 4 8 00

14-1   APPLICATION PROBLEM (LO2, 3), p. 434

Journalizing the adjusting entry for Allowance for Uncollectible Accounts

1.

Age Group	Amount	Percent	Uncollectible
Current	$20,489.15	2.0%	
1–30	16,487.20	6.0%	
31–60	8,415.29	15.0%	
61–90	6,218.47	50.0%	
Over 90	2,584.95	90.0%	
	$54,195.06		
Current Balance of Allowance for Uncollectible Accounts			
Estimated Addition to Allowance for Uncollectible Accounts			

2.

GENERAL JOURNAL   PAGE 13

	DATE	ACCOUNT TITLE	DOC. NO.	POST. REF.	DEBIT	CREDIT	
1							1
2							2
3							3
4							4

Recording entries related to uncollectible accounts receivable

1., 2.

GENERAL JOURNAL   PAGE 6

	DATE		ACCOUNT TITLE	DOC. NO.	POST. REF.	DEBIT	CREDIT	
1								1
2								2
3								3
4								4
5								5
6								6
7								7
8								8
9								9
10								10
11								11
12								12

1., 2.   **ACCOUNTS RECEIVABLE LEDGER**

ACCOUNT Durham Supply   CUSTOMER NO. 110

	DATE		ITEM	POST. REF.	DEBIT	CREDIT	DEBIT BALANCE	
	May	1	Balance	✔			9 4 8 50	

ACCOUNT Foley Corp.   CUSTOMER NO. 120

DATE		ITEM	POST. REF.	DEBIT	CREDIT	DEBIT BALANCE

14-2 APPLICATION PROBLEM (continued)

ACCOUNT Pennington Co.   CUSTOMER NO. 130

DATE		ITEM	POST. REF.	DEBIT	CREDIT	DEBIT BALANCE
20-- May	1	Balance	✔			4 8 8 93

ACCOUNT Suarez Consulting   CUSTOMER NO. 140

DATE		ITEM	POST. REF.	DEBIT	CREDIT	DEBIT BALANCE
20-- May	1	Balance	✔			1 6 4 8 11

2.   GENERAL LEDGER

ACCOUNT Accounts Receivable   ACCOUNT NO. 1130

DATE		ITEM	POST. REF.	DEBIT	CREDIT	BALANCE DEBIT	BALANCE CREDIT
20-- May	1	Balance	✔			19 4 8 2 58	

ACCOUNT Allowance for Uncollectible Accounts   ACCOUNT NO. 1135

DATE		ITEM	POST. REF.	DEBIT	CREDIT	BALANCE DEBIT	BALANCE CREDIT
20-- May	1	Balance	✔				3 4 5 0 00

1., 2.

CASH RECEIPTS JOURNAL

DATE	ACCOUNT TITLE	DOC. NO.	POST. REF.	GENERAL DEBIT	GENERAL CREDIT	ACCOUNTS RECEIVABLE CREDIT	SALES CREDIT	SALES TAX PAYABLE CREDIT	SALES DISCOUNT DEBIT	CASH DEBIT	
											1
											2
											3

14-3 APPLICATION PROBLEM (LO6, 7, 8), p. 435

Recording notes receivable

1.

Note	Date	Principal	Interest Rate	Time in Days	Interest	Maturity Date	Maturity Value
NR8	April 16	$25,000.00	8%	90			
NR9	May 3	$ 8,000.00	9%	180			

Calculations:

1.

Note	Maturity Date			Interest	Maturity Value
		Days from the Month	Days Remaining		
NR8			90		
	Term of the Note				
NR9		Days from the Month	Days Remaining		
			180		
	Term of the Note				

2.

GENERAL JOURNAL

PAGE 16

	DATE	ACCOUNT TITLE	DOC. NO.	POST. REF.	DEBIT	CREDIT	
10							10
11							11
12							12
13							13
14							14
15							15

2.

CASH RECEIPTS JOURNAL

PAGE 23

	DATE	ACCOUNT TITLE	DOC. NO.	POST. REF.	GENERAL DEBIT	GENERAL CREDIT	ACCOUNTS RECEIVABLE CREDIT	SALES CREDIT	SALES TAX PAYABLE CREDIT	SALES DISCOUNT DEBIT	CASH DEBIT	
					1	2	3	4	5	6	7	
22												22
23												23
24												24

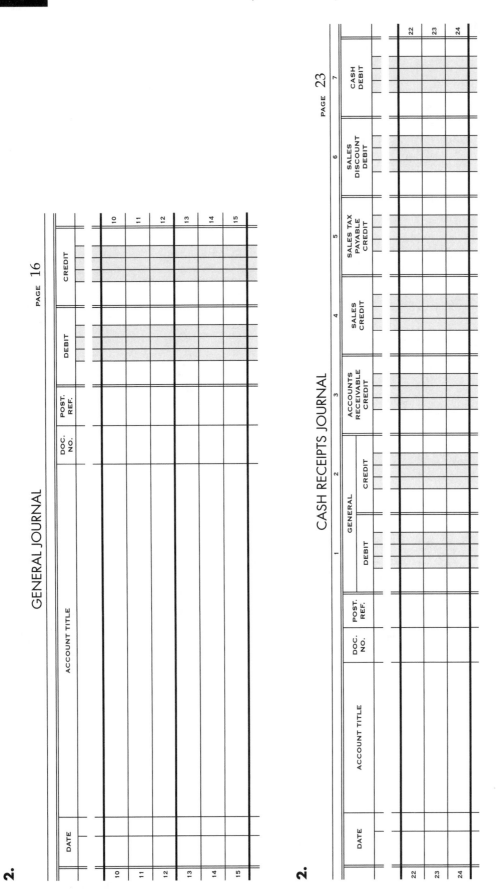

14-3 APPLICATION PROBLEM (concluded)

2., 3. ACCOUNTS RECEIVABLE LEDGER

ACCOUNT Daniel Burris   CUSTOMER NO. 110

DATE		ITEM	POST. REF.	DEBIT	CREDIT	DEBIT BALANCE
20-- June	1	Balance	✔			6 8 0 0 00

ACCOUNT Maggie Singer   CUSTOMER NO. 120

DATE		ITEM	POST. REF.	DEBIT	CREDIT	DEBIT BALANCE

3. GENERAL LEDGER

ACCOUNT Accounts Receivable   ACCOUNT NO. 1130

DATE		ITEM	POST. REF.	DEBIT	CREDIT	BALANCE DEBIT	BALANCE CREDIT
20-- June	1	Balance	✔			64 0 8 1 13	

ACCOUNT Notes Receivable   ACCOUNT NO. 1170

DATE		ITEM	POST. REF.	DEBIT	CREDIT	BALANCE DEBIT	BALANCE CREDIT
20-- June	1	Balance	✔			12 8 5 0 00	

ACCOUNT Interest Income   ACCOUNT NO. 7110

DATE		ITEM	POST. REF.	DEBIT	CREDIT	BALANCE DEBIT	BALANCE CREDIT
20-- June	1	Balance	✔				8 2 9 00

14-M MASTERY PROBLEM (LO4, 5, 6, 7, 8), p. 435

Recording entries for uncollectible accounts

1., 2.

GENERAL JOURNAL   PAGE 12

	DATE		ACCOUNT TITLE	DOC. NO.	POST. REF.	DEBIT	CREDIT	
1								1
2								2
3								3
4								4
5								5
6								6
7								7
8								8
9								9
10								10
11								11
12								12
13								13
14								14
15								15
16								16

3.

GENERAL JOURNAL   PAGE 13

	DATE		ACCOUNT TITLE	DOC. NO.	POST. REF.	DEBIT	CREDIT	
1								1
2								2
3								3
4								4
5								5

14-M MASTERY PROBLEM (continued)

1., 2.

CASH RECEIPTS JOURNAL

PAGE 22

	DATE	ACCOUNT TITLE	DOC. NO.	POST. REF.	GENERAL DEBIT	GENERAL CREDIT	ACCOUNTS RECEIVABLE CREDIT	SALES CREDIT	SALES TAX PAYABLE CREDIT	SALES DISCOUNT DEBIT	CASH DEBIT
1											
2											
3											
4											
5											
6											
7											

3.

Age Group	Amount	Percent	Uncollectible
Current	$ 52,271.96	1.0%	
1–30	32,581.28	2.5%	
31–60	12,849.15	7.5%	
61–90	9,418.25	25.0%	
Over 90	11,848.15	60.0%	
	$118,968.79		
Current Balance of Allowance for Uncollectible Accounts			
Estimated Addition to Allowance for Uncollectible Accounts			

1., 2., 3.   **ACCOUNTS RECEIVABLE LEDGER**

ACCOUNT Banda Company   CUSTOMER NO. 110

DATE	ITEM	POST. REF.	DEBIT	CREDIT	DEBIT BALANCE

ACCOUNT Broyles Industries   CUSTOMER NO. 120

DATE	ITEM	POST. REF.	DEBIT	CREDIT	DEBIT BALANCE

ACCOUNT Maples Corporation   CUSTOMER NO. 130

DATE	ITEM	POST. REF.	DEBIT	CREDIT	DEBIT BALANCE
20-- Dec. 1	Balance	✔			4 5 0 0 00

ACCOUNT Murrell, Inc.   CUSTOMER NO. 140

DATE	ITEM	POST. REF.	DEBIT	CREDIT	DEBIT BALANCE
20-- Dec. 1	Balance	✔			1 6 4 5 00

ACCOUNT Patel Corporation   CUSTOMER NO. 150

DATE	ITEM	POST. REF.	DEBIT	CREDIT	DEBIT BALANCE
20-- Dec. 1	Balance	✔			4 9 8 25

14-M MASTERY PROBLEM (concluded)

3.   GENERAL LEDGER

ACCOUNT Accounts Receivable   ACCOUNT NO. 1130

DATE		ITEM	POST. REF.	DEBIT	CREDIT	BALANCE	
						DEBIT	CREDIT
Dec. 20--	1	Balance	✔			120 7 1 6 04	

ACCOUNT Allowance for Uncollectible Accounts   ACCOUNT NO. 1135

DATE		ITEM	POST. REF.	DEBIT	CREDIT	BALANCE	
						DEBIT	CREDIT
Dec. 20--	1	Balance	✔				2 1 4 3 01

ACCOUNT Notes Receivable   ACCOUNT NO. 1170

DATE		ITEM	POST. REF.	DEBIT	CREDIT	BALANCE	
						DEBIT	CREDIT
Dec. 20--	1	Balance	✔			22 8 0 0 00	

ACCOUNT Uncollectible Accounts Expense   ACCOUNT NO. 6165

DATE		ITEM	POST. REF.	DEBIT	CREDIT	BALANCE	
						DEBIT	CREDIT

ACCOUNT Interest Income   ACCOUNT NO. 7110

DATE		ITEM	POST. REF.	DEBIT	CREDIT	BALANCE	
						DEBIT	CREDIT
Dec. 20--	1	Balance	✔				1 0 9 5 00

14-C CHALLENGE PROBLEM (LO2), p. 436

Estimating uncollectible accounts expense

1., 2.

	Wood Company Aging of Accounts Receivable 12/31/20--		
Age Group	**Amount**	**Percent**	**Uncollectible**
Current	$ 70,728.14		
1–30	30,438.99		
31–60	14,563.59		
61–90	8,090.34		
Over 90	14,574.76		
	$138,395.82		
Current Balance of Allowance for Uncollectible Accounts			
Estimated Addition to Allowance for Uncollectible Accounts			

3.

_____

_____

_____

_____

_____

_____

Study Guide 15

Name	Perfect Score	Your Score
Identifying Accounting Terms	17 Pts.	
Identifying Accounting Concepts and Practices	20 Pts.	
Analyzing Adjustments	12 Pts.	
Total	49 Pts.	

Part One—Identifying Accounting Terms

Directions: Select the one term in Column I that best fits each definition in Column II. Print the letter identifying your choice in the Answers column.

Column I	Column II	Answers
A. accrued interest income	**1.** A trial balance prepared before adjusting entries are posted. (p. 441)	1. _____
B. accrued revenue	**2.** The amount of inventory on hand at the beginning of a fiscal period. (p. 446)	2. _____
C. accumulated depreciation	**3.** The actual count of merchandise at the end of a fiscal period. (p. 446)	3. _____
D. adjusted trial balance	**4.** Revenue earned in one fiscal period but not received until a later fiscal period. (p. 447)	4. _____
E. beginning inventory	**5.** Interest earned but not yet received. (p. 448)	5. _____
F. book value of a plant asset	**6.** Cash and other assets expected to be exchanged for cash or consumed within a year. (p. 450)	6. _____
G. current assets	**7.** Physical assets that will be used for a number of years in the operation of a business. (p. 450)	7. _____
H. depreciation	**8.** A loss in the usefulness of a plant asset as a result of wear or obsolescence. (p. 450)	8. _____
I. depreciation expense	**9.** The portion of a plant asset's cost that is transferred to an expense account in each fiscal period during that asset's useful life. (p. 450)	9. _____
J. ending inventory	**10.** An estimate of the amount that will be received for an asset at the time of its disposal. (p. 450)	10. _____
K. marginal tax rate	**11.** The period of time over which an asset contributes to the earnings of a business. (p. 450)	11. _____
L. plant assets	**12.** Recording an equal amount of depreciation expense for a plant asset in each year of its useful life. (p. 451)	12. _____
M. salvage value	**13.** The total amount of depreciation expense that has been recorded since the purchase of a plant asset. (p. 451)	13. _____
N. straight-line method of depreciation	**14.** The original cost of a plant asset minus accumulated depreciation. (p. 451)	14. _____
O. tax bracket	**15.** A trial balance prepared after adjusting entries are posted. (p. 457)	15. _____
P. unadjusted trial balance	**16.** Each tax rate and taxable income amount on one line of a tax table. (p. 458)	16. _____
Q. useful life	**17.** The tax rate associated with a tax bracket. (p. 458)	17. _____

Part Two—Identifying Accounting Concepts and Practices

Directions: Place a *T* for True or an *F* for False in the Answers column to show whether each of the following statements is true or false.

1. Businesses must use a 12-month period, or fiscal year, ending on December 31 for reporting their financial performance. (p. 440)

  1. _____

2. The adjusting entry for Merchandise Inventory is unique to a merchandising business. (p. 440)

  2. _____

3. The first step in preparing adjusting entries is to prepare an unadjusted trial balance. (p. 441)

  3. _____

4. A trial balance provides a complete list of accounts that may need to be brought up to date. (p. 441)

  4. _____

5. Rather than using a worksheet, a business can use an unadjusted trial balance and record adjustments directly to a general journal. (p. 441)

  5. _____

6. The adjustment for the Supplies—Office account will result in a debit to Supplies Expense—Office. (p. 442)

  6. _____

7. The amount of the adjustment for Prepaid Insurance represents the value of insurance premium used during the fiscal period. (p. 444)

  7. _____

8. For a company using the periodic inventory method, the account balance of Merchandise Inventory changes during the fiscal year. (p. 446)

  8. _____

9. If ending inventory is less than the account balance of Merchandise Inventory, the inventory adjustment will include a credit to Income Summary. (p. 447)

  9. _____

10. The adjusting entry for accrued revenue increases a revenue account (a credit) and increases a receivable account (a debit). (p. 447)

  10. _____

11. Estimates of the cost, salvage value, and useful life of a plant asset are used to calculate its annual depreciation. (p. 450)

  11. _____

12. Functional depreciation occurs when a plant asset becomes inadequate or obsolete. (p. 450)

  12. _____

13. The annual straight-line depreciation of equipment costing $4,000.00 with a salvage value of $500.00 and a useful life of 5 years would be $700.00. (p. 451)

  13. _____

14. The adjustment for Accumulated Depreciation—Store Equipment includes a credit to Depreciation Expense—Store Equipment. (p. 452)

  14. _____

15. The annual straight-line depreciation of land costing $40,000.00 with a salvage value of $10,000.00 and a useful life of 20 years would be $1,500.00. (p. 452)

  15. _____

16. The adjustment for Federal Income Tax Payable and Federal Income Tax Expense is determined only after all other adjusting entries are posted and the net income before federal income tax is determined. (p. 457)

  16. _____

17. Corporations anticipating annual federal income taxes of $500.00 or more are required to pay estimated taxes each month. (p. 458)

  17. _____

18. A corporation using a 35% marginal tax rate must pay income taxes equal to 35% of its income before federal income taxes. (p. 458)

  18. _____

19. Tax rates for corporations can be changed by an act of Congress. (p. 458)

  19. _____

20. Any amount of federal income tax owed at the end of the fiscal year is debited to Federal Income Tax Payable. (p. 459)

  20. _____

Part Three—Analyzing Adjustments

Directions: For each of the following items, select the choice that best completes the statement. Print the letter identifying your choice in the Answers column.

Answers

1. The amount in the Supplies—Office account on an unadjusted trial balance represents the value of supplies (A) at the beginning of a fiscal period (B) used during a fiscal period (C) at the beginning of a fiscal period plus office supplies bought during the fiscal period (D) bought during a fiscal period. (p. 442)

1. _____

2. The two accounts used to adjust the Office Supplies account are (A) Supplies and Purchases (B) Supplies—Office and Income Summary (C) Supplies—Office and Supplies Expense—Office (D) Supplies Expense—Office and Income Summary. (p. 442)

2. _____

3. The portion of the insurance premiums that has expired during a fiscal period is classified as (A) a liability (B) an asset (C) an expense (D) capital. (p. 444)

3. _____

4. The two accounts used to adjust the Prepaid Insurance account are (A) Insurance Expense and Income Summary (B) Prepaid Insurance and Insurance Expense (C) Prepaid Insurance and Income Summary (D) Prepaid Insurance Expense and Income Summary. (p. 444)

4. _____

5. For a business using the periodic inventory method, the Merchandise Inventory amount on the unadjusted trial balance represents the merchandise inventory (A) at the end of a fiscal period (B) at the beginning of a fiscal period (C) purchased during a fiscal period (D) available during a fiscal period. (p. 446)

5. _____

6. The two accounts used to adjust the Merchandise Inventory account are (A) Merchandise Inventory and Supplies (B) Merchandise Inventory and Purchases (C) Merchandise Inventory and Income Summary (D) Merchandise Inventory and Sales. (pp. 446–447)

6. _____

7. A credit to Income Summary in the Merchandise Inventory adjustment represents the (A) decrease in Merchandise Inventory (B) increase in Merchandise Inventory (C) beginning Merchandise Inventory (D) ending Merchandise Inventory. (p. 447)

7. _____

8. Recording revenue in the accounting period in which the revenue is earned is an application of the accounting concept (A) Realization of Revenue (B) Consistent Reporting (C) Historical Cost (D) Adequate Disclosure. (p. 447)

8. _____

9. The two accounts used to adjust for interest income earned on notes receivable are (A) Interest Receivable and Interest Income (B) Accounts Receivable and Interest Income (C) Interest Receivable and Sales (D) Accounts Receivable and Sales. (p. 448)

9. _____

10. After recording the adjustment for accumulated depreciation, the book value of plant assets (A) remains unchanged, (B) increases, (C) decreases, (D) cannot be determined. (pp. 451–452)

10. _____

11. The two accounts used to adjust the depreciation of store equipment are (A) Store Equipment and Store Equipment Expense (B) Accumulated Depreciation—Store Equipment and Accumulated Depreciation Expense (C) Accumulated Depreciation—Store Equipment and Store Equipment Expense (D) Accumulated Depreciation—Store Equipment and Depreciation Expense—Store Equipment. (p. 452)

11. _____

12. The two accounts used to record the adjustment for federal income tax are (A) Federal Income Tax Expense and Prepaid Taxes (B) Federal Income Tax Payable and Federal Income Tax Expense (C) Federal Income Tax Expense and Allowance for Federal Tax Expense (D) Federal Income Tax Expense and Federal Income Tax Adjustments. (p. 459)

12. _____

Across

3. Physical assets that will be used for a number of years in the operation of a business.

6. Each tax rate and taxable income amount on one line of a tax table.

7. A trial balance prepared after adjusting entries are posted.

9. The period of time over which an asset contributes to the earnings of a business.

10. Transactions that are set up for automated entry in computerized accounting systems.

11. The amount of inventory on hand at the beginning of a fiscal period.

12. Cash and other assets expected to be exchanged for cash or consumed within a year.

13. The actual count of merchandise at the end of a fiscal period.

Down

1. The portion of a plant asset's cost that is transferred to an expense account in each fiscal period during that asset's useful life.

2. The tax rate associated with a tax bracket.

4. The amount that will be received for an asset at the time of its disposal.

5. Revenue earned in one fiscal period but not received until a later fiscal period.

8. A loss in the usefulness of a plant asset as a result of wear or obsolescence.

15-1 WORK TOGETHER, p. 445

Journalizing the adjusting entries for supplies and prepaid insurance

(Note: Working papers for 15-1 ON YOUR OWN begin on p. 439.)

1., 2.

ACCOUNT TITLE	DEBIT	CREDIT
Cash	24 1 9 4 34	
Petty Cash	2 5 0 00	
Accounts Receivable	38 5 1 8 56	
Merchandise Inventory	94 8 4 5 31	
Supplies—Office	3 1 0 8 08	
Supplies—Store		
Prepaid Insurance	11 2 0 0 00	
Notes Receivable	8 0 0 0 00	
Interest Receivable		
Office Equipment	6 9 4 8 88	
Store Equipment	22 4 6 1 95	
Accumulated Depreciation—Store Equipment		8 5 6 4 00
Accounts Payable		4 4 6 2 21
Sales Tax Payable		4 9 5 90
Employee Income Tax Payable—Federal		5 9 4 00
Social Security Tax Payable		1 2 6 6 80
Medicare Tax Payable		2 9 6 27
Health Insurance Premiums Payable		2 8 8 04
Retirement Benefits Payable		2 9 1 17
Unemployment Tax Payable—Federal		1 8 5 99
Unemployment Tax Payable—State		9 2 31
Federal Income Tax Payable		
Dividends Payable		3 0 0 0 00
Capital Stock		30 0 0 0 00
Retained Earnings		37 1 2 9 26
Dividends	12 0 0 0 00	

(Note: Trial balance is continued on the next page.)

Chapter 15 Preparing Adjusting Entries and a Trial Balance • **427**

ACCOUNT TITLE	DEBIT	CREDIT
Income Summary		
Sales		532 3 7 1 75
Sales Discount	2 1 8 10	
Sales Returns and Allowances	1 4 8 48	
Purchases	223 1 7 4 88	
Purchases Discount		9 2 2 14
Purchases Returns and Allowances		1 4 9 5 01
Advertising Expense	2 1 8 2 81	
Credit Card Fee Expense	3 9 5 42	
Depreciation Expense—Office Equipment		
Depreciation Expense—Store Equipment		
Miscellaneous Expense	2 3 8 2 80	
Payroll Taxes Expense	12 7 9 7 20	
Rent Expense	5 7 1 4 03	
Salary Expense	115 3 6 4 38	
Supplies Expense—Office		
Supplies Expense—Store		
Uncollectible Accounts Expense		
Utilities Expense	3 9 7 3 68	
Federal Income Tax Expense	32 0 0 0 00	
Interest Income		4 6 4 00

15-1, 15-2, 15-3, and 15-4   WORK TOGETHER, pp. 445, 449, 454, and 462

15-1 Journalizing the adjusting entries for supplies and prepaid insurance

15-2 Journalizing the adjusting entries for merchandise inventory and interest receivable

15-3 Journalizing the adjusting entries for accumulated depreciation

15-4 Preparing the adjusting entry for federal income tax and an adjusted trial balance

GENERAL JOURNAL   PAGE 15

	DATE		ACCOUNT TITLE	DOC. NO.	POST. REF.	DEBIT	CREDIT	
1			Adjusting Entries					1
2	20-- Dec.	31	Uncollectible Accounts Expense			3 4 1 5 00		2
3			Allowance for Uncollectible Accounts				3 4 1 5 00	3
4								4
5								5
6								6
7								7
8								8
9								9
10								10
11								11
12								12
13								13
14								14
15								15
16								16
17								17
18								18
19								19
20								20

1.

Original Cost	$ _____
Estimated Salvage Value	_____
Estimated Total Depreciation Expense	$ _____
Years of Estimated Useful Life	_____
Annual Depreciation Expense	$ _____

2.

Original Cost		$ _____
Depreciation: Year 1	$ _____	
Year 2	_____	_____
Book Value		$ _____

15-4 WORK TOGETHER, p. 462

GENERAL LEDGER

1., 4.

ACCOUNT Allowance for Uncollectible Accounts   ACCOUNT NO. 1135

DATE	ITEM	POST. REF.	DEBIT	CREDIT	BALANCE DEBIT	BALANCE CREDIT
20-- Dec. 1	Balance	✔				4 8 67

ACCOUNT Merchandise Inventory   ACCOUNT NO. 1140

DATE	ITEM	POST. REF.	DEBIT	CREDIT	BALANCE DEBIT	BALANCE CREDIT
20-- Dec. 1	Balance	✔			94 8 4 5 31	

ACCOUNT Supplies—Office   ACCOUNT NO. 1145

DATE	ITEM	POST. REF.	DEBIT	CREDIT	BALANCE DEBIT	BALANCE CREDIT
20-- Dec. 1	Balance	✔			3 1 0 8 08	

ACCOUNT Supplies—Store   ACCOUNT NO. 1150

DATE	ITEM	POST. REF.	DEBIT	CREDIT	BALANCE DEBIT	BALANCE CREDIT
20-- Dec. 1	Balance	✔			4 4 8 3 62	

ACCOUNT Prepaid Insurance   ACCOUNT NO. 1160

DATE	ITEM	POST. REF.	DEBIT	CREDIT	BALANCE DEBIT	BALANCE CREDIT
20-- Dec. 1	Balance	✔			11 2 0 0 00	

ACCOUNT Interest Receivable   ACCOUNT NO. 1175

DATE	ITEM	POST. REF.	DEBIT	CREDIT	BALANCE DEBIT	BALANCE CREDIT

ACCOUNT Accumulated Depreciation—Office Equipment   ACCOUNT NO. 1210

DATE	ITEM	POST. REF.	DEBIT	CREDIT	BALANCE DEBIT	BALANCE CREDIT
20-- Dec. 1	Balance	✔				2 3 9 5 00

ACCOUNT Accumulated Depreciation—Store Equipment   ACCOUNT NO. 1220

DATE	ITEM	POST. REF.	DEBIT	CREDIT	BALANCE DEBIT	BALANCE CREDIT
20-- Dec. 1	Balance	✔				8 5 6 4 00

ACCOUNT Federal Income Tax Payable   ACCOUNT NO. 2170

DATE	ITEM	POST. REF.	DEBIT	CREDIT	BALANCE DEBIT	BALANCE CREDIT

ACCOUNT Income Summary   ACCOUNT NO. 3150

DATE	ITEM	POST. REF.	DEBIT	CREDIT	BALANCE DEBIT	BALANCE CREDIT

ACCOUNT Depreciation Expense—Office Equipment   ACCOUNT NO. 6120

DATE	ITEM	POST. REF.	DEBIT	CREDIT	BALANCE DEBIT	BALANCE CREDIT

ACCOUNT Depreciation Expense—Store Equipment   ACCOUNT NO. 6125

DATE	ITEM	POST. REF.	DEBIT	CREDIT	BALANCE DEBIT	BALANCE CREDIT

15-4 WORK TOGETHER (continued)

ACCOUNT Insurance Expense   ACCOUNT NO. 6130

DATE	ITEM	POST. REF.	DEBIT	CREDIT	BALANCE DEBIT	BALANCE CREDIT

ACCOUNT Supplies Expense—Office   ACCOUNT NO. 6155

DATE	ITEM	POST. REF.	DEBIT	CREDIT	BALANCE DEBIT	BALANCE CREDIT

ACCOUNT Supplies Expense—Store   ACCOUNT NO. 6160

DATE	ITEM	POST. REF.	DEBIT	CREDIT	BALANCE DEBIT	BALANCE CREDIT

ACCOUNT Uncollectible Accounts Expense   ACCOUNT NO. 6165

DATE	ITEM	POST. REF.	DEBIT	CREDIT	BALANCE DEBIT	BALANCE CREDIT

ACCOUNT Federal Income Tax Expense   ACCOUNT NO. 6205

DATE	ITEM	POST. REF.	DEBIT	CREDIT	BALANCE DEBIT	BALANCE CREDIT
20-- Dec. 1	Balance	✔			32 000 00	

ACCOUNT Interest Income   ACCOUNT NO. 7110

DATE	ITEM	POST. REF.	DEBIT	CREDIT	BALANCE DEBIT	BALANCE CREDIT
20-- Dec. 1	Balance	✔				464 00

Chapter 15 Preparing Adjusting Entries and a Trial Balance • 433

3.

Total of income statement credit accounts .... $ _____

Less total of income statement debit accounts

    excluding federal income tax.. _____

Equals net income before federal income tax......................... $ _____

Net Income before Federal Income Tax	−	Of the Amount Over	=	Net Income Subject to Marginal Tax Rate	×	Marginal Tax Rate	=	Marginal Income Tax
$	−	$	=	$	×		=	$

Bracket Minimum Income Tax	+	Marginal Income Tax	=	Federal Income Tax
$	+	$	=	$

15-4 WORK TOGETHER (continued)

2., 5., 6.

ACCOUNT TITLE	DEBIT	CREDIT
Cash	24 1 9 4 34	
Petty Cash	2 5 0 00	
Accounts Receivable	38 5 1 8 56	
Allowance for Uncollectible Accounts		
Merchandise Inventory		
Supplies—Office		
Supplies—Store		
Prepaid Insurance		
Notes Receivable	8 0 0 0 00	
Interest Receivable		
Office Equipment	6 9 4 8 88	
Accumulated Depreciation—Office Equipment		
Store Equipment	22 4 6 1 95	
Accumulated Depreciation—Store Equipment		
Accounts Payable		4 4 6 2 21
Sales Tax Payable		4 9 5 90
Employee Income Tax Payable—Federal		5 9 4 00
Social Security Tax Payable		1 2 6 6 80
Medicare Tax Payable		2 9 6 27
Health Insurance Premiums Payable		2 8 8 04
Retirement Benefits Payable		2 9 1 17
Unemployment Tax Payable—Federal		1 8 5 99
Unemployment Tax Payable—State		9 2 31
Federal Income Tax Payable		
Dividends Payable		3 0 0 0 00
Capital Stock		30 0 0 0 00
Retained Earnings		37 1 2 9 26
Dividends	12 0 0 0 00	

(Note: Trial balance is continued on the next page.)

ACCOUNT TITLE	DEBIT	CREDIT
Income Summary		
Sales		532 3 7 1 75
Sales Discount	2 1 8 10	
Sales Returns and Allowances	1 4 8 48	
Purchases	223 1 7 4 88	
Purchases Discount		9 2 2 14
Purchases Returns and Allowances		1 4 9 5 01
Advertising Expense	2 1 8 2 81	
Credit Card Fee Expense	3 9 5 42	
Depreciation Expense—Office Equipment		
Depreciation Expense—Store Equipment		
Insurance Expense		
Miscellaneous Expense	2 3 8 2 80	
Payroll Taxes Expense	12 7 9 7 20	
Rent Expense	5 7 1 4 03	
Salary Expense	115 3 6 4 38	
Supplies Expense—Office		
Supplies Expense—Store		
Uncollectible Accounts Expense		
Utilities Expense	3 9 7 3 68	
Federal Income Tax Expense		
Interest Income		

15-1 ON YOUR OWN, p. 445

Journalizing the adjusting entries for supplies and prepaid insurance

1., 2.

ACCOUNT TITLE	DEBIT	CREDIT
Cash	18 4 3 1 35	
Petty Cash	2 0 0 00	
Accounts Receivable	38 1 4 8 21	
Merchandise Inventory	165 4 4 8 21	
Supplies—Store	5 4 9 1 19	
Prepaid Insurance	12 8 0 0 00	
Notes Receivable	7 5 0 0 00	
Interest Receivable		
Office Equipment	15 4 9 5 28	
Accumulated Depreciation—Office Equipment		6 1 4 9 00
Store Equipment	28 4 9 1 48	
Accounts Payable		8 4 9 1 04
Sales Tax Payable		4 9 1 5 22
Employee Income Tax Payable—Federal		7 4 3 00
Social Security Tax Payable		1 5 8 3 34
Medicare Tax Payable		3 7 0 30
Health Insurance Premiums Payable		3 6 0 02
Retirement Benefits Payable		3 6 3 93
Unemployment Tax Payable—Federal		2 3 2 46
Unemployment Tax Payable—State		1 1 5 38
Federal Income Tax Payable		
Dividends Payable		2 5 0 0 00
Capital Stock		50 0 0 0 00
Retained Earnings		103 8 0 7 14
Dividends	10 0 0 0 00	

(Note: Trial balance is continued on the next page.)

ACCOUNT TITLE	DEBIT	CREDIT
Income Summary		
Sales		768 1 9 4 26
Sales Discount	2 4 8 7 16	
Sales Returns and Allowances	3 1 4 9 25	
Purchases	395 4 1 9 20	
Purchases Discount		2 9 4 7 24
Purchases Returns and Allowances		3 4 9 8 11
Advertising Expense	24 2 0 0 00	
Credit Card Fee Expense	12 4 4 1 80	
Depreciation Expense—Office Equipment		
Depreciation Expense—Store Equipment		
Insurance Expense		
Miscellaneous Expense	6 8 4 7 14	
Payroll Taxes Expense	12 9 7 7 15	
Rent Expense	34 8 0 0 00	
Salary Expense	144 1 9 1 15	
Supplies Expense—Office		
Supplies Expense—Store		
Uncollectible Accounts Expense		
Utilities Expense	6 1 4 8 25	
Federal Income Tax Expense	18 0 0 0 00	

15-1, 15-2, 15-3, and 15-4 — ON YOUR OWN, pp. 445, 449, 454, and 462

15-1 Journalizing the adjusting entries for supplies and prepaid insurance
15-2 Journalizing the adjusting entries for merchandise inventory and interest receivable
15-3 Journalizing the adjusting entries for accumulated depreciation
15-4 Preparing the adjusting entry for federal income tax and an adjusted trial balance

GENERAL JOURNAL   PAGE 18

	DATE		ACCOUNT TITLE	DOC. NO.	POST. REF.	DEBIT	CREDIT	
1			Adjusting Entries					1
2	20-- Dec.	31	Uncollectible Accounts Expense			4 2 2 5 00		2
3			Allowance for Uncollectible Accounts				4 2 2 5 00	3
4								4
5								5
6								6
7								7
8								8
9								9
10								10
11								11
12								12
13								13
14								14
15								15
16								16
17								17
18								18
19								19
20								20

1.

Original Cost	$_____
Estimated Salvage Value	_____
Estimated Total Depreciation Expense	$_____
Years of Estimated Useful Life	_____
Annual Depreciation Expense	$_____

2.

Original Cost			$_____
Depreciation:	Year 1	$_____	
	Year 2	_____	_____
Book Value			$_____

15-4 ON YOUR OWN, p. 462

GENERAL LEDGER

1., 4.

ACCOUNT Allowance for Uncollectible Accounts   ACCOUNT NO. 1135

DATE	ITEM	POST. REF.	DEBIT	CREDIT	BALANCE DEBIT	BALANCE CREDIT
20-- Dec. 1	Balance	✔			2 08 50	

ACCOUNT Merchandise Inventory   ACCOUNT NO. 1140

DATE	ITEM	POST. REF.	DEBIT	CREDIT	BALANCE DEBIT	BALANCE CREDIT
20-- Dec. 1	Balance	✔			165 4 48 21	

ACCOUNT Supplies—Office   ACCOUNT NO. 1145

DATE	ITEM	POST. REF.	DEBIT	CREDIT	BALANCE DEBIT	BALANCE CREDIT
20-- Dec. 1	Balance	✔			4 1 48 12	

ACCOUNT Supplies—Store   ACCOUNT NO. 1150

DATE	ITEM	POST. REF.	DEBIT	CREDIT	BALANCE DEBIT	BALANCE CREDIT
20-- Dec. 1	Balance	✔			5 4 91 19	

ACCOUNT Prepaid Insurance   ACCOUNT NO. 1160

DATE	ITEM	POST. REF.	DEBIT	CREDIT	BALANCE DEBIT	BALANCE CREDIT
20-- Dec. 1	Balance	✔			12 8 00 00	

ACCOUNT Interest Receivable   ACCOUNT NO. 1175

DATE	ITEM	POST. REF.	DEBIT	CREDIT	BALANCE DEBIT	BALANCE CREDIT

ACCOUNT Accumulated Depreciation—Office Equipment   ACCOUNT NO. 1210

DATE		ITEM	POST. REF.	DEBIT	CREDIT	BALANCE DEBIT	BALANCE CREDIT
20-- Dec.	1	Balance	✔				6 1 4 9 00

ACCOUNT Accumulated Depreciation—Store Equipment   ACCOUNT NO. 1220

DATE		ITEM	POST. REF.	DEBIT	CREDIT	BALANCE DEBIT	BALANCE CREDIT
20-- Dec.	1	Balance	✔				12 4 9 5 00

ACCOUNT Federal Income Tax Payable   ACCOUNT NO. 2170

DATE	ITEM	POST. REF.	DEBIT	CREDIT	BALANCE DEBIT	BALANCE CREDIT

ACCOUNT Income Summary   ACCOUNT NO. 3150

DATE	ITEM	POST. REF.	DEBIT	CREDIT	BALANCE DEBIT	BALANCE CREDIT

ACCOUNT Depreciation Expense—Office Equipment   ACCOUNT NO. 6120

DATE	ITEM	POST. REF.	DEBIT	CREDIT	BALANCE DEBIT	BALANCE CREDIT

ACCOUNT Depreciation Expense—Store Equipment   ACCOUNT NO. 6125

DATE	ITEM	POST. REF.	DEBIT	CREDIT	BALANCE DEBIT	BALANCE CREDIT

15-4 ON YOUR OWN (continued)

ACCOUNT Insurance Expense   ACCOUNT NO. 6130

DATE	ITEM	POST. REF.	DEBIT	CREDIT	BALANCE DEBIT	BALANCE CREDIT

ACCOUNT Supplies Expense—Office   ACCOUNT NO. 6155

DATE	ITEM	POST. REF.	DEBIT	CREDIT	BALANCE DEBIT	BALANCE CREDIT

ACCOUNT Supplies Expense—Store   ACCOUNT NO. 6160

DATE	ITEM	POST. REF.	DEBIT	CREDIT	BALANCE DEBIT	BALANCE CREDIT

ACCOUNT Uncollectible Accounts Expense   ACCOUNT NO. 6165

DATE	ITEM	POST. REF.	DEBIT	CREDIT	BALANCE DEBIT	BALANCE CREDIT

ACCOUNT Federal Income Tax Expense   ACCOUNT NO. 6205

DATE	ITEM	POST. REF.	DEBIT	CREDIT	BALANCE DEBIT	BALANCE CREDIT
20-- Dec. 1	Balance	✔			18 0 0 0 00	

ACCOUNT Interest Income   ACCOUNT NO. 7110

DATE	ITEM	POST. REF.	DEBIT	CREDIT	BALANCE DEBIT	BALANCE CREDIT
20-- Dec. 1	Balance	✔				2 5 8 00

3.

Total of income statement credit accounts .... $ _____

Less total of income statement debit accounts

    excluding federal income tax .... _____

Equals net income before federal income tax .... $ _____

Net Income before Federal Income Tax	–	Of the Amount Over	=	Net Income Subject to Marginal Tax Rate	×	Marginal Tax Rate	=	Marginal Income Tax
$	–	$	=	$	×		=	$

Bracket Minimum Income Tax	+	Marginal Income Tax	=	Federal Income Tax
$	+	$	=	$

15-4 **ON YOUR OWN** (continued)

2., 5., 6.

ACCOUNT TITLE	DEBIT	CREDIT
Cash	18 4 3 1 35	
Petty Cash	2 0 0 00	
Accounts Receivable	38 1 4 8 21	
Allowance for Uncollectible Accounts		
Merchandise Inventory		
Supplies—Office		
Supplies—Store		
Prepaid Insurance		
Notes Receivable	7 5 0 0 00	
Interest Receivable		
Office Equipment	15 4 9 5 28	
Accumulated Depreciation—Office Equipment		
Store Equipment	28 4 9 1 48	
Accumulated Depreciation—Store Equipment		
Accounts Payable		8 4 9 1 04
Sales Tax Payable		4 9 1 5 22
Employee Income Tax Payable—Federal		7 4 3 00
Social Security Tax Payable		1 5 8 3 34
Medicare Tax Payable		3 7 0 30
Health Insurance Premiums Payable		3 6 0 02
Retirement Benefits Payable		3 6 3 93
Unemployment Tax Payable—Federal		2 3 2 46
Unemployment Tax Payable—State		1 1 5 38
Federal Income Tax Payable		
Dividends Payable		2 5 0 0 00
Capital Stock		50 0 0 0 00
Retained Earnings		103 8 0 7 14
Dividends	10 0 0 0 00	

(Note: Trial balance is continued on the next page.)

ACCOUNT TITLE	DEBIT	CREDIT
Income Summary		
Sales		768 1 9 4 26
Sales Discount	2 4 8 7 16	
Sales Returns and Allowances	3 1 4 9 25	
Purchases	395 4 1 9 20	
Purchases Discount		2 9 4 7 24
Purchases Returns and Allowances		3 4 9 8 11
Advertising Expense	24 2 0 0 00	
Credit Card Fee Expense	12 4 4 1 80	
Depreciation Expense—Office Equipment		
Depreciation Expense—Store Equipment		
Insurance Expense		
Miscellaneous Expense	6 8 4 7 14	
Payroll Taxes Expense	12 9 7 7 15	
Rent Expense	34 8 0 0 00	
Salary Expense	144 1 9 1 15	
Supplies Expense—Office		
Supplies Expense—Store		
Uncollectible Accounts Expense		
Utilities Expense	6 1 4 8 25	
Federal Income Tax Expense		
Interest Income		

15-1 APPLICATION PROBLEM (LO1, 2), p. 465

Preparing adjusting entries for supplies and prepaid insurance

1., 2.

ACCOUNT TITLE	DEBIT	CREDIT
Cash	16 4 4 8 28	
Petty Cash	3 0 0 00	
Accounts Receivable	28 4 1 9 36	
Allowance for Uncollectible Accounts		3 3 2 20
Supplies—Office	3 4 1 9 11	
Supplies—Store	4 1 1 6 25	
Prepaid Insurance	14 2 0 0 00	
Notes Receivable	4 2 0 0 00	
Interest Receivable		
Office Equipment	16 4 4 7 21	
Store Equipment	42 1 1 5 00	
Accumulated Depreciation—Store Equipment		18 4 4 1 48
Accounts Payable		7 5 1 0 94
Sales Tax Payable		2 4 4 8 11
Employee Income Tax Payable—Federal		5 9 0 00
Social Security Tax Payable		1 1 9 1 20
Medicare Tax Payable		2 7 8 59
Health Insurance Premiums Payable		2 7 0 85
Retirement Benefits Payable		2 7 3 80
Unemployment Tax Payable—Federal		1 7 4 89
Unemployment Tax Payable—State		8 6 80
Federal Income Tax Payable		
Dividends Payable		1 0 0 0 00
Capital Stock		20 0 0 0 00
Retained Earnings		72 6 4 9 37
Dividends	4 0 0 0 00	

(Note: Trial balance is continued on the next page.)

ACCOUNT TITLE	DEBIT	CREDIT
Income Summary		
Sales		574 80 1 40
Sales Discount	3 1 4 0 84	
Sales Returns and Allowances	2 4 7 9 20	
Purchases	294 4 1 8 26	
Purchases Discount		1 8 4 7 16
Purchases Returns and Allowances		2 8 4 6 51
Advertising Expense	18 2 0 0 00	
Credit Card Fee Expense	8 4 4 5 63	
Depreciation Expense—Store Equipment		
Insurance Expense		
Miscellaneous Expense	8 1 1 4 10	
Payroll Taxes Expense	12 9 1 8 25	
Rent Expense	18 2 0 0 00	
Salary Expense	108 4 7 9 50	
Supplies Expense—Office		
Supplies Expense—Store		
Utilities Expense	7 1 1 9 21	
Federal Income Tax Expense	10 0 0 0 00	
Interest Income		3 5 6 00

15-1, 15-2, 15-3, and 15-4 APPLICATION PROBLEMS, pp. 465–466

15-1 Preparing adjusting entries for supplies and prepaid insurance (LO1, 2)

15-2 Journalizing the adjusting entries for merchandise inventory and interest receivable (LO3, 4)

15-3 Journalizing the adjusting entries for accumulated depreciation (LO5, 6)

15-4 Preparing the adjusting entry for federal income tax and an adjusted trial balance (LO7, 8, 9)

GENERAL JOURNAL

PAGE 20

	DATE		ACCOUNT TITLE	DOC. NO.	POST. REF.	DEBIT	CREDIT	
1			Adjusting Entries					1
2	Dec.	31	Uncollectible Accounts Expense			4 2 2 5 00		2
3			Allowance for Uncollectible Accounts				4 2 2 5 00	3
4								4
5								5
6								6
7								7
8								8
9								9
10								10
11								11
12								12
13								13
14								14
15								15
16								16
17								17
18								18
19								19
20								20

1.

Original Cost	$ _____
Estimated Salvage Value	_____
Estimated Total Depreciation Expense	$ _____
Years of Estimated Useful Life	_____
Annual Depreciation Expense	$ _____

2.

Original Cost		$ _____
Depreciation: Year 1	$ _____	
Year 2	_____	_____
Book Value		$ _____

15-4 APPLICATION PROBLEM, p. 466

GENERAL LEDGER

1., 4.

ACCOUNT Allowance for Uncollectible Accounts   ACCOUNT NO. 1135

DATE	ITEM	POST. REF.	DEBIT	CREDIT	BALANCE DEBIT	BALANCE CREDIT
20-- Dec. 1	Balance	✔				3 3 2 20

ACCOUNT Merchandise Inventory   ACCOUNT NO. 1140

DATE	ITEM	POST. REF.	DEBIT	CREDIT	BALANCE DEBIT	BALANCE CREDIT
20-- Dec. 1	Balance	✔			85 1 1 4 10	

ACCOUNT Supplies—Office   ACCOUNT NO. 1145

DATE	ITEM	POST. REF.	DEBIT	CREDIT	BALANCE DEBIT	BALANCE CREDIT
20-- Dec. 1	Balance	✔			3 4 1 9 11	

ACCOUNT Supplies—Store   ACCOUNT NO. 1150

DATE	ITEM	POST. REF.	DEBIT	CREDIT	BALANCE DEBIT	BALANCE CREDIT
20-- Dec. 1	Balance	✔			4 1 1 6 25	

ACCOUNT Prepaid Insurance   ACCOUNT NO. 1160

DATE	ITEM	POST. REF.	DEBIT	CREDIT	BALANCE DEBIT	BALANCE CREDIT
20-- Dec. 1	Balance	✔			14 2 0 0 00	

ACCOUNT Interest Receivable   ACCOUNT NO. 1175

DATE	ITEM	POST. REF.	DEBIT	CREDIT	BALANCE DEBIT	BALANCE CREDIT

ACCOUNT Accumulated Depreciation—Office Equipment ACCOUNT NO. 1210

DATE	ITEM	POST. REF.	DEBIT	CREDIT	BALANCE DEBIT	BALANCE CREDIT
20-- Dec. 1	Balance	✔				5 1 9 5 00

ACCOUNT Accumulated Depreciation—Store Equipment ACCOUNT NO. 1220

DATE	ITEM	POST. REF.	DEBIT	CREDIT	BALANCE DEBIT	BALANCE CREDIT
20-- Dec. 1	Balance	✔				18 4 4 1 48

ACCOUNT Federal Income Tax Payable ACCOUNT NO. 2170

DATE	ITEM	POST. REF.	DEBIT	CREDIT	BALANCE DEBIT	BALANCE CREDIT

ACCOUNT Income Summary ACCOUNT NO. 3150

DATE	ITEM	POST. REF.	DEBIT	CREDIT	BALANCE DEBIT	BALANCE CREDIT

ACCOUNT Depreciation Expense—Office Equipment ACCOUNT NO. 6120

DATE	ITEM	POST. REF.	DEBIT	CREDIT	BALANCE DEBIT	BALANCE CREDIT

ACCOUNT Depreciation Expense—Store Equipment ACCOUNT NO. 6125

DATE	ITEM	POST. REF.	DEBIT	CREDIT	BALANCE DEBIT	BALANCE CREDIT

15-4 APPLICATION PROBLEM (continued)

ACCOUNT Insurance Expense   ACCOUNT NO. 6130

DATE	ITEM	POST. REF.	DEBIT	CREDIT	BALANCE DEBIT	BALANCE CREDIT

ACCOUNT Supplies Expense—Office   ACCOUNT NO. 6155

DATE	ITEM	POST. REF.	DEBIT	CREDIT	BALANCE DEBIT	BALANCE CREDIT

ACCOUNT Supplies Expense—Store   ACCOUNT NO. 6160

DATE	ITEM	POST. REF.	DEBIT	CREDIT	BALANCE DEBIT	BALANCE CREDIT

ACCOUNT Uncollectible Accounts Expense   ACCOUNT NO. 6165

DATE	ITEM	POST. REF.	DEBIT	CREDIT	BALANCE DEBIT	BALANCE CREDIT

ACCOUNT Federal Income Tax Expense   ACCOUNT NO. 6205

DATE	ITEM	POST. REF.	DEBIT	CREDIT	BALANCE DEBIT	BALANCE CREDIT
20-- Dec.	1	Balance	✔			10 0 0 0 00	

ACCOUNT Interest Income   ACCOUNT NO. 7110

DATE	ITEM	POST. REF.	DEBIT	CREDIT	BALANCE DEBIT	BALANCE CREDIT
20-- Dec.	1	Balance	✔				3 5 6 00

3.

Total of income statement credit accounts .... $ _____

Less total of income statement debit accounts

   excluding federal income tax.. _____

Equals net income before federal income tax.......................... $ _____

Net Income before Federal Income Tax	−	Of the Amount Over	=	Net Income Subject to Marginal Tax Rate	×	Marginal Tax Rate	=	Marginal Income Tax
$	−	$	=	$	×		=	$

Bracket Minimum Income Tax	+	Marginal Income Tax	=	Federal Income Tax
$	+	$	=	$

15-4 APPLICATION PROBLEM (continued)

2., 5., 6.

ACCOUNT TITLE	DEBIT	CREDIT
Cash	16 4 4 8 28	
Petty Cash	3 0 0 00	
Accounts Receivable	28 4 1 9 36	
Allowance for Uncollectible Accounts		
Merchandise Inventory		
Supplies—Office		
Supplies—Store		
Prepaid Insurance		
Notes Receivable	4 2 0 0 00	
Interest Receivable		
Office Equipment	16 4 4 7 21	
Accumulated Depreciation—Office Equipment		
Store Equipment	42 1 1 5 00	
Accumulated Depreciation—Store Equipment		
Accounts Payable		7 5 1 0 94
Sales Tax Payable		2 4 4 8 11
Employee Income Tax Payable—Federal		5 9 0 00
Social Security Tax Payable		1 1 9 1 20
Medicare Tax Payable		2 7 8 59
Health Insurance Premiums Payable		2 7 0 85
Retirement Benefits Payable		2 7 3 80
Unemployment Tax Payable—Federal		1 7 4 89
Unemployment Tax Payable—State		8 6 80
Federal Income Tax Payable		
Dividends Payable		1 0 0 0 00
Capital Stock		20 0 0 0 00
Retained Earnings		72 6 4 9 37
Dividends	4 0 0 0 00	

(Note: Trial balance is continued on the next page.)

ACCOUNT TITLE	DEBIT	CREDIT
Income Summary		
Sales		574 8 0 1 40
Sales Discount	3 1 4 0 84	
Sales Returns and Allowances	2 4 7 9 20	
Purchases	294 4 1 8 26	
Purchases Discount		1 8 4 7 16
Purchases Returns and Allowances		2 8 4 6 51
Advertising Expense	18 2 0 0 00	
Credit Card Fee Expense	8 4 4 5 63	
Depreciation Expense—Office Equipment		
Depreciation Expense—Store Equipment		
Insurance Expense		
Miscellaneous Expense	8 1 1 4 10	
Payroll Taxes Expense	12 9 1 8 25	
Rent Expense	18 2 0 0 00	
Salary Expense	108 4 7 9 50	
Supplies Expense—Office		
Supplies Expense—Store		
Uncollectible Accounts Expense		
Utilities Expense	7 1 1 9 21	
Federal Income Tax Expense		
Interest Income		

15-M MASTERY PROBLEM (LO2, 3, 4, 6, 7, 8, 9), p. 466

Journalizing adjusting entries and preparing an adjusted trial balance

1., 2., 4., 5.

GENERAL JOURNAL

PAGE 16

	DATE		ACCOUNT TITLE	DOC. NO.	POST. REF.	DEBIT	CREDIT	
1								1
2								2
3								3
4								4
5								5
6								6
7								7
8								8
9								9
10								10
11								11
12								12
13								13
14								14
15								15
16								16
17								17
18								18
19								19
20								20
21								21
22								22
23								23
24								24
25								25
26								26
27								27
28								28

3., 6.

ACCOUNT TITLE	DEBIT	CREDIT
Cash	42 4 8 9 25	
Petty Cash	2 0 0 00	
Accounts Receivable	16 4 1 8 50	
Allowance for Uncollectible Accounts		
Merchandise Inventory		
Supplies—Office		
Supplies—Store		
Prepaid Insurance		
Notes Receivable	3 2 0 0 00	
Interest Receivable		
Office Equipment	12 4 9 1 00	
Accumulated Depreciation—Office Equipment		
Store Equipment	62 1 9 4 00	
Accumulated Depreciation—Store Equipment		
Accounts Payable		4 9 8 1 26
Sales Tax Payable		2 1 0 9 05
Employee Income Tax Payable—Federal		7 2 0 00
Social Security Tax Payable		1 5 2 5 00
Medicare Tax Payable		3 5 6 82
Health Insurance Premiums Payable		3 4 6 92
Retirement Benefits Payable		3 5 0 60
Unemployment Tax Payable—Federal		2 2 4 00
Unemployment Tax Payable—State		1 1 1 18
Federal Income Tax Payable		
Dividends Payable		10 0 0 0 00
Capital Stock		20 0 0 0 00
Retained Earnings		52 8 2 6 35
Dividends	40 0 0 0 00	

(Note: Trial balance is continued on the next page.)

15-M MASTERY PROBLEM (continued)

ACCOUNT TITLE	DEBIT	CREDIT
Income Summary		
Sales		501 810 98
Sales Discount	2 148 52	
Sales Returns and Allowances	2 948 36	
Purchases	124 893 50	
Purchases Discount		2 489 14
Purchases Returns and Allowances		3 749 51
Advertising Expense	6 200 00	
Credit Card Fee Expense	6 148 25	
Depreciation Expense—Office Equipment		
Depreciation Expense—Store Equipment		
Insurance Expense		
Miscellaneous Expense	12 495 05	
Payroll Taxes Expense	16 218 18	
Rent Expense	24 800 00	
Salary Expense	138 945 50	
Supplies Expense—Office		
Supplies Expense—Store		
Uncollectible Accounts Expense		
Utilities Expense	9 482 25	
Federal Income Tax Expense		
Interest Income		

GENERAL LEDGER

2., 5.

ACCOUNT Allowance for Uncollectible Accounts   ACCOUNT NO. 1135

DATE		ITEM	POST. REF.	DEBIT	CREDIT	BALANCE DEBIT	BALANCE CREDIT
20-- Dec.	1	Balance	✔				2 5 60

ACCOUNT Merchandise Inventory   ACCOUNT NO. 1140

DATE		ITEM	POST. REF.	DEBIT	CREDIT	BALANCE DEBIT	BALANCE CREDIT
20-- Dec.	1	Balance	✔			51 8 4 3 50	

ACCOUNT Supplies—Office   ACCOUNT NO. 1145

DATE		ITEM	POST. REF.	DEBIT	CREDIT	BALANCE DEBIT	BALANCE CREDIT
20-- Dec.	1	Balance	✔			4 2 1 9 36	

ACCOUNT Supplies—Store   ACCOUNT NO. 1150

DATE		ITEM	POST. REF.	DEBIT	CREDIT	BALANCE DEBIT	BALANCE CREDIT
20-- Dec.	1	Balance	✔			5 1 4 8 19	

ACCOUNT Prepaid Insurance   ACCOUNT NO. 1160

DATE		ITEM	POST. REF.	DEBIT	CREDIT	BALANCE DEBIT	BALANCE CREDIT
20-- Dec.	1	Balance	✔			17 0 0 0 00	

ACCOUNT Interest Receivable   ACCOUNT NO. 1175

DATE		ITEM	POST. REF.	DEBIT	CREDIT	BALANCE DEBIT	BALANCE CREDIT

15-M **MASTERY PROBLEM (continued)**

ACCOUNT Accumulated Depreciation—Office Equipment   ACCOUNT NO. 1210

DATE		ITEM	POST. REF.	DEBIT	CREDIT	BALANCE DEBIT	BALANCE CREDIT
20-- Dec.	1	Balance	✔				5 1 9 5 00

ACCOUNT Accumulated Depreciation—Store Equipment   ACCOUNT NO. 1220

DATE		ITEM	POST. REF.	DEBIT	CREDIT	BALANCE DEBIT	BALANCE CREDIT
20-- Dec.	1	Balance	✔				22 4 4 8 00

ACCOUNT Federal Income Tax Payable   ACCOUNT NO. 2170

DATE		ITEM	POST. REF.	DEBIT	CREDIT	BALANCE DEBIT	BALANCE CREDIT

ACCOUNT Income Summary   ACCOUNT NO. 3150

DATE		ITEM	POST. REF.	DEBIT	CREDIT	BALANCE DEBIT	BALANCE CREDIT

ACCOUNT Depreciation Expense—Office Equipment   ACCOUNT NO. 6120

DATE		ITEM	POST. REF.	DEBIT	CREDIT	BALANCE DEBIT	BALANCE CREDIT

ACCOUNT Depreciation Expense—Store Equipment   ACCOUNT NO. 6125

DATE		ITEM	POST. REF.	DEBIT	CREDIT	BALANCE DEBIT	BALANCE CREDIT

ACCOUNT Insurance Expense   ACCOUNT NO. 6130

DATE	ITEM	POST. REF.	DEBIT	CREDIT	BALANCE DEBIT	BALANCE CREDIT

ACCOUNT Supplies Expense—Office   ACCOUNT NO. 6155

DATE	ITEM	POST. REF.	DEBIT	CREDIT	BALANCE DEBIT	BALANCE CREDIT

ACCOUNT Supplies Expense—Store   ACCOUNT NO. 6160

DATE	ITEM	POST. REF.	DEBIT	CREDIT	BALANCE DEBIT	BALANCE CREDIT

ACCOUNT Uncollectible Accounts Expense   ACCOUNT NO. 6165

DATE	ITEM	POST. REF.	DEBIT	CREDIT	BALANCE DEBIT	BALANCE CREDIT

ACCOUNT Federal Income Tax Expense   ACCOUNT NO. 6205

DATE	ITEM	POST. REF.	DEBIT	CREDIT	BALANCE DEBIT	BALANCE CREDIT
20-- Dec. 1	Balance	✔			30 0 0 0 00	

ACCOUNT Interest Income   ACCOUNT NO. 7110

DATE	ITEM	POST. REF.	DEBIT	CREDIT	BALANCE DEBIT	BALANCE CREDIT
20-- Dec. 1	Balance	✔				2 1 4 00

15-M **MASTERY PROBLEM (concluded)**

4.

Total of income statement credit accounts .... $ _____

Less total of income statement debit accounts

　excluding federal income tax.. _____

Equals net income before federal income tax.......................... $ _____

Net Income before Federal Income Tax	−	Of the Amount Over	=	Net Income Subject to Marginal Tax Rate	×	Marginal Tax Rate	=	Marginal Income Tax
$	−	$	=	$	×		=	$

Bracket Minimum Income Tax	+	Marginal Income Tax	=	Federal Income Tax
$	+	$	=	$

Journalizing adjusting entries

1., 2., 3.

GENERAL JOURNAL

	DATE	ACCOUNT TITLE	DOC. NO.	POST. REF.	DEBIT	CREDIT	
1							1
2							2
3							3
4							4
5							5
6							6
7							7
8							8
9							9
10							10
11							11
12							12
13							13
14							14
15							15
16							16
17							17
18							18
19							19
20							20
21							21
22							22
23							23
24							24
25							25
26							26
27							27
28							28

Name	Perfect Score	Your Score
Identifying Accounting Terms	11 Pts.	
Preparing Financial Statements for a Merchandising Business Organized as a Corporation	12 Pts.	
Analyzing Financial Statements for a Merchandising Business	30 Pts.	
Total	53 Pts.	

Part One—Identifying Accounting Terms

Directions: Select the one term in Column I that best fits each definition in Column II. Print the letter identifying your choice in the Answers column.

Column I	Column II	Answers
A. current liabilities	**1.** The revenue earned by a business from its normal business operations. (p. 475)	**1.** _____
B. cost of merchandise sold	**2.** The amount of sales, less sales discounts and sales returns and allowances. (p. 475)	**2.** _____
C. gross profit	**3.** The original price of all merchandise sold during a fiscal period. (p. 476)	**3.** _____
D. income from operations	**4.** The revenue remaining after cost of merchandise sold has been deducted. (p. 476)	**4.** _____
E. long-term liabilities	**5.** The expenses incurred by a business in its normal operations. (p. 478)	**5.** _____
F. net sales	**6.** The operating revenue remaining after the cost of merchandise sold and operating expenses have been deducted. (p. 478)	**6.** _____
G. operating expenses	**7.** A financial statement that shows changes in a corporation's ownership for a fiscal period. (p. 482)	**7.** _____
H. operating revenue	**8.** A value assigned to a share of stock and printed on the stock certificate. (p. 483)	**8.** _____
I. par value	**9.** Liabilities due within a short time, usually within a year. (p. 489)	**9.** _____
J. statement of stockholders' equity	**10.** Liabilities owed for more than a year. (p. 489)	**10.** _____
K. supporting schedule	**11.** A report prepared to give details about an item on a principal financial statement. (p. 492)	**11.** _____

Part Two—Preparing Financial Statements for a Merchandising Business Organized as a Corporation

Directions: Write a number from 1 to 12 to the left of each step to indicate the correct sequence of all the steps in the accounting cycle. (p. 504)

Answers

1. _____ An adjusted trial balance is prepared from the general ledger.

2. _____ A post-closing trial balance is prepared from the general ledger.

3. _____ Journal entries are posted to the accounts payable ledger, the accounts receivable ledger, and the general ledger.

4. _____ Closing entries are journalized.

5. _____ An unadjusted trial balance is prepared from the general ledger.

6. _____ Source documents are checked for accuracy, and transactions are analyzed into debit and credit parts.

7. _____ Adjusting entries are journalized.

8. _____ Financial statements are prepared from the adjusted trial balance.

9. _____ Schedules of accounts payable and accounts receivable are prepared from the subsidiary ledgers.

10. _____ Closing entries are posted to the general ledger.

11. _____ Transactions, from information on source documents, are recorded in journals.

12. _____ Adjusting entries are posted to the general ledger.

Part Three—Analyzing Financial Statements for a Merchandising Business

Directions: Place a *T* for True or an *F* for False in the Answers column to show whether each of the following statements is true or false.

Answers

1. Financial statements provide the primary source of information needed by owners and managers to make decisions on the future activity of a business. (p. 472)   1. _____

2. Reporting financial information the same way from one fiscal period to the next is an application of the accounting concept Adequate Disclosure. (p. 472)   2. _____

3. An income statement for a merchandising business has four main sections: operating revenue, cost of merchandise sold, operating expenses, and other revenue. (p. 473)   3. _____

4. The amount of sales, less sales discounts, returns, and allowances is called gross profit. (p. 475)   4. _____

5. Cost of merchandise sold is also known as cost of goods sold. (p. 476)   5. _____

6. Operating revenue less cost of merchandise sold equals net income. (p. 476)   6. _____

7. Calculating a ratio between gross profit and net sales enables management to compare its performance to prior fiscal periods. (p. 476)   7. _____

8. To calculate vertical analysis percentages on an income statement, each amount is divided by net sales. (p. 477)   8. _____

9. Interest earned on notes receivable is reported in the Operating Expenses section of an income statement. (p. 478)   9. _____

10. Total operating expenses on an income statement are deducted from gross profit to determine income from operations. (p. 478)   10. _____

11. Federal income tax expense is an example of an operating expense. (pp. 478–479)   11. _____

12. All the information required to prepare a statement of stockholders' equity is obtained from the income statement and the adjusted trial balance. (p. 482)   12. _____

13. A statement of stockholders' equity contains two major sections: (1) Capital Stock and (2) Retained Earnings. (p. 483)   13. _____

14. The beginning balance of the capital stock account is the amount of capital stock issued as of the beginning of the year. (p. 483)   14. _____

15. The amounts in the capital stock section of the statement of stockholders' equity are obtained from the general ledger account, Capital Stock. (p. 483)   15. _____

16. Net income is shown on the last line of a statement of stockholders' equity. (p. 484)   16. _____

17. The amount of dividends reported on a statement of stockholders' equity is obtained from the adjusted trial balance. (p. 484)   17. _____

18. Data needed to prepare the liabilities section of a balance sheet are obtained from an adjusted trial balance. (p. 486)   18. _____

19. The difference between an asset's account balance and its related contra account balance is known as its book value. (p. 487)   19. _____

20. A mortgage payable is an example of a current liability. (p. 489)   20. _____

21. The amount of dividends paid during the year is presented on the balance sheet. (p. 490)   21. _____

22. The amounts reported on the balance sheet in the stockholders' equity section are obtained directly from general ledger accounts. (p. 490)   22. _____

23. The amount owed to a certain vendor would appear on a supporting schedule. (p. 492)   23. _____

24. Amounts needed for the closing entries are obtained from the adjusted trial balance and from the statement of stockholders' equity. (p. 494)

24. _____

25. The Income Summary account has a normal credit balance. (p. 494)

25. _____

26. A closing entry that results in credit to Income Summary would close sales, contra purchase, and other revenue accounts. (p. 495)

26. _____

27. Closing a contra revenue account results in a credit to Income Summary. (p. 496)

27. _____

28. A corporation with net income would post a closing entry that credits Retained Earnings. (p. 498)

28. _____

29. The Dividends account is closed by recording a debit to Retained Earnings. (p. 498)

29. _____

30. In the accounting cycle, adjusting entries are posted to the general ledger prior to the preparation of the financial statements. (p. 504)

30. _____

16-1 WORK TOGETHER, p. 481

Preparing an income statement for a merchandising business

Superior Corporation

Adjusted Trial Balance

December 31, 20--

ACCOUNT TITLE	DEBIT	CREDIT
Cash	43 3 5 5 47	
Petty Cash	2 0 0 00	
Accounts Receivable	16 3 0 5 45	
Allowance for Uncollectible Accounts		2 4 8 4 22
Merchandise Inventory	81 0 1 7 26	
Supplies—Office	7 7 7 65	
Supplies—Store	5 1 6 36	
Prepaid Insurance	2 8 0 0 00	
Notes Receivable	4 9 6 0 00	
Interest Receivable	9 5 00	
Office Equipment	19 9 1 6 14	
Accumulated Depreciation—Office Equipment		12 4 3 6 20
Store Equipment	47 3 1 8 49	
Accumulated Depreciation—Store Equipment		16 6 2 6 00
Accounts Payable		13 1 9 1 28
Sales Tax Payable		2 8 5 9 71
Employee Income Tax Payable		7 6 0 00
Social Security Tax Payable		1 6 1 8 45
Medicare Tax Payable		3 7 8 51
Health Insurance Premiums Payable		3 6 8 00
Retirement Benefits Payable		3 7 2 00
Unemployment Tax Payable—Federal		2 3 7 62
Unemployment Tax Payable—State		1 1 7 94
Federal Income Tax Payable		3 8 7 9 69
Dividends Payable		3 0 0 0 00
Capital Stock		82 5 0 0 00
Retained Earnings		15 2 8 3 40
Dividends	12 0 0 0 00	

(Note: Adjusted trial balance is continued on next page.)

Superior Corporation

Adjusted Trial Balance

December 31, 20--

ACCOUNT TITLE	DEBIT	CREDIT
Income Summary	5 7 7 1 89	
Sales		505 8 9 7 40
Sales Discount	1 3 1 8 55	
Sales Returns and Allowances	3 1 5 3 26	
Purchases	203 8 8 1 01	
Purchases Discount		7 3 7 71
Purchases Returns and Allowances		1 1 9 6 01
Advertising Expense	3 7 4 4 00	
Credit Card Fee Expense	5 4 7 3 76	
Depreciation Expense—Office Equipment	7 4 8 5 00	
Depreciation Expense—Store Equipment	9 8 3 0 00	
Insurance Expense	6 0 0 0 00	
Miscellaneous Expense	2 7 9 6 03	
Payroll Taxes Expense	14 3 7 5 91	
Rent Expense	6 7 2 0 00	
Salary Expense	131 9 7 8 76	
Supplies Expense—Office	2 8 6 0 89	
Supplies Expense—Store	3 5 2 3 33	
Uncollectible Accounts Expense	2 3 8 4 10	
Utilities Expense	3 9 7 2 34	
Federal Income Tax Expense	19 8 7 9 69	
Interest Income		4 6 6 20
Totals	664 4 1 0 34	664 4 1 0 34

16-1 WORK TOGETHER (concluded)

1., 2.

						% OF NET SALES

Preparing an income statement for a merchandising business

Eastern Imports

Adjusted Trial Balance

December 31, 20--

ACCOUNT TITLE	DEBIT	CREDIT
Cash	19 0 1 9 92	
Petty Cash	1 8 0 00	
Accounts Receivable	34 6 7 4 91	
Allowance for Uncollectible Accounts		2 6 5 0 00
Merchandise Inventory	122 4 6 1 80	
Supplies—Office	7 8 0 00	
Supplies—Store	1 3 2 3 00	
Prepaid Insurance	2 6 0 0 00	
Notes Receivable	4 4 6 4 00	
Interest Receivable	8 2 00	
Office Equipment	17 9 2 4 53	
Accumulated Depreciation—Office Equipment		11 9 4 1 08
Store Equipment	42 5 8 6 64	
Accumulated Depreciation—Store Equipment		15 9 4 6 40
Accounts Payable		14 8 7 2 15
Sales Tax Payable		2 5 7 3 74
Employee Income Tax Payable		6 8 4 00
Social Security Tax Payable		1 4 5 6 61
Medicare Tax Payable		3 4 0 66
Health Insurance Premiums Payable		3 3 1 20
Retirement Benefits Payable		3 3 4 80
Unemployment Tax Payable—Federal		2 1 3 86
Unemployment Tax Payable—State		1 0 6 15
Federal Income Tax Payable		1 6 1 7 90
Dividends Payable		2 7 0 0 00
Capital Stock		136 0 0 0 00
Retained Earnings		29 4 7 4 56
Dividends	24 0 0 0 00	

(Note: Adjusted trial balance is continued on next page.)

16-1 ON YOUR OWN (continued)

Eastern Imports

Adjusted Trial Balance

December 31, 20--

ACCOUNT TITLE	DEBIT	CREDIT
Income Summary	5 6 4 8 44	
Sales		432 4 3 2 64
Sales Discount	1 1 8 6 70	
Sales Returns and Allowances	2 8 3 7 93	
Purchases	193 4 9 2 91	
Purchases Discount		6 6 3 94
Purchases Returns and Allowances		1 0 7 6 41
Advertising Expense	3 3 6 9 60	
Credit Card Fee Expense	4 9 2 6 38	
Depreciation Expense—Office Equipment	8 4 8 5 00	
Depreciation Expense—Store Equipment	8 8 3 0 00	
Insurance Expense	5 1 2 0 00	
Miscellaneous Expense	2 5 1 6 43	
Payroll Taxes Expense	12 9 3 8 32	
Rent Expense	6 0 4 8 00	
Salary Expense	109 4 8 5 25	
Supplies Expense—Office	2 4 9 4 69	
Supplies Expense—Store	2 5 1 2 72	
Uncollectible Accounts Expense	2 6 5 0 00	
Utilities Expense	3 5 7 5 11	
Federal Income Tax Expense	9 6 1 7 90	
Interest Income		4 1 6 08
Totals	655 8 3 2 18	655 8 3 2 18

1., 2.

					% OF NET SALES

16-2 **WORK TOGETHER, p. 485**

Preparing a statement of stockholders' equity

Preparing a statement of stockholders' equity

16-3 WORK TOGETHER, p. 493

Preparing a balance sheet for a corporation

Preparing a balance sheet for a corporation

16-4 WORK TOGETHER, p. 501

Journalizing closing entries

GENERAL JOURNAL

PAGE ____

	DATE		ACCOUNT TITLE	DOC. NO.	POST. REF.	DEBIT	CREDIT	
1								1
2								2
3								3
4								4
5								5
6								6
7								7
8								8
9								9
10								10
11								11
12								12
13								13
14								14
15								15
16								16
17								17
18								18
19								19
20								20
21								21
22								22
23								23
24								24
25								25
26								26
27								27
28								28
29								29
30								30
31								31

Journalizing closing entries

GENERAL JOURNAL

PAGE

	DATE	ACCOUNT TITLE	DOC. NO.	POST. REF.	DEBIT	CREDIT	
1							1
2							2
3							3
4							4
5							5
6							6
7							7
8							8
9							9
10							10
11							11
12							12
13							13
14							14
15							15
16							16
17							17
18							18
19							19
20							20
21							21
22							22
23							23
24							24
25							25
26							26
27							27
28							28
29							29
30							30
31							31

Name _____ Date _____ Class _____

Preparing a post-closing trial balance

ACCOUNT TITLE	DEBIT	CREDIT

Preparing a post-closing trial balance

ACCOUNT TITLE	DEBIT	CREDIT

16-1 APPLICATION PROBLEM (LO1), p. 509

Preparing an income statement for a merchandising business

Top-Light Corporation

Adjusted Trial Balance

December 31, 20--

ACCOUNT TITLE	DEBIT	CREDIT
Cash	14 024 81	
Petty Cash	3 000 00	
Accounts Receivable	16 957 67	
Allowance for Uncollectible Accounts		2 107 00
Merchandise Inventory	88 142 54	
Supplies—Office	3 900 00	
Supplies—Store	7 500 00	
Prepaid Insurance	2 000 00	
Notes Receivable	6 110 00	
Interest Receivable	48 88	
Office Equipment	23 814 00	
Accumulated Depreciation—Office Equipment		18 609 25
Store Equipment	51 948 65	
Accumulated Depreciation—Store Equipment		23 507 84
Accounts Payable		13 718 93
Sales Tax Payable		2 574 10
Employee Income Tax Payable		790 00
Social Security Tax Payable		1 683 19
Medicare Tax Payable		393 65
Health Insurance Premiums Payable		380 00
Retirement Benefits Payable		420 00
Unemployment Tax Payable—Federal		247 13
Unemployment Tax Payable—State		122 66
Federal Income Tax Payable		907 37
Dividends Payable		4 600 00
Capital Stock		57 500 00
Retained Earnings		50 403 31

(Note: Adjusted trial balance is continued on next page.)

Top-Light Corporation

Adjusted Trial Balance

December 31, 20--

ACCOUNT TITLE	DEBIT	CREDIT
Dividends	17 2 0 0 00	
Income Summary	2 1 1 8 18	
Sales		557 9 0 0 50
Sales Discount	1 3 7 1 30	
Sales Returns and Allowances	3 2 7 9 39	
Purchases	260 0 3 6 25	
Purchases Discount		2 2 1 8 16
Purchases Returns and Allowances		3 1 1 9 45
Advertising Expense	18 4 1 1 32	
Credit Card Fee Expense	5 6 9 2 71	
Depreciation Expense—Office Equipment	5 4 6 0 00	
Depreciation Expense—Store Equipment	8 4 4 0 00	
Insurance Expense	12 0 0 0 00	
Miscellaneous Expense	4 1 5 9 31	
Payroll Taxes Expense	14 0 1 9 64	
Rent Expense	8 4 0 0 00	
Salary Expense	155 7 7 3 80	
Supplies Expense—Office	2 4 8 1 72	
Supplies Expense—Store	3 6 4 5 81	
Uncollectible Accounts Expense	1 4 9 4 12	
Utilities Expense	4 9 9 5 14	
Federal Income Tax Expense	7 9 0 7 37	
Interest Income		1 7 0 07
Totals	741 3 7 2 61	741 3 7 2 61

16-1 APPLICATION PROBLEM (concluded)

1., 2.

							% OF NET SALES

16-2 APPLICATION PROBLEM (LO2), p. 509

Preparing a statement of stockholders' equity

16-3 APPLICATION PROBLEM (LO3), p. 509

Preparing a balance sheet for a corporation

APPLICATION PROBLEM (LO4), p. 510

Journalizing closing entries

GENERAL JOURNAL   PAGE

	DATE	ACCOUNT TITLE	DOC. NO.	POST. REF.	DEBIT	CREDIT	
1							1
2							2
3							3
4							4
5							5
6							6
7							7
8							8
9							9
10							10
11							11
12							12
13							13
14							14
15							15
16							16
17							17
18							18
19							19
20							20
21							21
22							22
23							23
24							24
25							25
26							26
27							27
28							28
29							29
30							30
31							31

16-5 APPLICATION PROBLEM (LO5), p. 510

Preparing a post-closing trial balance

ACCOUNT TITLE	DEBIT	CREDIT

Preparing financial statements and closing entries

Paulson Corporation

Adjusted Trial Balance

December 31, 20--

ACCOUNT TITLE	DEBIT	CREDIT
Cash	28 3 6 2 11	
Petty Cash	2 0 0 00	
Accounts Receivable	21 1 9 7 09	
Allowance for Uncollectible Accounts		2 5 1 4 26
Merchandise Inventory	107 1 7 7 46	
Supplies—Office	1 7 4 5 76	
Supplies—Store	1 7 2 8 27	
Prepaid Insurance	2 8 0 0 00	
Notes Receivable	8 9 0 0 00	
Interest Receivable	7 1 20	
Office Equipment	25 8 9 0 98	
Accumulated Depreciation—Office Equipment		23 9 2 1 56
Store Equipment	61 5 1 4 04	
Accumulated Depreciation—Store Equipment		28 6 6 4 80
Accounts Payable		17 1 4 8 66
Sales Tax Payable		3 2 1 7 62
Employee Income Tax Payable		9 8 8 00
Social Security Tax Payable		2 1 0 3 99
Medicare Tax Payable		4 9 2 06
Health Insurance Premiums Payable		4 7 8 40
Retirement Benefits Payable		4 8 3 60
Unemployment Tax Payable—Federal		3 0 8 91
Unemployment Tax Payable—State		1 5 3 32
Federal Income Tax Payable		1 5 1 9 82
Dividends Payable		5 0 0 0 00
Capital Stock		50 0 0 0 00
Retained Earnings		66 2 5 9 31

(Note: Adjusted trial balance is continued on next page.)

16-M MASTERY PROBLEM (continued)

Paulson Corporation

Adjusted Trial Balance

December 31, 20--

ACCOUNT TITLE	DEBIT	CREDIT
Dividends	20 0 0 0 00	
Income Summary	5 6 4 8 44	
Sales		697 3 7 5 62
Sales Discount	1 7 1 4 12	
Sales Returns and Allowances	4 0 9 9 24	
Purchases	325 0 4 5 31	
Purchases Discount		1 9 5 9 02
Purchases Returns and Allowances		2 5 5 4 81
Advertising Expense	4 8 6 7 20	
Credit Card Fee Expense	7 1 1 5 89	
Depreciation Expense—Office Equipment	7 8 8 5 00	
Depreciation Expense—Store Equipment	9 4 3 0 00	
Insurance Expense	8 6 4 0 00	
Miscellaneous Expense	3 6 3 4 84	
Payroll Taxes Expense	18 6 8 8 68	
Rent Expense	8 7 3 6 00	
Salary Expense	184 7 7 0 26	
Supplies Expense—Office	2 9 8 4 34	
Supplies Expense—Store	3 5 2 3 33	
Uncollectible Accounts Expense	2 3 8 4 10	
Utilities Expense	5 1 6 4 04	
Federal Income Tax Expense	21 5 1 9 82	
Interest Income		2 9 3 76
Totals	905 4 3 7 52	905 4 3 7 52

1., 2.

																	% OF NET SALES

16-M MASTERY PROBLEM (continued)

3.

4.

16-M **MASTERY PROBLEM (concluded)**

5.

GENERAL JOURNAL

PAGE _____

	DATE		ACCOUNT TITLE	DOC. NO.	POST. REF.	DEBIT	CREDIT	
1								1
2								2
3								3
4								4
5								5
6								6
7								7
8								8
9								9
10								10
11								11
12								12
13								13
14								14
15								15
16								16
17								17
18								18
19								19
20								20
21								21
22								22
23								23
24								24
25								25
26								26
27								27
28								28
29								29
30								30
31								31

Preparing an income statement

KLT Corporation

Adjusted Trial Balance

December 31, 20--

ACCOUNT TITLE	DEBIT	CREDIT
Cash	54 1 9 4 34	
Accounts Receivable	20 3 8 1 81	
Allowance for Uncollectible Accounts		2 5 0 9 25
Merchandise Inventory	64 3 2 2 59	
Income Summary	2 6 4 2 37	
Domestic Sales		252 4 6 6 34
International Sales		325 4 3 6 34
Internet Sales		264 2 4 5 22
Sales Discount	5 2 1 4 32	
Sales Returns and Allowances	6 5 2 3 23	
Purchases	364 3 2 4 25	
Purchases Discount		6 5 4 2 16
Purchases Returns and Allowances		3 8 7 9 85
Advertising Expense	32 4 0 0 00	
Credit Card Fee Expense	7 5 3 4 23	
Depreciation Expense—Office Equipment	6 9 0 0 00	
Depreciation Expense—Store Equipment	12 5 0 0 00	
Insurance Expense	13 0 0 0 00	
Miscellaneous Expense	19 3 2 7 34	
Payroll Taxes Expense	36 2 3 0 85	
Rent Expense	24 0 0 0 00	
Salary Expense	262 5 4 2 36	
Supplies Expense	6 2 6 2 95	
Uncollectible Accounts Expense	5 3 9 0 65	
Utilities Expense	4 1 6 8 96	
Federal Income Tax Expense	6 5 6 0 99	
Interest Expense	4 3 3 96	
Interest Income		5 6 5 50
Totals	987 2 5 3 61	987 2 5 3 61

16-C CHALLENGE PROBLEM (concluded)

1., 2.

						% OF NET SALES

Name		Perfect Score	Your Score
	Identifying Accounting Terms	20 Pts.	
	Analyzing Financial Ratios	19 Pts.	
	Calculating Financial Ratios	11 Pts.	
	Total	50 Pts.	

Part One—Identifying Accounting Terms

Directions: Select the one term in Column I that best fits each definition in Column II. Print the letter identifying your choice in the Answers column.

Column I	Column II	Answers
A. benchmark	**1.** A ratio that measures the ability of a business to generate income. (p. 516)	**1.** _____
B. comparative financial statements	**2.** A standard used to evaluate financial performance. (p. 516)	**2.** _____
C. current ratio	**3.** Financial statements that provide information for multiple fiscal periods. (p. 517)	**3.** _____
D. debt ratio	**4.** An analysis of changes over time. (p. 517)	**4.** _____
E. dividend yield	**5.** Net income after federal income tax as a percent of net sales. (p. 517)	**5.** _____
F. earnings per share	**6.** Gross profit as a percent of net sales. (p. 518)	**6.** _____
G. gross margin	**7.** Income from operations as a percent of net sales. (p. 519)	**7.** _____
H. horizontal analysis	**8.** Total operating expenses as a percent of net sales. (p. 519)	**8.** _____
I. liquidity ratio	**9.** A ratio that measures the ability of a business to pay its long-term liabilities. (p. 526)	**9.** _____
J. market ratio	**10.** Total Liabilities divided by Total Assets. (p. 526)	**10.** _____
K. operating expense ratio	**11.** A comparison of one item on a financial statement with the same item on a previous period's financial statement. (p. 528)	**11.** _____
L. operating margin	**12.** Net income after federal income tax divided by the number of outstanding shares of stock. (p. 533)	**12.** _____
M. price-earnings ratio	**13.** A ratio that measures a corporation's financial performance in relation to the market value of its stock. (p. 534)	**13.** _____
N. profit margin	**14.** The relationship between dividends per share and market price per share. (p. 534)	**14.** _____
O. profitability ratio	**15.** The relationship between the market value per share and earnings per share of a stock. (p. 534)	**15.** _____
P. quick assets	**16.** A ratio that measures the ability of a business to pay its current financial obligations. (p. 535)	**16.** _____
Q. quick ratio	**17.** The amount of total current assets less total current liabilities. (p. 535)	**17.** _____
R. solvency ratio	**18.** A ratio that measures the relationship of current assets to current liabilities. (p. 535)	**18.** _____
S. trend analysis	**19.** Cash and other current assets that can be quickly converted into cash. (p. 535)	**19.** _____
T. working capital	**20.** A ratio that measures the relationship of quick assets to current liabilities. (p. 535)	**20.** _____

Part Two—Analyzing Financial Ratios

Directions: Place a *T* for True or an *F* for False in the Answers column to show whether each of the following statements is true or false.

Answers

1. Vertical analysis ratios are an example of a profitability ratio. (p. 516)

   1. _____

2. A benchmark ratio can be stated as a single value or a target range. (p. 516)

   2. _____

3. To perform vertical analysis on an income statement, each amount is divided by net sales. (p. 516)

   3. _____

4. An increase in merchandise costs reduces the gross margin. (p. 518)

   4. _____

5. Gross profit is also referred to as the rate of return on sales. (p. 518)

   5. _____

6. The operating margin gives investors the best indication of how effectively a business is earning a profit from its normal business operations. (p. 519)

   6. _____

7. Best Company's benchmark operating expense ratio is between 29.0% and 31.0%. A decline in its operating expense ratio from 34.5% to 33.6% is a favorable trend. (p. 519)

   7. _____

8. Reducing the amount of operating expenses always has a positive impact on a business. (p. 520)

   8. _____

9. A business should never make a business decision for the sole purpose of meeting a benchmark ratio. (p. 524)

   9. _____

10. A vertical analysis ratio for accounts receivable above the target range may indicate that ThreeGreen is too restrictive in extending credit to its customers. (p. 524)

    10. _____

11. Investors use the debt ratio to rate the ability of the business to pay its current and long-term liabilities. (p. 526)

    11. _____

12. The debt ratio is an example of a solvency ratio. (p. 526)

    12. _____

13. Best Company's target range for its debt ratio is 20.0% to 25.0%. The company's debt ratio decreased from 34.5% to 26.7%. This is an unfavorable trend. (p. 526)

    13. _____

14. A horizontal analysis ratio is calculated by dividing the difference between the current and prior period amounts by the current period amount. (p. 528)

    14. _____

15. EPS is the most widely recognized measure of a corporation's financial performance. (p. 533)

    15. _____

16. A corporation's earnings per share can only be compared to the earnings per share of other corporations in the same industry. (p. 533)

    16. _____

17. The dividend yield is an example of a market ratio. (p. 534)

    17. _____

18. Investors are willing to pay a higher P/E ratio for income stocks than for growth stocks. (p. 534)

    18. _____

19. The income statement is the primary source of data to calculate liquidity ratios. (p. 535)

    19. _____

Part Three—Calculating Financial Ratios

Directions: For each of the following items, select the choice that best completes the statement. Print the letter identifying your choice in the Answers column.

Selected financial information for Lambert Company is presented below.

Sales	$840,000.00
Cost of Merchandise Sold	$400,000.00
Total Operating Expenses	$360,000.00
Net Income after Federal Income Taxes	$68,000.00
Quick Assets	$38,000.00
Current Assets	$95,000.00
Total Assets	$175,000.00
Total Liabilities (all current)	$25,000.00
Dividends per Share	$3.00
Market Price	$60.00
Number of Shares Outstanding	10,000

Answers

1. The earnings per share is
   (A) $3.00   (C) $6.80
   (B) $14.70   (D) 8.1%   (p. 533)

   1. _____

2. The debt ratio is
   (A) 26.3%   (C) 7.00
   (B) 14.3%   (D) 17.0%   (p. 526)

   2. _____

3. The current ratio is
   (A) $70,000.00   (C) 54.3%
   (B) 0.74   (D) 3.80   (p. 535)

   3. _____

4. The dividend yield is
   (A) 5.00%   (C) 20.00%
   (B) 0.03%   (D) 10.00%   (p. 534)

   4. _____

5. The gross margin is
   (A) 42.9%   (C) 52.4%
   (B) 9.5%   (D) 54.3%   (p. 518)

   5. _____

6. The price-earnings ratio is
   (A) 8.8   (C) 5.0%
   (B) 17.6   (D) 11.3%   (p. 534)

   6. _____

7. The operating margin is
   (A) 19.0%   (C) 54.3%
   (B) 42.9%   (D) 9.5%   (p. 519)

   7. _____

8. The working capital is
   (A) $95,000.00   (C) $120,000.00
   (B) $70,000.00   (D) 26.3%   (p. 535)

   8. _____

9. The operating expense ratio is
   (A) 54.3%   (C) 42.9%
   (B) 47.6%   (D) 9.5%   (p. 519)

   9. _____

10. The gross profit margin is
    (A) 52.4%   (C) 47.6%
    (B) 54.3%   (D) 42.9%   (p. 518)

    10. _____

11. The quick ratio is
    (A) 0.4   (C) 0.2
    (B) 1.5   (D) 2.5   (p. 535)

    11. _____

Across

3. A standard used to evaluate financial performance.

7. Total liabilities divided by total assets.

8. A ratio that measures a corporation's financial performance in relation to the market value of its stock.

10. Gross profit as a percent of net sales.

12. The amount of total current assets less total current liabilities.

13. The movement of funds from one qualified retirement plan to another.

14. Cash and other current assets that can be quickly converted into cash.

15. Net income after federal income tax as a percent of net sales.

16. A ratio that measures the ability of a business to generate income.

17. A ratio that measures the ability of a business to pay its current financial obligations.

Down

1. Net income after federal income tax divided by the number of outstanding shares of stock.

2. The relationship between dividends per share and market price per share.

4. A ratio that measures the relationship of current assets to current liabilities.

5. The amount of dividends divided by net income.

6. An analysis of changes over time.

9. A ratio that measures the relationship of quick assets to current liabilities.

11. A ratio that measures the ability of a business to pay its long-term liabilities.

17-1 WORK TOGETHER, p. 521

Analyzing an income statement

1.

Tri-State Pipe

Comparative Income Statement

For Years Ended December 31, 20-- and 20--

	Current Year		Prior Year	
	Amount	Percent	Amount	Percent
Net Sales	659 4 7 0 53	100.0	642 1 8 9 81	100.0
Cost of Merchandise Sold	321 0 3 4 21		301 8 4 3 28	
Gross Profit	338 4 3 6 32		340 3 4 6 53	
Operating Expenses:				
Advertising Expense	24 9 8 1 05	3.8	23 1 4 9 84	3.6
Credit Card Fee Expense	6 9 7 7 95	1.1	6 8 1 9 25	1.1
Depreciation Expense—Office Equipment	7 8 5 0 00	1.2	7 6 5 0 00	1.2
Depreciation Expense—Store Equipment	6 4 9 0 00	1.0	6 0 8 0 00	0.9
Insurance Expense	8 4 0 0 00	1.3	8 2 0 0 00	1.3
Miscellaneous Expense	3 8 2 6 79	0.6	4 1 9 4 19	0.7
Payroll Taxes Expense	8 2 9 8 94	1.3	8 5 6 8 54	1.3
Rent Expense	8 4 4 7 55	1.3	8 4 0 0 00	1.3
Salary Expense	92 1 9 4 99		95 1 9 0 11	
Supplies Expense—Office	3 9 4 9 22	0.6	4 1 0 9 28	0.6
Supplies Expense—Store	4 9 8 9 92	0.8	4 2 1 9 10	0.7
Uncollectible Accounts Expense	16 4 8 7 08	2.5	12 1 9 7 16	1.9
Utilities Expense	5 2 6 9 69	0.8	4 9 1 0 82	0.8
Total Operating Expenses	198 1 6 3 18		193 6 8 8 29	
Income from Operations	140 2 7 3 14		146 6 5 8 24	
Other Revenue	5 9 8 78	0.1	4 4 9 14	0.1
Net Income before Federal Income Tax	140 8 7 1 92	21.4	147 1 0 7 38	22.9
Less Federal Income Tax Expense	38 1 9 0 05	5.8	40 6 2 1 88	6.3
Net Income after Federal Income Tax	102 6 8 1 87	15.6	106 4 8 5 50	16.6

2.

Ratio	Target Range		Actual Ratio		Favorable Trend	Favorable Result
	Low	High	Current Year	Prior Year		
Gross margin	50.4%	52.0%				
Operating expenses	27.0%	29.0%				
Operating margin	21.4%	25.0%				

Analyzing an income statement

1.

PBH Corporation

Comparative Income Statement

For Years Ended December 31, 20-- and 20--

	Current Year		Prior Year	
	Amount	Percent	Amount	Percent
Net Sales	747 923 57	100.0	694 841 18	100.0
Cost of Merchandise Sold	339 418 69		318 189 99	
Gross Profit	408 504 88		376 651 19	
Operating Expenses:				
Advertising Expense	9 655 70	1.3	11 084 92	1.6
Credit Card Fee Expense	7 467 60	1.0	5 914 81	0.9
Depreciation Expense—Office Equipment	4 550 00	0.6	4 250 00	0.6
Depreciation Expense—Store Equipment	6 830 00	0.9	6 710 00	1.0
Insurance Expense	13 126 68	1.8	13 014 92	1.9
Miscellaneous Expense	4 192 71	0.6	5 148 61	0.7
Payroll Taxes Expense	9 627 46	1.3	8 765 28	1.3
Rent Expense	8 447 55	1.1	7 848 00	1.1
Salary Expense	106 953 84		97 375 74	
Supplies Expense—Office	4 396 25	0.6	4 184 19	0.6
Supplies Expense—Store	5 353 08	0.7	5 019 71	0.7
Uncollectible Accounts Expense	8 042 78	1.1	7 319 36	1.1
Utilities Expense	9 823 69	1.3	9 220 08	1.3
Total Operating Expenses	198 467 34		185 855 62	
Income from Operations	210 037 54		190 795 57	
Other Revenue	475 33	0.1	662 08	0.1
Net Income before Federal Income Tax	210 512 87	28.1	191 457 65	27.6
Less Federal Income Tax Expense	65 350 02	8.7	57 918 48	8.3
Net Income after Federal Income Tax	145 162 85	19.4	133 539 17	19.2

2.

Ratio	Target Range		Actual Ratio		Favorable Trend	Favorable Result
	Low	High	Current Year	Prior Year		
Gross margin	54.2%	54.9%				
Operating expenses	25.0%	26.0%				
Operating margin	28.2%	29.9%				

17-2 WORK TOGETHER, p. 527

Analyzing a balance sheet

1.

Tri-State Pipe

Comparative Balance Sheet

December 31, 20-- and 20--

	Current Year Amount	Current Year Percent	Prior Year Amount	Prior Year Percent
ASSETS				
Current Assets:				
Cash	27 4 1 3 71	12.7	25 2 3 8 46	14.0
Petty Cash	2 5 0 0 00	0.1	2 0 0 0 00	0.1
Accounts Receivable (net)	18 5 4 3 50		16 1 9 8 38	
Merchandise Inventory	105 1 1 1 94		99 1 9 4 10	
Supplies—Office	6 2 3 58	0.3	6 9 5 18	0.4
Supplies—Store	4 8 7 52	0.2	4 4 7 15	0.2
Prepaid Insurance	2 8 0 0 00	1.3	1 2 0 0 00	0.7
Notes Receivable	6 3 5 5 00	2.9	2 4 0 0 00	1.3
Interest Receivable	9 5 65	0.0	6 2 50	0.0
Total Current Assets	161 6 8 0 90		145 6 3 5 77	
Plant Assets:				
Office Equipment (net)	11 9 7 8 55	5.5	12 9 1 8 64	7.2
Store Equipment (net)	42 4 1 0 83	19.6	21 9 4 8 39	12.2
Total Plant Assets	54 3 8 9 38		34 8 6 7 03	
Total Assets	216 0 7 0 28	100.0	180 5 0 2 80	100.0
LIABILITIES				
Current Liabilities:				
Accounts Payable	16 6 3 3 44	7.7	11 8 8 9 95	6.6
Sales Tax Payable	3 5 8 9 68	1.7	3 2 8 1 18	1.8
Employee Income Tax Payable	9 8 8 00	0.5	9 2 6 00	0.5
Social Security Tax Payable	2 0 7 1 04	1.0	1 9 4 6 78	1.1
Medicare Tax Payable	4 8 4 36	0.2	4 5 5 30	0.3
Health Insurance Premiums Payable	4 6 3 00	0.2	4 3 5 00	0.2
Retirement Benefits Payable	4 6 5 00	0.2	4 3 7 00	0.2
Unemployment Tax Payable—Federal	3 0 4 06	0.1	2 8 5 82	0.2
Unemployment Tax Payable—State	1 5 0 92	0.1	1 4 1 86	0.1
Federal Income Tax Payable	3 6 8 3 00	1.7	6 1 4 8 00	3.4
Dividends Payable	20 0 0 0 00	9.3	10 0 0 0 00	5.5
Total Liabilities	48 8 3 2 50		35 9 4 6 89	
STOCKHOLDERS' EQUITY				
Capital Stock	25 0 0 0 00	11.6	25 0 0 0 00	13.9
Retained Earnings	142 2 3 7 78	65.8	119 5 5 5 91	66.2
Total Stockholders' Equity	167 2 3 7 78		144 5 5 5 91	
Total Liabilities and Stockholders' Equity	216 0 7 0 28	100.0	180 5 0 2 80	100.0

2.

	Target Range		Actual Ratio		Favorable Trend	Favorable Result
	Low	High	Current Year	Prior Year		
Accounts receivable	12.0%	14.0%				
Merchandise inventory	50.0%	55.0%				
Total current assets	73.0%	76.0%				
Total plant assets	24.0%	27.0%				
Total liabilities	20.0%	25.0%				
Total stockholders' equity	75.0%	80.0%				

17-2 ON YOUR OWN, p. 527

Analyzing a balance sheet

1.

PBH Corporation

Comparative Balance Sheet

December 31, 20-- and 20--

	Current Year Amount	Current Year Percent	Prior Year Amount	Prior Year Percent
ASSETS				
Current Assets:				
Cash	42 250 56	12.6	22 965 32	9.2
Petty Cash	500 00	0.1	500 00	0.2
Accounts Receivable (net)	24 918 33		22 918 35	
Merchandise Inventory	142 894 19		109 718 25	
Supplies—Office	624 00	0.2	258 00	0.1
Supplies—Store	995 00	0.3	1 095 00	0.4
Prepaid Insurance	3 400 00	1.0	3 200 00	1.3
Notes Receivable	10 950 00	3.3	6 498 00	2.6
Interest Receivable	109 50	0.0	88 25	0.0
Total Current Assets	226 641 58		167 241 17	
Plant Assets:				
Office Equipment (net)	44 918 10	13.4	36 991 18	14.8
Store Equipment (net)	62 988 14	18.8	45 194 99	18.1
Total Plant Assets	107 906 24		82 186 17	
Total Assets	334 547 82	100.0	249 427 34	100.0
LIABILITIES				
Current Liabilities:				
Accounts Payable	14 379 90	4.3	36 198 74	14.5
Sales Tax Payable	6 562 36	2.0	6 129 19	2.5
Employee Income Tax Payable	1 852 00	0.6	1 703 00	0.7
Social Security Tax Payable	3 893 56	1.2	3 582 07	1.4
Medicare Tax Payable	910 60	0.3	837 75	0.3
Health Insurance Premiums Payable	870 00	0.3	800 40	0.3
Retirement Benefits Payable	874 00	0.3	804 08	0.3
Unemployment Tax Payable—Federal	571 64	0.2	525 90	0.2
Unemployment Tax Payable—State	283 72	0.1	261 02	0.1
Federal Income Tax Payable	296 00	0.1	8 194 00	3.3
Dividends Payable	8 000 00	2.4	7 500 00	3.0
Total Liabilities	38 493 78		66 536 15	
STOCKHOLDERS' EQUITY				
Capital Stock	150 000 00	44.8	150 000 00	60.1
Retained Earnings	146 054 04	43.7	32 891 19	13.2
Total Stockholders' Equity	296 054 04		182 891 19	
Total Liabilities and Stockholders' Equity	334 547 82	100.0	249 427 34	100.0

2.

	Target Range		Actual Ratio		Favorable Trend	Favorable Result
	Low	High	Current Year	Prior Year		
Accounts receivable	12.0%	14.0%				
Merchandise inventory	40.0%	45.0%				
Total current assets	60.0%	68.0%				
Total plant assets	32.0%	40.0%				
Total liabilities	25.0%	30.0%				
Total stockholders' equity	70.0%	75.0%				

17-3 WORK TOGETHER, p. 532

Analyzing financial statements using horizontal analysis

1.

Tri-State Pipe

Comparative Income Statement

For Years Ended December 31, 20-- and 20--

	Current Year	Prior Year	Increase (Decrease) Amount	Percent
Net Sales	659 4 7 0 53	642 1 8 9 81		
Cost of Merchandise Sold	321 0 3 4 21	301 8 4 3 28		
Gross Profit	338 4 3 6 32	340 3 4 6 53		
Operating Expenses:				
Advertising Expense	24 9 8 1 05	23 1 4 9 84		
Credit Card Fee Expense	6 9 7 7 95	6 8 1 9 25	1 5 8 70	2.3
Depreciation Expense—Office Equipment	7 8 5 0 00	7 6 5 0 00	2 0 0 00	2.6
Depreciation Expense—Store Equipment	6 4 9 0 00	6 0 8 0 00	4 1 0 00	6.7
Insurance Expense	8 4 0 0 00	8 2 0 0 00	2 0 0 00	2.4
Miscellaneous Expense	3 8 2 6 79	4 1 9 4 19	(3 6 7 40)	(8.8)
Payroll Taxes Expense	8 2 9 8 94	8 5 6 8 54	(2 6 9 60)	(3.1)
Rent Expense	8 4 4 7 55	8 4 0 0 00	4 7 55	0.6
Salary Expense	92 1 9 4 99	95 1 9 0 11		
Supplies Expense—Office	3 9 4 9 22	4 1 0 9 28	(1 6 0 06)	(3.9)
Supplies Expense—Store	4 9 8 9 92	4 2 1 9 10	7 7 0 82	18.3
Uncollectible Accounts Expense	16 4 8 7 08	12 1 9 7 16		
Utilities Expense	5 2 6 9 69	4 9 1 0 82	3 5 8 87	7.3
Total Operating Expenses	198 1 6 3 18	193 6 8 8 29	4 4 7 4 89	2.3
Income from Operations	140 2 7 3 14	146 6 5 8 24		
Other Revenue	5 9 8 78	4 4 9 14	1 4 9 64	33.3
Net Income before Federal Income Tax	140 8 7 1 92	147 1 0 7 38	(6 2 3 5 46)	(4.2)
Less Federal Income Tax Expense	38 1 9 0 05	40 6 2 1 88	(2 4 3 1 83)	(6.0)
Net Income after Federal Income Tax	102 6 8 1 87	106 4 8 5 50	(3 8 0 3 63)	(3.6)

Analyzing financial statements using horizontal analysis

1.

PBH Corporation

Comparative Balance Sheet

December 31, 20-- and 20--

	Current Year	Prior Year	Increase (Decrease) Amount	Percent
ASSETS				
Current Assets:				
Cash	27 4 1 3 71	25 2 3 8 46	2 1 7 5 25	8.6
Petty Cash	2 5 0 00	2 0 0 00	5 0 00	25.0
Accounts Receivable (net)	18 5 4 3 50	16 1 9 8 38		
Merchandise Inventory	105 1 1 1 94	99 1 9 4 10		
Supplies—Office	6 2 3 58	6 9 5 18	(7 1 60)	(10.3)
Supplies—Store	4 8 7 52	4 4 7 15	4 0 37	9.0
Prepaid Insurance	2 8 0 0 00	1 2 0 0 00	1 6 0 0 00	133.3
Notes Receivable	6 3 5 5 00	2 4 0 0 00	3 9 5 5 00	164.8
Interest Receivable	9 5 65	6 2 50	3 3 15	53.0
Total Current Assets	161 6 8 0 90	145 6 3 5 77		
Plant Assets:				
Office Equipment (net)	11 9 7 8 55	12 9 1 8 64	(9 4 0 09)	(7.3)
Store Equipment (net)	42 4 1 0 83	21 9 4 8 39	20 4 6 2 44	93.2
Total Plant Assets	54 3 8 9 38	34 8 6 7 03		
Total Assets	216 0 7 0 28	180 5 0 2 80	35 5 6 7 48	19.7
LIABILITIES				
Current Liabilities:				
Accounts Payable	16 6 3 3 44	11 8 8 9 95	4 7 4 3 49	39.9
Sales Tax Payable	3 5 8 9 68	3 2 8 1 18	3 0 8 50	9.4
Employee Income Tax Payable	9 8 8 00	9 2 6 00	6 2 00	6.7
Social Security Tax Payable	2 0 7 1 04	1 9 4 6 78	1 2 4 26	6.4
Medicare Tax Payable	4 8 4 36	4 5 5 30	2 9 06	6.4
Health Insurance Premiums Payable	4 6 3 00	4 3 5 00	2 8 00	6.4
Retirement Benefits Payable	4 6 5 00	4 3 7 00	2 8 00	6.4
Unemployment Tax Payable—Federal	3 0 4 06	2 8 5 82	1 8 24	6.4
Unemployment Tax Payable—State	1 5 0 92	1 4 1 86	9 06	6.4
Federal Income Tax Payable	3 6 8 3 00	6 1 4 8 00	(2 4 6 5 00)	(40.1)
Dividends Payable	20 0 0 0 00	10 0 0 0 00	10 0 0 0 00	100.0
Total Liabilities	48 8 3 2 50	35 9 4 6 89		
STOCKHOLDERS' EQUITY				
Capital Stock	25 0 0 0 00	25 0 0 0 00	—	0.0
Retained Earnings	142 2 3 7 78	119 5 5 5 91	22 6 8 1 87	19.0
Total Stockholders' Equity	167 2 3 7 78	144 5 5 5 91		
Total Liabilities and Stockholders' Equity	216 0 7 0 28	180 5 0 2 80	35 5 6 7 48	19.7

17-4 WORK TOGETHER, p. 537

Analyzing financial statements using financial ratios

1., 2.

	Current Year	Prior Year	Increase over Prior Year (Yes or No)	Evaluation
Earnings per share		$3.26		
Dividend yield		6.63%		
Price-earnings ratio		9.5		

3., 4.

	Target Range		Actual Ratio	Favorable Result
	Low	High		
Working capital	$150,000.00	$200,000.00		
Current ratio	1.50	2.00		
Quick ratio	1.00	1.50		

17-4 ON YOUR OWN, p. 537

Analyzing financial statements using financial ratios

1., 2.

	Current Year	Prior Year	Increase over Prior Year (Yes or No)	Evaluation
Earnings per share		$0.56		
Dividend yield		0.12%		
Price-earnings ratio		44.7		

3., 4.

	Target Range		Actual Ratio	Favorable Result
	Low	High		
Working capital	$1,200,000.00	$1,800,000.00		
Current ratio	1.30	1.70		
Quick ratio	1.00	1.40		

17-1 APPLICATION PROBLEM (LO1), p. 541

Analyzing an income statement

1.

TR's Quik Mart

Comparative Income Statement

For Years Ended December 31, 20-- and 20--

	Current Year		Prior Year	
	Amount	Percent	Amount	Percent
Net Sales	979 2 9 2 15	100.0	951 8 4 8 08	100.0
Cost of Merchandise Sold	703 7 7 9 06		673 1 8 4 19	
Gross Profit	275 5 1 3 09		278 6 6 3 89	
Operating Expenses:				
Advertising Expense	3 1 0 1 00	0.3	15 4 8 1 18	1.6
Credit Card Fee Expense	14 9 1 4 28	1.5	13 4 9 8 09	1.4
Depreciation Expense—Office Equipment	3 4 1 8 00	0.3	2 1 8 0 00	0.2
Depreciation Expense—Store Equipment	4 1 9 8 00	0.4	3 2 2 0 00	0.3
Insurance Expense	6 2 0 0 00	0.6	6 0 0 0 00	0.6
Miscellaneous Expense	12 7 4 8 14	1.3	14 1 8 8 07	1.5
Payroll Taxes Expense	8 8 3 4 84	0.9	8 0 2 7 91	0.8
Rent Expense	18 0 0 0 00	1.8	18 0 0 0 00	1.9
Salary Expense	98 1 4 8 50		89 1 8 4 08	
Supplies Expense—Office	2 1 4 8 21	0.2	1 8 4 8 66	0.2
Supplies Expense—Store	9 4 1 8 19	1.0	10 1 9 8 17	1.1
Uncollectible Accounts Expense	1 4 8 0 00	0.2	9 1 4 00	0.1
Utilities Expense	6 8 4 8 89	0.7	6 8 7 1 09	0.7
Total Operating Expenses	189 4 5 8 05		189 6 1 1 25	
Income from Operations	86 0 5 5 04		89 0 5 2 64	
Other Revenue	9 2 00	0.0	2 2 50	0.0
Net Income before Federal Income Tax	86 1 4 7 04	8.8	89 0 7 5 14	9.4
Less Federal Income Tax Expense	17 5 3 9 99	1.8	18 5 2 7 90	1.9
Net Income after Federal Income Tax	68 6 0 7 05	7.0	70 5 4 7 24	7.4

2.

Ratio	Target Range		Actual Ratio		Favorable Trend	Favorable Result
	Low	High	Current Year	Prior Year		
Gross margin	27.5%	28.0%				
Operating expenses	18.8%	19.5%				
Operating margin	8.0%	9.2%				

Analyzing a balance sheet

1.

TR's Quick Mart

Comparative Balance Sheet

December 31, 20-- and 20--

	Current Year		Prior Year	
	Amount	Percent	Amount	Percent
ASSETS				
Current Assets:				
Cash	33 1 7 8 76	8.6	40 2 1 7 86	10.8
Petty Cash	3 0 0 00	0.1	3 0 0 00	0.1
Accounts Receivable (net)	7 9 9 2 17	2.1	6 4 8 9 38	1.7
Merchandise Inventory	248 9 1 1 08		231 9 4 4 19	
Supplies—Office	1 4 9 0 00	0.4	1 6 9 0 00	0.5
Supplies—Store	3 4 8 9 00	0.9	3 3 2 0 00	0.9
Prepaid Insurance	2 6 0 0 00	0.7	2 5 0 0 00	0.7
Notes Receivable	6 1 8 4 00	1.6	1 8 4 0 00	0.5
Interest Receivable	9 5 00	0.0	1 0 50	0.0
Total Current Assets	304 2 4 0 01		288 3 1 1 93	
Plant Assets:				
Office Equipment (net)	14 7 2 0 50	3.8	16 9 4 8 50	4.5
Store Equipment (net)	66 6 9 1 25	17.3	68 1 9 4 25	18.3
Total Plant Assets	81 4 1 1 75		85 1 4 2 75	
Total Assets	385 6 5 1 76	100.0	373 4 5 4 68	100.0
LIABILITIES				
Current Liabilities:				
Accounts Payable	32 1 7 8 04	8.3	15 9 1 8 91	4.3
Sales Tax Payable	4 1 9 4 24	1.1	4 0 9 8 99	1.1
Employee Income Tax Payable	1 0 2 0 00	0.3	9 9 9 00	0.3
Social Security Tax Payable	2 1 8 0 44	0.6	2 1 3 6 83	0.6
Medicare Tax Payable	5 0 9 95	0.1	4 9 9 74	0.1
Health Insurance Premiums Payable	4 8 8 00	0.1	4 7 8 24	0.1
Retirement Benefits Payable	4 7 4 00	0.1	4 6 4 52	0.1
Unemployment Tax Payable—Federal	3 2 0 13	0.1	3 1 3 72	0.1
Unemployment Tax Payable—State	1 5 8 89	0.0	1 5 5 71	0.0
Federal Income Tax Payable	4 9 8 0 00	1.3	1 8 4 8 00	0.5
Dividends Payable	20 0 0 0 00	5.2	16 0 0 0 00	4.3
Total Liabilities	66 5 0 3 69		42 9 1 3 66	
STOCKHOLDERS' EQUITY				
Capital Stock	200 0 0 0 00	51.9	200 0 0 0 00	53.6
Retained Earnings	119 1 4 8 07	30.9	130 5 4 1 02	35.0
Total Stockholders' Equity	319 1 4 8 07		330 5 4 1 02	
Total Liabilities and Stockholders' Equity	385 6 5 1 76	100.0	373 4 5 4 68	100.0

17-2 APPLICATION PROBLEM (concluded)

2.

	Target Range		Actual Ratio		Favorable Trend	Favorable Result
	Low	High	Current Year	Prior Year		
Merchandise inventory	65.0%	68.0%				
Total current assets	76.0%	78.0%				
Total plant assets	22.0%	24.0%				
Total liabilities	15.0%	20.0%				
Total stockholders' equity	80.0%	85.0%				

Analyzing financial statements using horizontal analysis

1.

Vector Industries

Comparative Income Statement

For Years Ended December 31, 20-- and 20--

	Current Year	Prior Year	Increase (Decrease) Amount	Percent
Net Sales	721 199 15	558 365 40		
Cost of Merchandise Sold	348 117 38	228 424 84		
Gross Profit	373 081 77	329 940 56		
Operating Expenses:				
Advertising Expense	25 002 23	24 719 24	282 99	1.1
Credit Card Fee Expense	7 247 31	5 607 40	1 639 91	29.2
Depreciation Expense—Office Equipment	8 030 00	7 850 00	180 00	2.3
Depreciation Expense—Store Equipment	6 920 00	6 750 00	170 00	2.5
Insurance Expense	8 868 04	8 129 78	738 26	9.1
Miscellaneous Expense	3 996 67	5 474 82		
Payroll Taxes Expense	15 214 27	15 418 58		
Rent Expense	24 000 00	24 000 00		
Salary Expense	169 019 10	166 138 42		
Supplies Expense—Office	4 245 08	3 517 48	727 60	20.7
Supplies Expense—Store	5 273 77	5 028 48	245 29	4.9
Uncollectible Accounts Expense	17 045 17	13 481 04	3 564 13	26.4
Utilities Expense	5 539 80	6 207 75	(6 67 95)	(10.8)
Total Operating Expenses	300 401 44	292 322 99	8 078 45	2.8
Income from Operations	72 680 33	37 617 57	35 062 76	93.2
Other Revenue	1 58 39	1 48 18	10 21	6.9
Net Income before Federal Income Tax	72 838 72	37 765 75		
Less Federal Income Tax Expense	13 209 68	5 664 86		
Net Income after Federal Income Tax	59 629 04	32 100 89		

17-3 APPLICATION PROBLEM (concluded)

2.

Vector Industries

Comparative Balance Sheet

December 31, 20-- and 20--

	Current Year	Prior Year	Increase (Decrease) Amount	Increase (Decrease) Percent
ASSETS				
Current Assets:				
Cash	51 989 62	15 445 82	36 543 80	236.6
Petty Cash	500 00	300 00	200 00	66.7
Accounts Receivable (net)	16 489 18	13 198 18		
Merchandise Inventory	121 843 06	116 164 49		
Supplies—Office	521 00	552 00		
Supplies—Store	411 00	348 00	63 00	18.1
Prepaid Insurance	2 800 00	2 400 00	400 00	16.7
Notes Receivable	1 850 00	3 200 00	(1 350 00)	(42.2)
Interest Receivable	14 00	26 00	(12 00)	(46.2)
Total Current Assets	196 417 86	151 634 49	44 783 37	29.5
Plant Assets:				
Office Equipment (net)	24 918 18	21 894 18	3 024 00	13.8
Store Equipment (net)	32 194 48	36 914 13	(4 719 65)	
Total Plant Assets	57 112 66	58 808 31	(1 695 65)	(2.9)
Total Assets	253 530 52	210 442 80	43 087 72	20.5
LIABILITIES				
Current Liabilities:				
Accounts Payable	10 808 04	18 486 17		
Sales Tax Payable	4 030 07	3 249 25		
Employee Income Tax Payable	982 00	920 00		
Social Security Tax Payable	2 319 18	2 108 18	211 00	10.0
Medicare Tax Payable	489 27	444 75	44 52	10.0
Health Insurance Premiums Payable	466 00	424 00	42 00	9.9
Retirement Benefits Payable	418 00	380 00	38 00	10.0
Unemployment Tax Payable—Federal	282 57	256 86	25 71	10.0
Unemployment Tax Payable—State	140 25	127 49	12 76	10.0
Federal Income Tax Payable	6 148 00	228 00	5 920 00	2,596.5
Dividends Payable	400 00	400 00	——	0.0
Total Liabilities	30 083 38	30 624 70	(541 32)	(1.8)
STOCKHOLDERS' EQUITY				
Capital Stock	50 000 00	50 000 00	——	0.0
Retained Earnings	173 447 14	129 818 10	43 629 04	33.6
Total Stockholders' Equity	223 447 14	179 818 10	43 629 04	24.3
Total Liabilities and Stockholders' Equity	253 530 52	210 442 80	43 087 72	20.5

Analyzing financial statements using financial ratios

1., 2.

	Current Year	Prior Year	Increase over Prior Year (Yes or No)	Evaluation
Earnings per share		$3.29		
Dividend yield		5.87%		
Price-earnings ratio		12.4		

3., 4.

	Target Range		Actual Ratio	Favorable Result
	Low	High		
Working capital	$900,000.00	$1,100,000.00		
Current ratio	1.40	1.60		
Quick ratio	1.00	1.30		

17-M **MASTERY PROBLEM (LO1, 2, 3, 4, 5, 6, 7, 8), p. 542**

Analyzing financial statements

1.

Aqua Products, Inc.

Comparative Income Statement

For Years Ended December 31, 20-- and 20--

	Current Year		Prior Year	
	Amount	Percent	Amount	Percent
Net Sales	838 9 4 1 16		774 8 2 7 66	
Cost of Merchandise Sold	391 4 9 1 71		366 6 0 8 74	
Gross Profit	447 4 4 9 45		408 2 1 8 92	
Operating Expenses:				
Depreciation Expense	24 6 0 0 00		22 5 6 0 00	
Office Expense	10 4 9 1 18		9 7 4 2 49	
Salaries and Payroll Tax Expense	204 1 8 4 58		192 9 1 9 43	
Store Expense	169 1 8 4 15		170 1 9 4 55	
Total Operating Expenses	408 4 5 9 91		395 4 1 6 47	
Income from Operations	38 9 8 9 54		12 8 0 2 45	
Other Revenue	6 4 2 00		2 2 8 00	
Net Income before Federal Income Tax	39 6 3 1 54		13 0 3 0 45	
Less Federal Income Tax Expense	5 9 4 4 73		1 9 5 4 57	
Net Income after Federal Income Tax	33 6 8 6 81		11 0 7 5 88	

Aqua Products, Inc.

Comparative Balance Sheet

December 31, 20-- and 20--

	Current Year		Prior Year	
	Amount	Percent	Amount	Percent
ASSETS				
Current Assets:				
Cash	23 9 0 5 98		8 0 2 9 57	
Accounts Receivable (net)	18 1 4 2 15		17 9 1 5 63	
Merchandise Inventory	98 1 4 2 36		82 1 9 4 38	
Other Current Assets	9 1 4 8 25		8 1 4 3 37	
Total Current Assets	149 3 3 8 74		116 2 8 2 95	
Plant Assets:				
Office Equipment (net)	32 9 8 9 04		38 1 9 5 52	
Store Equipment (net)	35 1 8 4 47		40 9 1 4 83	
Total Plant Assets	68 1 7 3 51		79 1 1 0 35	
Total Assets	217 5 1 2 25		195 3 9 3 30	
LIABILITIES				
Current Liabilities:				
Accounts Payable	14 1 8 9 10		26 4 9 1 11	
Dividends Payable	2 0 0 0 00		1 8 0 0 00	
Other Current Liabilities	9 4 8 1 76		10 9 4 7 61	
Total Liabilities	25 6 7 0 86		39 2 3 8 72	
STOCKHOLDERS' EQUITY				
Capital Stock	100 0 0 0 00		90 0 0 0 00	
Retained Earnings	91 8 4 1 39		66 1 5 4 58	
Total Stockholders' Equity	191 8 4 1 39		156 1 5 4 58	
Total Liabilities and Stockholders' Equity	217 5 1 2 25		195 3 9 3 30	

17-M MASTERY PROBLEM (continued)

2.

Aqua Products, Inc.

Comparative Income Statement

For Years Ended December 31, 20-- and 20--

	Current Year	Prior Year	Increase (Decrease)	
			Amount	Percent
Net Sales	838 941 16	774 827 66		
Cost of Merchandise Sold	391 491 71	366 608 74		
Gross Profit	447 449 45	408 218 92		
Operating Expenses:				
Depreciation Expense	24 600 00	22 560 00		
Office Expense	10 491 18	9 742 49		
Salaries and Payroll Taxes Expense	204 184 58	192 919 43		
Store Expense	169 184 15	170 194 55		
Total Operating Expenses	408 459 91	395 416 47		
Income from Operations	38 989 54	12 802 45		
Other Revenue	642 00	228 00		
Net Income before Federal Income Tax	39 631 54	13 030 45		
Less Federal Income Tax Expense	5 944 73	1 954 57		
Net Income after Federal Income Tax	33 686 81	11 075 88		

Aqua Products, Inc.
Comparative Balance Sheet
December 31, 20-- and 20--

	Current Year	Prior Year	Increase (Decrease) Amount	Increase (Decrease) Percent
ASSETS				
Current Assets:				
Cash	23 9 0 5 98	8 0 2 9 57		
Accounts Receivable (net)	18 1 4 2 15	17 9 1 5 63		
Merchandise Inventory	98 1 4 2 36	82 1 9 4 38		
Other Current Assets	9 1 4 8 25	8 1 4 3 37		
Total Current Assets	149 3 3 8 74	116 2 8 2 95		
Plant Assets:				
Office Equipment (net)	32 9 8 9 04	38 1 9 5 52		
Store Equipment (net)	35 1 8 4 47	40 9 1 4 83		
Total Plant Assets	68 1 7 3 51	79 1 1 0 35		
Total Assets	217 5 1 2 25	195 3 9 3 30		
LIABILITIES				
Current Liabilities:				
Accounts Payable	14 1 8 9 10	26 4 9 1 11		
Dividends Payable	2 0 0 0 00	1 8 0 0 00		
Other Current Liabilities	9 4 8 1 76	10 9 4 7 61		
Total Liabilities	25 6 7 0 86	39 2 3 8 72		
STOCKHOLDERS' EQUITY				
Capital Stock	100 0 0 0 00	90 0 0 0 00		
Retained Earnings	91 8 4 1 39	66 1 5 4 58		
Total Stockholders' Equity	191 8 4 1 39	156 1 5 4 58		
Total Liabilities and Stockholders' Equity	217 5 1 2 25	195 3 9 3 30		

17-M MASTERY PROBLEM (concluded)

3.

Ratio	Target Range		Actual Ratio		Favorable Trend	Favorable Result
	Low	High	Current Year	Prior Year		
Gross margin	53.0%	54.0%				
Total operating expenses	46.0%	48.0%				
Operating margin	5.0%	8.0%				
Merchandise inventory	40.0%	42.0%				
Total plant assets	30.0%	35.0%				
Total liabilities	12.0%	15.0%				

4.

	Current Year	Prior Year	Increase over Prior Year (Yes or No)	Evaluation
Earnings per share		$1.23		
Dividend yield		0.82%		
Price-earnings ratio		26.6		

5.

	Target Range		Actual Ratio	Favorable Result
	Low	High		
Working capital	$125,000.00	$145,000.00		
Current ratio	4.50	5.00		
Quick ratio	1.00	2.00		

CHALLENGE PROBLEM (LO1, 3, 8), p. 542

Analyzing industry standards

A. _____

B. _____

C. _____

D. _____

E. _____

REINFORCEMENT ACTIVITY 2, Part B, p. 545

An Accounting Cycle for a Corporation: End-of-Fiscal-Period Work

11.

GENERAL JOURNAL						PAGE 13

	DATE	ACCOUNT TITLE	DOC. NO.	POST. REF.	DEBIT	CREDIT	
1							1
2							2
3							3
4							4
5							5
6							6
7							7

12.

_____

_____

13.

Gulf Uniform Supply, Inc.

Unadjusted Trial Balance

December 31, 20--

ACCOUNT TITLE	DEBIT	CREDIT
Cash		
Petty Cash		
Accounts Receivable		
Allowance for Uncollectible Accounts		
Merchandise Inventory		
Supplies—Office		
Supplies—Store		
Prepaid Insurance		
Notes Receivable		
Interest Receivable		
Office Equipment		
Accumulated Depreciation—Office Equipment		
Store Equipment		
Accumulated Depreciation—Store Equipment		
Accounts Payable		
Sales Tax Payable		
Employee Income Tax Payable		
Social Security Tax Payable		
Medicare Tax Payable		
Health Insurance Premiums Payable		
Retirement Benefits Payable		
Unemployment Tax Payable—Federal		
Unemployment Tax Payable—State		
Federal Income Tax Payable		
Dividends Payable		
Capital Stock		
Retained Earnings		

(Note: Unadjusted trial balance is continued on next page.)

REINFORCEMENT ACTIVITY 2, Part B (continued)

Gulf Uniform Supply, Inc.

Unadjusted Trial Balance

December 31, 20--

ACCOUNT TITLE	DEBIT	CREDIT
Dividends		
Income Summary		
Sales		
Sales Discount		
Sales Returns and Allowances		
Purchases		
Purchases Discount		
Purchases Returns and Allowances		
Advertising Expense		
Cash Short and Over		
Credit Card Fee Expense		
Depreciation Expense—Office Equipment		
Depreciation Expense—Store Equipment		
Insurance Expense		
Miscellaneous Expense		
Payroll Taxes Expense		
Rent Expense		
Salary Expense		
Supplies Expense—Office		
Supplies Expense—Store		
Uncollectible Accounts Expense		
Utilities Expense		
Federal Income Tax Expense		
Interest Income		

REINFORCEMENT ACTIVITY 2, Part B (continued)

14.

Age Group	Amount	Percent	Uncollectible
Current	$13,232.18	2.0%	
1–30	811.50	4.5%	
31–60	1,470.75	10.0%	
61–90	5,824.25	30.0%	
Over 90	1,489.15	60.0%	
	$22,827.83	———	
Current Balance of Allowance for Uncollectible Accounts			
Estimated Addition to Allowance for Uncollectible Accounts			

14., 15., 16., 19.

GENERAL JOURNAL

PAGE 14

	DATE	ACCOUNT TITLE	DOC. NO.	POST. REF.	DEBIT	CREDIT	
1							1
2							2
3							3
4							4
5							5
6							6
7							7
8							8
9							9
10							10
11							11
12							12
13							13
14							14
15							15
16							16
17							17
18							18
19							19

REINFORCEMENT ACTIVITY 2, Part B (continued)

17., 20.

Gulf Uniform Supply, Inc.
Adjusted Trial Balance
December 31, 20--

ACCOUNT TITLE	DEBIT	CREDIT
Cash		
Petty Cash		
Accounts Receivable		
Allowance for Uncollectible Accounts		
Merchandise Inventory		
Supplies—Office		
Supplies—Store		
Prepaid Insurance		
Notes Receivable		
Interest Receivable		
Office Equipment		
Accumulated Depreciation—Office Equipment		
Store Equipment		
Accumulated Depreciation—Store Equipment		
Accounts Payable		
Sales Tax Payable		
Employee Income Tax Payable		
Social Security Tax Payable		
Medicare Tax Payable		
Health Insurance Premiums Payable		
Retirement Benefits Payable		
Unemployment Tax Payable—Federal		
Unemployment Tax Payable—State		
Federal Income Tax Payable		
Dividends Payable		
Capital Stock		
Retained Earnings		

(Note: Adjusted trial balance is continued on next page.)

Gulf Uniform Supply, Inc.

Adjusted Trial Balance

December 31, 20--

ACCOUNT TITLE	DEBIT	CREDIT
Dividends		
Income Summary		
Sales		
Sales Discount		
Sales Returns and Allowances		
Purchases		
Purchases Discount		
Purchases Returns and Allowances		
Advertising Expense		
Cash Short and Over		
Credit Card Fee Expense		
Depreciation Expense—Office Equipment		
Depreciation Expense—Store Equipment		
Insurance Expense		
Miscellaneous Expense		
Payroll Taxes Expense		
Rent Expense		
Salary Expense		
Supplies Expense—Office		
Supplies Expense—Store		
Uncollectible Accounts Expense		
Utilities Expense		
Federal Income Tax Expense		
Interest Income		

REINFORCEMENT ACTIVITY 2, Part B (continued)

18.

Total of income statement credit accounts................................. $ _____

Less total of income statement debit accounts

   excluding federal income tax .... _____

Equals net income before federal income tax .... $ _____

Net Income before Federal Income Tax	−	Of the Amount Over	=	Net Income Subject to Marginal Tax Rate	×	Marginal Tax Rate	=	Marginal Income Tax
$	−	$	=	$	×		=	$

Bracket Minimum Income Tax	+	Marginal Income Tax	=	Federal Income Tax
$	+	$	=	$

21.

										% OF NET SALES

REINFORCEMENT ACTIVITY 2, Part B (continued)

22.

_____

_____

23.

REINFORCEMENT ACTIVITY 2, Part B (continued)

24.

GENERAL JOURNAL

	DATE		ACCOUNT TITLE	DOC. NO.	POST. REF.	DEBIT	CREDIT	
1								1
2								2
3								3
4								4
5								5
6								6
7								7
8								8
9								9
10								10
11								11
12								12
13								13
14								14
15								15
16								16
17								17
18								18
19								19
20								20
21								21
22								22
23								23
24								24
25								25
26								26
27								27
28								28
29								29
30								30
31								31

25.

Health Fashions, Inc.

Comparative Income Statement

For Years Ended December 31, 20-- and 20--

	Current Year		Prior Year	
	Amount	Percent	Amount	Percent
Net Sales	349 1 8 4 81		329 1 1 4 71	
Cost of Merchandise Sold	149 7 8 4 15		141 4 1 4 31	
Gross Profit	199 4 0 0 66		187 7 0 0 40	
Operating Expenses:				
Depreciation Expense	12 1 9 4 64		11 9 4 4 39	
Office Expense	12 4 9 1 22		10 9 1 4 72	
Salaries and Payroll Tax Expense	74 9 1 8 15		73 1 4 8 39	
Store Expense	39 4 8 1 19		37 4 9 4 08	
Total Operating Expenses	139 0 8 5 20		133 5 0 1 58	
Income from Operations	60 3 1 5 46		54 1 9 8 82	
Other Revenue	2 3 5 00		1 9 4 00	
Net Income before Federal Income Tax	60 5 5 0 46		54 3 9 2 82	
Less Federal Income Tax Expense	10 1 3 7 62		8 5 9 8 21	
Net Income after Federal Income Tax	50 4 1 2 84		45 7 9 4 61	

Health Fashions, Inc.

Comparative Balance Sheet

December 31, 20-- and 20--

	Current Year		Prior Year	
	Amount	**Percent**	**Amount**	**Percent**
ASSETS				
Current Assets:				
Cash	24 8 9 6 33		8 4 1 4 46	
Accounts Receivable (net)	25 1 9 5 49		16 4 8 4 39	
Merchandise Inventory	45 8 8 4 46		34 1 1 8 17	
Other Current Assets	17 9 4 8 28		16 4 8 1 27	
Total Current Assets	113 9 2 4 56		75 4 9 8 29	
Plant Assets:				
Office Equipment (net)	22 4 9 4 65		18 4 9 5 17	
Store Equipment (net)	25 9 4 8 69		24 9 1 4 71	
Total Plant Assets	48 4 4 3 34		43 4 0 9 88	
Total Assets	162 3 6 7 90		118 9 0 8 17	
LIABILITIES				
Current Liabilities:				
Accounts Payable	13 4 4 8 34		12 4 9 8 17	
Dividends Payable	2 0 0 0 00		2 0 0 0 00	
Other Current Liabilities	1 7 4 4 99		1 6 4 8 27	
Total Liabilities	17 1 9 3 33		16 1 4 6 44	
STOCKHOLDERS' EQUITY				
Capital Stock	50 0 0 0 00		50 0 0 0 00	
Retained Earnings	95 1 7 4 57		52 7 6 1 73	
Total Stockholders' Equity	145 1 7 4 57		102 7 6 1 73	
Total Liabilities and Stockholders' Equity	162 3 6 7 90		118 9 0 8 17	

26.

Health Fashions, Inc.

Comparative Income Statement

For Years Ended December 31, 20-- and 20--

	Current Year	Prior Year	Increase (Decrease) Amount	Increase (Decrease) Percent
Net Sales	349 1 8 4 81	329 1 1 4 71		
Cost of Merchandise Sold	149 7 8 4 15	141 4 1 4 31		
Gross Profit	199 4 0 0 66	187 7 0 0 40		
Operating Expenses:				
Depreciation Expense	12 1 9 4 64	11 9 4 4 39		
Office Expense	12 4 9 1 22	10 9 1 4 72		
Salaries and Payroll Tax Expense	74 9 1 8 15	73 1 4 8 39		
Store Expense	39 4 8 1 19	37 4 9 4 08		
Total Operating Expenses	139 0 8 5 20	133 5 0 1 58		
Income from Operations	60 3 1 5 46	54 1 9 8 82		
Other Revenue	2 3 5 00	1 9 4 00		
Net Income before Federal Income Tax	60 5 5 0 46	54 3 9 2 82		
Less Federal Income Tax Expense	10 1 3 7 62	8 5 9 8 21		
Net Income after Federal Income Tax	50 4 1 2 84	45 7 9 4 61		

REINFORCEMENT ACTIVITY 2, Part B (continued)

Health Fashions, Inc.

Comparative Balance Sheet

December 31, 20-- and 20--

	Current Year	Prior Year	Increase (Decrease) Amount	Increase (Decrease) Percent
ASSETS				
Current Assets:				
Cash	24 8 9 6 33	8 4 1 4 46		
Accounts Receivable (net)	25 1 9 5 49	16 4 8 4 39		
Merchandise Inventory	45 8 8 4 46	34 1 1 8 17		
Other Current Assets	17 9 4 8 28	16 4 8 1 27		
Total Current Assets	113 9 2 4 56	75 4 9 8 29		
Plant Assets:				
Office Equipment (net)	22 4 9 4 65	18 4 9 5 17		
Store Equipment (net)	25 9 4 8 69	24 9 1 4 71		
Total Plant Assets	48 4 4 3 34	43 4 0 9 88		
Total Assets	162 3 6 7 90	118 9 0 8 17		
LIABILITIES				
Current Liabilities:				
Accounts Payable	13 4 4 8 34	12 4 9 8 17		
Dividends Payable	2 0 0 0 00	2 0 0 0 00		
Other Current Liabilities	1 7 4 4 99	1 6 4 8 27		
Total Liabilities	17 1 9 3 33	16 1 4 6 44		
STOCKHOLDERS' EQUITY				
Capital Stock	50 0 0 0 00	50 0 0 0 00		
Retained Earnings	95 1 7 4 57	52 7 6 1 73		
Total Stockholders' Equity	145 1 7 4 57	102 7 6 1 73		
Total Liabilities and Stockholders' Equity	162 3 6 7 90	118 9 0 8 17		

27.

Ratio	Target Ranges for GUS		Actual Ratios for HFI		Favorable Trend	Favorable Result
	Low	High	Current Year	Prior Year		
Gross margin	57.0%	58.0%				
Total operating expenses	38.0%	40.0%				
Operating margin	17.0%	20.0%				
Merchandise inventory	26.0%	28.0%				
Total plant assets	25.0%	30.0%				
Total liabilities	12.0%	15.0%				

28.

	Current Year	Prior Year	Increase over Prior Year (Yes or No)	Evaluation
Earnings per share				
Dividend yield				
Price-earnings ratio				

29.

	Target Ranges for GUS		Actual Ratios for HFI	Favorable Result
	Low	High		
Working capital	$75,000.00	$100,000.00		
Current ratio	5.00	7.00		
Quick ratio	2.00	4.00		